MEL GIBSON
MAN ON A MISSION

MEL GIBSON
MAN ON A MISSION

WENSLEY CLARKSON

BLAKE

Published by BlakePublishing Ltd,
3, Bramber Court, 2 Bramber Road,
London W14 9PB, England

www.blake.co.uk

First published in hardback in 2004

ISBN 1 85782 537 3

British Library Cataloguing-in-Publication Data:

A catalogue record for this book is available from the British Library.

Design by www.envydesign.co.uk

Printed in Great Britain by Creative Print and Design

1 3 5 7 9 10 8 6 4 2

Pictures reproduced by kind permission of Rex Features

Papers used by Blake Publishing are natural, recyclable products made from
wood grown in sustainable forests. The manufacturing processes conform to the
environmental regulations of the country of origin.

Every attempt has been made to contact the relevant copyright-holders,
but some were unobtainable. We would be grateful if the appropriate people
could contact us.

ACKNOWLEDGEMENTS

My thanks, above all, to Anthony Bolton who aided and abetted me with this book so comprehensively, as well as providing me with so many friendly faces to call upon in Australia and America. Also to Victor Escandon Prada, John Blake, Pat Lovell, Mark Sandelson, Louise Johnson, Jonathan Margolis, Joan Wong, Tina Rothwell, Charlie Sungkawess, Som Pot Sungkawess, John Bremmer, Peter Nowlan, Graham Fowler, Ed Stinson, Carol Rowell, Ralph McCoach, Kathleen Lyons, Pat Grasso, Don McClennan, Maeva Salmon, Hare Salmon, Coco Dexter, Tevaite Vernette, Maimiti Kinnander, Irene Fuller, George Logue, Noetia Guy, Maco Roometua, Daphne Fuller, Scan Denis, Maurice Lenoir, Andrew Urban, Lisa Offord, Mitch Matthews, Michelle Adamson, Monroe Reimers, Emil Minty, Yvonne Perotette, Jeremy Connolly, Carmel Smith, Eileen Leiden, Tim Burstall, Jon Dowding, Don Bennetts, Scott Murray, Dan McDonnell, Robert Lawrence

MC, Peter Wilson, Rhonda Schepisi, Robert Menzies, Mark Griffin, Rea Francis, Hugh Keays-Byrne, Mark McGinnity, Judy Holst, Linda Newton, Deborah Foreman, Miranda Brewin, Chris O'Mara, Terri DePaolo, John Phillip Law, Phil Avalon, John Bell, Wendy Kane, John McShane, Bunty Avieson and every other person who agreed to be interviewed for this book, but requested that I do not reveal their identities. Also Globe Library, Associated Newspapers Library, News International Library and the Motion Picture Library, Los Angeles.

In addition, Mel Gibson by Keith McKay (Sidgwick and Jackson 1986), Mel Gibson by David Ragan (W.H. Allen 1985) and Reluctant Star by James Oram (Fontana 1991) provided some invaluable information about Mel Gibson and I am extremely grateful to them.

Stars are essentially worthless – and absolutely essential.
Adventures in the Screen Trade by William Goldman

To be or not to be, that is the question;
whether 'tis nobler in the mind to suffer the slings and
arrows of outrageous fortune or take arms against a sea
of troubles, and by opposing end them? ... For who would
bear the whips and scorns of time, the oppressor's wrong,
the proud man's contumely, the pangs of despised love,
the law's delay, the insolence of office ...
Hamlet by William Shakespeare

Write a book? Ha ha ha! Hell, what would I write about?
My life as a movie star? Actors only write books when
they run out of money.
Anyway, there's enough people writing about me.
There is someone doing it even as we speak. Does it get
on my nerves?
There's a sense of outrage that somebody's wandering
about talking to everyone I've ever known.
Mel Gibson

PROLOGUE

IF YOU HAVE NO GREAT EXPECTATIONS, YOU'RE NOT
GOING TO BE DISAPPOINTED.

Let me upstage a star and beat him to the draw in stating
something: you are starting a study which is bound to
disturb, distress and infuriate its subject, Mel Columbcille
Gerard Gibson.

For the great paradox of one of the screen's best-known
men is that hardly anyone knows him. Stonewalling his way
through reluctantly granted interviews or dancing out of
range behind smokescreens of ingenuous charm and
engagingly mocking flippancy, Mel Gibson is intent on
keeping it that way. The upfront guy of the movies is a
fiercely private person.

Accordingly, and strangely, Gibson will resent disclosure of
a record in which most people would take pride: a child
growing up in hard times, under an equally hard paternal
regime, with virtually no material advantages, who has
triumphed in the most competitive, least forgiving arena on
earth – Hollywood.

This book is clear-eyed rather than rose-tinted, certainly. You must decide whether Gibson emerges as its hero, anti-hero or merely the central character. For him, such findings are irrelevant. Refusing to write his own life story, he resents anyone else daring to ... simply because it is about him, and that's enough to rankle with an embattled man who loathes undue scrutiny and is almost superstitiously anxious to keep himself to himself and his family circle.

Mel would be extremely happy if the printing press had not been invented. Partly because he has managed to persuade himself that he's pretty good at just another job, as it might be plumbing or running a supermarket. The customers ought to be content to judge him on whether the taps have been fixed, the produce is fresh – or if they have been taken out of themselves by his latest picture. Leave it at that, huh?

Ain't never going to happen, as the modern American proverb goes. Having elevated the Ordinary Joe to titanic stature, or at least, wide-screen scale, Mel Gibson suffers from the iron law that anyone kindling the imaginations of untold millions is bound to ignite their curiosity as well. What's he *really* like ... what makes him tick?

Good questions, especially since he guards the answers. Depressingly few Great Big Stars are very interesting people. Many bear the hallmarks of a conventional, dull family background; either their college major was performing arts, leading on to theatre work, or they had high school dreams and broke through via modelling or TV soaps and ... ho-hum. Mel Gibson, thank God – to whom his extremist, vastly influential father, 'Red' Gibson, believes he may have a direct line, by the way – isn't like that.

Yes, he went to drama school, more or less by accident and not particularly willingly, either. That's the only suggestion of

Hollywood cookie-cutter uniformity. This man is a true original, a one-off on two legs.

Little about the erstwhile Mad Max is stereotyped, predictable. Even his hell-raising, while its wine, women and song trail was blazed by bygones like Errol Flynn, has unique ingredients of flinty honesty and good, old-fashioned Catholic guilt.

Other megastars drive themselves to get bigger or, at worst, cling to their rung on the platinum ladder. Mel Gibson dreams of giving it all up, to farm beef-cattle full time. His peers prattle, between one divorce and the next, of family values and their wonderful wife and kids. The one sure bet about Mel Gibson is that, if forced to choose between fame and career or his adored family, he'd be out of there and back home for good, the moment the choice was presented.

Movie-making is much like war, which has been said to be 90 per cent boredom while waiting for 10 per cent of frenetic activity. Making movies outside a studio, often right off the map, is worse, through offering fewer home comforts. Steam needs letting off, empty evenings must be filled – when it comes to disgraceful behaviour, the main difference between a film team and a rock group, out on the road, is that the band generally sings in key ...

This has led to a conscience-salving aphorism: 'On location, it doesn't count.' In other words, when the cameras stop rolling and the picture is over, so are the affairs.

Given Mel Gibson's tendency to run off the rails, one would expect him to have taken full advantage of being on location. Not so – he seems consciously to distance himself from the actresses and female technicians, many of whom would love to hang his celebrity scalp from their suspender-belts.

The message seems to be that Mel prefers the company of non-industry people, especially on occasions when he has lost self-control and gone over the high side. Intriguingly, he has only ever been tempted when away from film business territory. Apart from a genuine, unpatronising liking for 'real people', Mel still does not really trust Hollywood, or the motives of its denizens when they are eager to be his buddies.

As we shall see, his doubts are well founded.

Until Christmas of 1990, he fought a losing battle against alcoholism – one unfortunate side-effect being a string of brief, generally boozy, encounters with women outside the business.

Astonishingly, none of these women has anything unkind or even reproachful to say about him. He was, they could argue, deceiving nobody – except his wife. It's likely that Mel Gibson subscribes to the philosophy that what a wife doesn't know can't hurt her. Certainly, his strict Catholic upbringing at Gibson Senior's hands appears to have given him some highly reactionary views on women.

Modesto, California, in 1990, saw the watershed of his off-the-leash relationships with pretty, dazzled but undemanding girls. For the first time, Mel had been literally caught in the act … well, captured on film in mildly compromising, candid-camera action.

But, as his advisers stress, all that was before Mel gave up drinking. So while it reaped a sensational harvest of embarrassing publicity, worsened by a ham-fisted hush-up operation which didn't help things, Modesto-gate could well have been a farewell performance.

To the sneerers, Mel Gibson – the American who conquered Hollywood, or perhaps it hi-jacked him, by way of Australia – is a typical Aussie bloke who enjoys a beer and a barbie, glorified by an overdose of raw sex appeal. When it suits him, he encourages that misconception.

Even when complimented on his performance in *Hamlet* (lauded by more than one critic, while grudging ones conceded that the Action Man and sex-symbol was a genuine actor), all you got from him was a shrug and a deadpan refusal to admit that he's smarter and more gifted than the average hunk. 'Good … I've fooled another one.'

In recent years, Mel has become adept at telling journalists everything and nothing. He's a naturally reticent person and that is his *modus vivendi*, keeping contractual obligations to promote and publicise his films, while restricting personal data ... hugging something of himself, to himself.

Burned not once but several times, Mel Gibson is a hundred times shy these days. Many intimates whom I approached for help insisted on checking with him or his family first. They were all strongly discouraged from speaking to me. One relative was even 'instructed' not to loan out some innocuous photographs of the actor as a child. I tried to contact Mel's Hollywood agent, Ed Limato, but never got past his fax machine.

Then one of Mel's oldest friends advised me, 'Drop the project altogether.' Gibson, he warned, would oppose me very vigorously if I tried delving into his background. In Los Angeles, at least half-a-dozen people who had worked with or for Mel's production company (tellingly named Icon Productions, which Mel proudly announces stands for 'I con ...') retreated into total silence. A former employee explained, 'I would be finished in Hollywood if I gave you so much as the time of day.'

Thankfully, I eventually met a number of refreshingly open men and women who were happy to speak their minds and defy Tinseltown rules.

Obviously, many witnesses were mindful of what happened over that tabloid exposé of Mel's raffish romp with a trio of nubile women in Modesto. Heavy-hitter lawyers started pursuing them with 'confidentiality contracts' in a bid to seal the girls' mouths. It's likely that Mel's regiment of attorneys will suggest a similar damage-control exercise concerning this book, trying to discount, deny and cover up its findings.

But, if they do that, they will entirely miss the point of this biography. Mel is no better or worse than the guy next door. Which is exactly what he has maintained from the start, when accused of mega-star glamour. He's a fine, concerned father and loving, good-provider husband who has occasionally erred. In fairness, countless less gifted or famous players have made utter pigs of themselves after hitting the gusher of big bucks and bigger adulation. By contrast, Mel Gibson has hardly dipped a toe in the trough … and often scorned temptation.

The real reason for this unauthorised biography is that no one has written a comprehensive book about him. Strings of facts, not all accurate, for sure. Fan-magazine-cum-filmography essays, sure. But there's been no attempt to address the paradoxes and strokes of fortune, the interplay of genes and environment, the sheer believe-it-or-not quality of an obscure outsider's charge to the top of his profession.

I am an unreconstructed admirer. If for no other reason, I would have been bound to tell the Mel Gibson story because I feel such empathy with him. It may be imagination, but at moments I have sensed what has been going through his mind.

Let me explain: we are both the same age, both married young and have stayed with the same partner ever since, and both of us have raised a multitude of children, with all that means.

Use 20-20 hindsight and it's easy to say that Mel's time would have come, whether or not he had won the roles of Max Rockatansky or Martin Riggs. He was a virile, macho youngster with that elusive quality of making an audience take notice, just at the time of a great sea-change and renaissance of the arts, especially film-making, in Australia. Of course, as an All-American kid who, a few years before, seemed rooted in a flyspeck-on-the-map corner of upper New York State, Mel Gibson had no business being in Australia ... for an overt fatalist insisting that he's never expected much and thus avoids disappointment, he has had an unusual share of luck.

Maybe Mel isn't kidding about indifference to stardom, and his impatience to hand it back and get on with his real life.

Stardom has to be the most over-used and under-defined word in any actor's dictionary. It means everything and nothing. Great acting? Great popularity? Skill and charisma? Sexiness? Is it torment and self-destruction, as with Garland and Clift, or highprofile, excessive consumption, like Burton and Taylor in their lurid heyday? If so, and if craft and art need not be involved, where do fallen idols such as Olivier, Gielgud and, most recently, Brando fit in?

Thus, the crown Mel wears, so carelessly and frequently unwillingly, is invisible and indefinable. The one sure thing about stardom is that *every* actor, whatever they say, dreams of achieving it. Many famous people fear that, if that dream is taken away, the initiative goes with it.

Include Mel Gibson out of that. His dream, fully realised, was to have a good wife and lots of children, and look after them. The guy has no *right* to have got where he is!

And, as you will have gathered by now, he is not the easiest subject to analyse. He has none of that glib, manufactured charm of most Men-About-the-Movies. He's been described as shy but his taciturnity owes less to diffidence than a constant campaign to hide his real feelings.

Mel has been called handsome, but he's better than that. He is actually attractive, which is more accessible and less threatening. Significantly, female fans love him and, far from resenting and scoffing at him for it, their men like, admire and wish they were Mel. That is the rarest of cross-overs, a wild talent that cannot be learned, bought or simulated.

And just when you begin to think you've got a handle on this Extrovert-Introvert-Superstar-Family Man, he goes and blows all assumptions out of the water, and reinvents – or reveals for the first time – another facet of his wildly unpredictable talent. *The Passion of the Christ* saw him take the highly controversial reins of a major motion picture, casting himself not as leading man, but as co-writer, producer and director. With that movie, Mel Gibson sailed unapologetically headlong into a storm of controversy that has yet to die down. Whatever the film was – whether ultimately a project for Good or Evil, depending on your perspective – *The Passion of the Christ* was guaranteed to generate one of the biggest reactions to a film in recent decades for all sorts of reasons. Whether you loved or hated it, you couldn't ignore it ... because of its subject matter, and because it was a Mel Gibson film.

Whether in front of the camera or behind it, whether writing the script or delivering it, Mel Gibson is really only ever being himself. For all his striving, Mel Gibson does not have to persuade you that he is anybody else but Mel. The screen likes actors, but it adores stars.

The snag is that stars are deceptive, unknowable. Simplest

proof of that – Mad Max and madder Marty Riggs are extroverts, and then some. Mel Gibson, despite putting on a show, is much more of an introvert.

Yet there is a bond and, as this book will demonstrate, the one common factor between Max, Marty and Mel is intriguing, engaging and uncommonly worth attention ... all three are magnificent mavericks and they prove that Mel truly is a man on a mission.

ONE

IF YOU HAVE NO GREAT EXPECTATIONS,
YOU'RE NOT GOING TO BE DISAPPOINTED.

S he had the audience in the palm of her hand.
They demanded encore after encore. The Sydney Town
Hall was packed to capacity for the farewell concert of famed
contralto Eva Mylott. If there are such things as show
business genes, then it must have been Eva who passed them
on to her grandson Mel Gibson.

In February 1902, Eva, then 27, was giving her last
performance before setting off for Europe, a land of hope and
opportunity which – naturally – she intended to take by
storm. Australia had been good to her and her family ever
since Eva's father Patrick Mylott escaped the Great Potato
Famine and British repression in Ireland to head Down Under.
Eva became renowned as a free spirit in a land where society
was a bastion of male domination. She wanted the sort of
artistic freedom and licence that everyone had told her existed
in Europe. It was a huge risk for a single woman, but that was
typical of Eva Mylott.

Eva spent a total of five years in Europe. The black clouds of World War I were not yet on the horizon and the emphasis was on living well and playing hard. She fell in and out of love as regularly as her emotions decreed. The artistic opportunities of cities like Paris, Rome and Madrid made them even more seductive places to Eva. She had so much to learn.

But there was an even bigger, more exciting land of opportunity beckoning from across the Atlantic and she grew ever more inquisitive about America. There was growing interest in opera in the United States and travellers spoke of vast concert halls and enthusiastic crowds desperate to welcome entertainers. When another love affair crumbled, Eva found the appeal of America too hard to resist. It was a perfect time, once again, to start afresh.

In the summer of 1907, she entered Upper New York Bay, sailed past the Statue of Liberty and stood on the upper deck for the final three-quarters-of-a-mile towards Ellis Island. Eva's eyes were dazzled as she stared out at her new home and unknown future.

Within months, Eva was winning rave notices for her performances at concerts in Chicago, Boston, Philadelphia and Montreal. She was rapidly gaining a reputation as a superb contralto. Over in Europe, Nellie Melba was proud of her success. She pored over every word of each letter Eva sent her. Her prodigy had well and truly made it.

Life in America could not have been kinder to Eva. She swept audiences up with her magnetism.

'She had a way of handling crowds. They adored her,' explained old Gibson family friend Ed Stinson.

Eva also had those incredible blue eyes that movie audiences across the globe have found so irresistible in her grandson. Child behavioural experts have long been convinced that personality patterns frequently skip a generation. In other words, you are more likely to resemble your grandparents than your own mother and father. Eva Mylott was a warm, attractive, hypnotic personality, scornful of risks and capable of grabbing attention in a crowded room. Little wonder that Mel Gibson found his calling in Hollywood's movie industry.

But in 1914, Eva – who was then nearly 40 and still unmarried – met millionaire businessman John Hutton Gibson after a sellout concert in Chicago. Gibson, a shy, reserved, handsome man, was, perhaps not surprisingly, bowled over by the beautiful, exotic Eva. She, in turn, felt attracted to him because he was the exact opposite of the flighty, flirty men whom she usually encountered during life on the road. Too many love affairs had crumbled after Eva fell for predatory fellows interested only in a brief liaison with a spirited opera star.

In Gibson, she found a man who truly cared for her – and, as partner in a successful Chicago metal foundry, he could provide her with the security she desperately craved. It was a last chance for Eva. She had lived life in the fast lane but now it was dawning on her that she had so little to show for it. No husband. No children.

Marriage to Gibson brought her more happiness than a thousand encores. She helped raise money to send medical supplies to Australian hospitals during World War I, spurred on by her family links Down Under. The couple moved to the tranquillity of Montclair in New York State where, at the age of 43, Eva's dream came true in 1918 when she gave birth to Hutton Peter Gibson, father of Mel.

Typically, Eva defied doctors in the first place by getting pregnant at an age when many women were about to become grandmothers. But she angered medics even further by trying for more children after the birth of Hutton. Fifteen months later, just weeks after giving birth to her second son, Alexander Mylott, serious post-natal complications set in.

Eva knew she was dying, and, according to family lore, she grasped her heartbroken husband's hand as he sat by her hospital bedside and told him, 'It is God's will. We have two wonderful boys. The Gibson name will carry on.'

A month after giving birth to Alexander, Eva died. Gibson was understandably distraught at the funeral service in Chicago held a few days later. He felt betrayed to have found love late in life, only to have it snatched away so cruelly. In a pledge of loyalty that would become characteristic of his son and grandson, he swore that he would never marry again. No one could replace Eva in his affections and the very suggestion of another woman entering his life brought an indignant response. Widower Gibson turned to the Roman Catholic Church for his solace and strove to ensure that his two sons did likewise.

Hutton and his baby brother were, as is often the case, as different as chalk and cheese. For the first few years after their mother's death, they led a wealthy if not exactly inspiring existence in the Gibson mansion.

Hutton Gibson was barely into his early teens when the Depression hit the family very badly. Gibson senior's income halved; eventually, he lost his stake in the metal foundry and suffered poor health for the remainder of his life. The Gibsons were no longer the richest kids on the block and a paper round became an important source of income for young Hutton. He rose at four every morning to complete not one, but two rounds in a desperate effort to augment the family income. His doggedness has become a hallmark of his clan.

In the evenings, Hutton Gibson accepted the lack of attention from his father and threw himself into Catholicism, often reading avidly until the early hours. His deep commitment to the faith was growing by the day. Like many before and since, he used his unswerving beliefs to feed eternal optimism that everything would once again be fine in the world. He studied devotedly and, years later, still insisted, 'The greatest benefit anyone can have is to be a Catholic. You have the lifelong satisfaction of being right.'

Hutton got back to his sombre family home each night, increasingly disillusioned by this futility. His spare time dominated by religious exploration, he sensed that his vocation lay elsewhere – the Church.

Chicago's Society of the Divine Word was a dour, imposing place but, as combined college and recruit-barracks for the priesthood, seminaries are supposed to be that way and Hutton was undaunted. He thrived in an ascetic, intellectually demanding regime. Catholicism was his calling, his new home. He had no qualms about the vow of celibacy; temptations tripping most hot-blooded kids were mere hurdles to be vaulted for Hutton.

His initial year went well enough. An ideal seminarian at first, Hutton welcomed the discipline, structure and, above all, the company of like-minded men on the same road. At home, there had been tension and friction with his sprightlier young brother, and the implicit gloom generated by his father's declining health and spirits. At last, he had a clearly defined goal and means of reaching it.

But, as the would-be priest adjusted to seminary restrictions and routine, his questioning began. It wasn't a matter of the yoke of self-denial starting to chafe. Quite the reverse – young Hutton's distaste was for the Roman Catholic Church's belated, very mild and minor attempts to move with the times. His attitude did not go down well. Many priests at the seminary were in favour of reform and he was regarded as something of a pest.

More than 20 years later, Hutton's unbending religious creed captured headlines, but, at that time, it simply convinced the softly spoken yet stubborn American that the priesthood was not for him. Freed from celibacy, he might better serve Christ by fathering children who would be trained in the good old, true old faith. So, just after the outbreak of World War II, Hutton abandoned the seminary.

Weeks later, his father died and Hutton became doubly orphaned, parents and vocation lost. Whether it was patriotism or panic at being rootless and aimless, young Hutton opted for another all-male, highly structured society – he joined the Army. Enlisting in the infantry may have been the most illuminating and shocking move of his life. It wasn't the grisly, hand-to-hand conflict in the Pacific that shook Hutton Gibson, but fellow GIs' total disdain for God.

'There are no atheists in foxholes' was a wartime saying, but such was not soldier Hutton's experience. As he saw it, he was surrounded by blasphemers, unbelievers, modern pagans. They might die at any moment, unshriven, *and so many of them didn't care*. The teachings of Our Lord did not extend to the killing fields and that baffled and disturbed him, far more than the very likely prospect of dying in tropical mud.

It was a crucial insight, not only for the World War II warrior but, one of his sons, whose birth lay years ahead. Because Hutton – Second Lieutenant Gibson by then, a combat veteran – made up his mind that *his* children would never abuse God in the cause and course of war. And, when Hutton Gibson reaches a decision, it's set in concrete, so, long afterwards, he took his vast family halfway around the world, a modern Moses leading his tribe in flight from Pentagon Pharaohs, rather than allow his boys to be conscripted.

In Ireland, towards the turn of the century, the Reilly family was experiencing, as far as they were concerned, the horrors of British rule. The notorious Black and Tans were an army of ex-servicemen sent over from the mainland to 'teach the Irish a lesson'. Paid just 10s (50p) a day, the Tans (named after their mix of army and police uniforms) were first sent to Ireland in March 1920. Beyond doubt, many of the Auxiliaries were out of control on occasions, behaving in such a brutal and heartless fashion that the locals held them in complete contempt as well as healthy fear. Not only IRA propagandists believe that the Black and Tans were a significant element of a wind that, as in the Bible, was being reaped as the whirlwind on the streets and in Bandit Country fields of Northern Ireland and the border, until very recently.

Longtime family friend Ed Stinson says that the behaviour of the British towards the family of Mel's mother Anne (and especially her own mother) remains unforgotten to this day.

'There was and still is great resentment towards the English. The Black and Tans came to Ireland when Mel's grandmother lived there. They were nothing more than thugs and they attacked many women over there. Mel's mother in particular hated the English. Anne told me that women in her family were raped by the Black and Tans; those stories have been handed down over the years.'

Certainly, Mel and the rest of the Gibson clan share a distrust of the British as a result of whatever did actually occur. And Mel himself has talked in interviews about his feelings towards the British for the way they handled America and then Australia.

'Both countries started for the same reason. They were places where Mother England put her cast-offs, her undesirables – a lot of Irish and English criminals. Then you guys [the Americans] got strong enough to sort of say to the British, "Get lost, we don't want you around here any more.

You got rid of us … we're doing something good here … leave us alone." But the Australians never did that.'

Mel's mother's family, the Reillys, settled in the Bushwick section of Brooklyn, New York. Ironically, Anne Patricia Reilly actually ended up being born in the home country after her mother returned to Ireland to visit her own mother who had refused to move to the New World despite the horrors inflicted on her by the dreaded Black and Tans.

Anne's grandmother was a widow suffering from regular bouts of ill health and living in the picturesque country area of Marley, in County Longford. But the pregnant mother's visit to Ireland coincided with some of the worst outbreaks of civil unrest and she witnessed the full, horrifying impact of the Black and Tans. In the middle of all this violence, Anne was born.

Eventually, they arrived back safely in New York. Mel's mother attended a parochial school in the parish of Our Lady of Lourdes and then went on to graduate from Bushwick High, a state school. Anne showed a particular talent for drawing and she was greatly interested in photography. Later, she even attended art school in Manhattan.

Anne was a homely sort of girl, enjoying a fine relationship with her parents. And, like any good Catholic girl, she continued living at home after getting a job at a photographic firm near Penn Station, on Seventh Avenue. Anne relished family life and happily obeyed the rigid rules of a traditional Catholic household. That was something which definitely made her a good catch for the deeply religious Hutton Gibson when they eventually met and fell in love.

At that time, Anne's elder sister Kathleen married a young man who worked for the New York transit company as a motorman on trolley cars. One of his best friends was fellow worker Harold Cardello, who came from the Flatbush area of

Brooklyn. When Cardello enlisted in the infantry, he was sent to Fort Benning, Georgia, where he became acquainted with Hutton Gibson, a fellow GI.

'At first, I might say, he did not seem a very lovable person, not until you got to know him,' says Mel's aunt Kathleen. 'I didn't think too much of him and, seeing he seemed likely to marry my sister, there was some defensive mechanism early in the piece. He seemed strong and single-minded.'

But then Hutton was in his early twenties, with no parents and a wild kid brother who had taken off to do his own thing years earlier. He was unsure how to handle friendships, let alone actual relationships.

Earnest, worthy Hutton started being called 'Red' by his newly adopted family. It was a name that was to stick for the rest of his life. But, at Gibson's insistence, only his family could call him that. To the rest of the world, he was 'Hutt'.

Hutton Gibson hardly swept Anne Reilly off her feet. He quietly got to know her. Family members say that he wanted to make sure she shared his religious beliefs before they even so much as held hands.

A few months later, Hutton was sent to officer cadet school in the Signal Corps at nearby Fort Monmouth, New Jersey. It was the perfect transfer for the young soldier. His affection for Anne was slowly but surely growing.

Almost inevitably, Hutton – whose own mother had been too old to have more than just two children – had already decided that he wanted a huge family. In some ways, it might recompense him for missing out on all the fun of being part of a big family when he was a child. He went out of his way to play with Kathleen's children to make up for what he had forfeited. Interestingly, Mel Gibson appears to have been equally adept at handling his relatives' children, even when still in his teens.

'Mel loved children even when he was still at drama school. He was always talking about his nieces and nephews. He was the sort of uncle who would take them all to the park,' said one of Mel's former girlfriends from student days.

It was during World War II that Hutton Gibson made his first visit to Australia. He and brother Alexander had hoped to visit their mother's birthplace but they were both recalled to active service before they had a chance to organise the trip. Hutton made a pledge, there and then, to return one day. The vow altered many lives.

Towards the end of the war, Gibson was wounded in the battle of Guadalcanal and sent home. Anne Reilly was there to greet him when he set foot on American soil. Hutton did not hesitate in asking her to marry him that very day but he made her make one solemn promise.

'Hutt told Anne she had to read up on all the Catholic writings on birth control and the marriage vows before they could wed,' explained Ed Stinson.

Once again, the Hutton Gibson black-or-white philosophy prevailed. Life was uncompromising, not to mention the fact that he made it clear he would only marry a virgin – an attitude he appears to have passed down to many of his children, including Mel.

The happy couple were married in a simple ceremony at the church of Our Lady of Good Counsel in Brooklyn, on the morning of 1 May 1944.

'We're going to have ten children,' announced Hutton with a mischievous smile to the assembled guests. Just like every word he ever speaks, Hutton meant it.

A few weeks before his wedding, Hutton had taken a job on the New York Central Railroad. Strange career choice for a well-educated man from a fine middle-class background, but the wages were better than average and that would give Hutton the freedom to start the family he longed to raise.

The newlyweds set up home in a large sunny apartment near 212th Street, Manhattan. It was a fine, safe area and Hutton felt that, for the first time in his life, things were going his way. Both he and Anne were thrilled when their first child, Patricia, was born on April Fool's Day in 1945. Anne was just 24 years old when that baby was born – almost 20 years younger than Hutton's tragic mother had been when she gave birth to him. He was determined that he and Anne would live to enjoy the growing up of all the children they were planning to have. So far, everything had gone precisely to plan.

More babies followed with the sort of regularity that alarmed friends and colleagues but delighted Anne and Hutton. There was Sheila, then Mary, Kevin and Maura Louise.

Wisely, Hutton decided that the city was no place to bring up an ever-growing family so they moved 30 miles north of the city to Croton-on-Hudson. It was a quiet, friendly little community and Hutton managed to transfer to working on the freight trains travelling to and from the huge Croton-Harmon railroad yard. With the arrival of baby number four, Kevin, Hutton's family soon outgrew their small, one-storey home so they headed for the peaceful hamlet of Verplanck nearby.

Verplanck's Point, to give it its full name, is one of several historic villages on the eastern bank of the Hudson River, settled by the Dutch in the late seventeenth century. Nestled on the banks of this vast river, with the shadow of Dunderberg Mountain and its cliff-edge roads to the north and other mountains to the south, it is hard to imagine that the sprawling metropolis of New York lies just 40 miles to the south.

This now predominantly Irish–Italian town looks across the

river to Tomkins Cove and Stony Point. It is girdled by thick forest and, during winter, snow-clad roads and lush pastures have definite picture-postcard appeal. Winter in these parts is by far the longest season and the Gibsons spent many months huddled in front of their one and only fireplace while the dozen or so streets in Verplanck remained deserted for much of the day and night.

Home was a modest, shingled, one-storey house on Seventh Street. The property was right next to the entrance to the Sun Oil Company depot, which meant that a steady procession of heavy tanker trucks thundered past the Gibson front door, day and night.

Hutton's outgoings at this time were rapidly overtaking his salary, yet it would take a tragedy long after the birth of five more children finally to help him realise his true potential.

TWO

I DON'T GO IN FOR PERSONAL HEROES BUT
I DO HAVE ONE – MY OLD MAN. MY ADMIRATION FOR
HIM CANNOT BE MEASURED.

'A son to Mr and Mrs Hutton Gibson, of Verplanck, at the Peekskill Hospital, 4.45pm, January 3.'

It was a simple announcement, typical of Hutton. No fuss, plain and to the point. The year was 1956 and the births column of the *Peekskill Evening Star* (cost 5 cents) the following day contained only one other announcement. The paper's front page revealed vital up-to-the-minute news such as the fractured wrist suffered by nine-year-old Diane Wyatt and the ten stitches required by ten-year-old Anne Mason after she put her arm through a window.

Hutton Gibson whisked Anne and latest arrival Mel away from hospital in the family's scruffy blue station wagon just a day after the birth. 'They never had good cars and, often, whatever one they did have would be broken down and they'd all have to walk,' recalled family friend Ed Stinson.

And, as the family grew, it became more and more taxing to

fit mother, father and the children all in the car at the same time. Then there was Hutton Gibson's professed distrust of the medical profession. Mainly fuelled by the high cost of medicine in the United States, it was also influenced by a natural suspicion about non-Catholic doctors and a reluctance to part with any of his hard-earned cash.

The end result of this was that Hutton shovelled vitamin pills into his children at an astonishing daily rate. He also tried to grow organic vegetables. He firmly believed that, by keeping his children fit, he could avoid doctors completely.

'In all the years I knew them, I never saw a doctor at the house. That is pretty amazing when you raise that number of kids,' Ed Stinson points out.

This obsession with vitamin pills is yet another habit that Hutton passed down to Mel, who swallows at least 30 different brands each day. He even made a commercial for American television, for free, to tell viewers that vitamins are healthy.

In January 1956, Mel was baptised at St Patrick's in Verplanck by Reverend Monsignor Daniel Dougherty. He was christened Mel Columbcille Gerard Gibson.

Columbcille – pronounced 'Colum-kill' – is the name of the rural diocese in Ireland where Mel's mother was born. Columba of Iona – sometimes called Columbcille – is one of the best-loved Irish saints, a descendant of Niall, the first high king of Ireland. Gerard is for Saint Gerard, an Italian saint of the eighteenth century, the patron saint of expectant mothers, to whom Anne Gibson prayed each time she was expecting another child.

And it wasn't long before her constant prayers were answered. She provided Mel with four younger brothers and sisters – twins Danny and Chris, Donal and Ann. The house in Verplanck was becoming a bit of a tight squeeze to say the least, so Hutton – already working 16-hour shifts on the railroad – set about extending the property, single-handedly. It was mid-July and seemingly the correct time to be ripping the roof off to enlarge the attic. The only problem was that the Gibson clan had nowhere else to stay, so they slept under the stars – literally.

Then Hutton Gibson went off to work in New York City one evening, leaving Anne and the ten children roofless in Verplanck. Good friend and neighbour Ed Stinson takes up the story.

'Early one morning, a huge clap of thunder woke me up. It began raining buckets and I knew the kids were there alone with their mother. I jumped in my car and got down to the house as fast as I could. The house was flooding and all the kids – big and little – were running around with pots trying to catch the water, but they were fighting a losing battle.

'I pulled them all out and took them to my office nearby and got some tarpaulins to put over what was left. But there was a lot of damage.'

Now some wives might have been really annoyed at their husbands leaving them in the lurch like that – but not Anne Gibson. She had, according to Ed Stinson, an inborn gift for 'riding the tide'. He says, 'Anne went along with practically everything Hutt said. It takes a good woman to go through something like that and come up laughing, but Anne did. We always laugh about that experience.'

Predictably, the stresses and strains of living a hand-to-mouth existence with ten children did fire Hutton Gibson's temper at times. Forty years ago, child abuse was a term restricted to battering and sexual molestation. The rule of the stick was common in most households and there was certainly nothing illegal (or even immoral) about inflicting corporal punishment on a child who misbehaved. These days, it sometimes seems as if shouting at your child in the street can spark a child abuse charge.

Ed Stinson recalls, 'Hutt was very, very strict with his family. He had them toeing the mark the whole time. He was a stern person. When he had to do his duty, he was right there as far as discipline was concerned. But they still adored him. Believe me, he was not bashful at dusting them off. He let them know every now and again if they were being bad. Hutt believed in the power of the hand. If the children did not behave, they got hit. But he also believed he was doing it for the good of the family.'

More than 20 years later, Mel admitted that he was a chip off the old block, saying that sometimes he smacks his own children to make them behave. This was yet another example of the influence that his father has had on him.

Life in Verplanck sounds very insular by today's standards. Hutton the old-time religionist naturally banned all television in the house and comics were hidden under mattresses like contraband for fear that father Gibson might find them and let fly with his explosive temper.

The children were brought up on a staple diet of reading the classics. Cursing was strictly forbidden and punishable with a right-hander. Smoking and drinking were (and still are) considered two of the deadliest sins. Human nature has ensured that nearly all the Gibson offspring – including Mel – have enjoyed their fair share of booze and cigarettes over the years.

'I never saw Hutt have a drink, ever. Even at Christmas, there was no alcohol in the house,' says Ed Stinson. In fact, the most popular beverage in the Gibson household was tea.

By all accounts, the children excelled at amusing themselves. There were few toys in the Gibson household. Hutton laid the law down partly because he could not afford to buy many possessions but also because he distrusted the outside, materialistic world and all its 'evil' influences.

But there was a downside to his overbearing personality. While Christmas sounded a solemn affair, birthdays seem to have been positively depressing occasions. 'They got a cake and that was it,' says Ed Stinson. 'Virtually no presents. That was Hutton's way.'

There was another underlying motive for this apparent obsession with not enjoying oneself. Hutton was a very tight-fisted fellow, and was seriously stretched financially. Some years ago, Hutton, mellowed with age and free of the cashflow problems associated with bringing up such a large family, made a candid confession that he is so mean he 'can squeeze an American dime until the Indian on one side ends up riding the buffalo on the other side',

Back in Verplanck, the Gibsons' social life was bounded by church, school and family. Occasionally, they would visit relatives in Brooklyn. Movies were a very rare occurrence. Hutton Gibson's strict regime meant that films were out of bounds for the most part.

Sometimes, if the kids were well behaved and did their homework, they were allowed to go round to a school pal's home to watch *The Mickey Mouse Club* on television. But that tended to be a treat given, on the most part, after Hutton had set off for a nightshift on the railroad. He would most certainly not have approved of such hedonistic behaviour from his offspring.

Vacations just did not exist in the Gibson household; too many kids and not enough money. However, the surrounding countryside in Upstate New York was the backdrop for many juvenile adventures – swimming in the river, sledging on nearby hillsides, skating and ice hockey on the lake, walks through the forest. And, despite their lack of spare cash, Anne

Gibson managed to keep herself and her family well fed – in fact, by today's standards, some of the children would undoubtedly be classified as overweight. But then Mom liked eating as well as cooking.

'Anne was not what you would call thin,' explained Ed Stinson. 'She took up two seats whenever the family went out in their automobile.'

Even Mel at the age of five was hardly wasting away. His chunky physique more than made up for his lack of inches. And it wasn't until his early twenties and fame had struck that he managed to lose weight – which he proudly tells friends he has never regained since.

'We always had enough to eat. My mother would stuff us full of Irish soda bread, flan with raisins, or stews, pies and hotpots,' said Mel many years later.

Margaret Smith Saladino was Mel's first babysitter when she was a 16-year-old schoolgirl in Verplanck. She remembers the family vividly. 'It was not long after Mel was born, but he was always giggling and smiling even then. My mom was great friends with the Gibsons. They were always pitching in like big families do and my younger sister Eileen was close friends with Patricia.'

To most of the residents of Verplanck, the Gibsons are unforgettable for two notable reasons: the unusual size of the family and their overt religious beliefs. 'They were a very strong family unit. I think their religious faith kept them very close,' Margaret believes.

Her sister Eileen, Patricia's special friend, has even fonder memories of Mel. 'Mel was always my favourite … I don't know why. Probably because of his personality. He was kind of a happy-go-lucky kid. All smiles. The kind of kid you enjoy having around. He may have been kind of a little devil, but he was the sort who could get away with it because he was so cute.'

There seems little doubt that Mel's mischievous ways were signalling something special, even in Verplanck. 'He was like a comedian, always doing different kinds of comic things, making fun of this or that. Mel was very smart, sharp as a tack ... and he was a little devil,' says Aunt Kathleen.

Mel loved to act the clown, even when aged just five. He adored entertaining anyone who happened to be around, with fake falls from scooters and bikes and by walking into doors and walls. He was a disciple of his favourites, the Three Stooges, without knowing about them. Sometimes, his brothers and sisters would try and emulate his pratfalls.

'But they were never as good as Mel,' chuckles Ed Stinson. 'If he made you smile, or laugh, he was happy. There was never any malice in Mel's heart and I don't think there ever will be.'

Years later, Mel confirmed, 'Of course I enjoy entertaining people. I have been doing that since I was little. You know how little kids do it. They love the attention – especially if they come from a big family. I used to get a kick out of affecting people, no matter what sort of effect. That is what drives you on.'

Many members of the Gibson clan look on their 11 years in Verplanck as the happiest times of their lives. But for Hutton Gibson, that timespan represented an intensely hard period of work on the railroad during which he strove to keep the family unit afloat, financially. Finally, he became a freight conductor.

In the spring of 1961, Hutton announced to his family and friends that he had found the perfect property among the white wooden houses and picket fences of Mount Vision, a community of just a few thousand nestled in the high country between mountains and lakes, almost 200 miles north of New

York. So the family set off in their newly purchased bone-shaker of a Volkswagen van for a better life.

The farmhouse itself was a picturesque, two-storey, double-fronted property with more rooms and space than any of the Gibson children had imagined living in. Ten acres of wilderness backed on to the main building. The site looked down on to the village of Laurens, three miles across a small valley, and the little-used Highway 205. The hamlet was exactly halfway between the bustling towns of Oneonta and Cooperstown, in a stretch of unspoiled landscape. To Hutton Gibson, this was paradise, the sort of place he had been looking for to fulfil his dreams since those distant days when he promised himself he would some day have a huge, happy family.

One of the first problems encountered by the Gibsons was the sheer solitude of life in Mount Vision. Hutton would take off at dawn most Mondays in the Volkswagen van for work on the railroad and, more often than not, end up sleeping over weekdays at his sister-in-law's in New York City, only returning late Friday to his family.

With Anne unable to drive, this left her and the children completely stranded. Even Anne's easygoing nature found it hard to accept that this was, as Hutton claimed, a better life. Just a visit to the village store was a major operation and, with all those mouths to feed three times a day, she spent much of her time on the winding road down to Mount Vision.

Luckily, a steady stream of visiting relatives and friends broke the monotony, but other children were struck by the lack of activities at the rambling house. There were no horses to ride, no motorbikes to explore the hilly trails. Some of the Gibson clan did not even own bicycles.

But Mel and his five older brothers and sisters did manage to take younger visitors over to some of the swimming holes in nearby Ostego Creek and, in those days, youngsters could safely thumb a ride into the village to buy sticks of penny candy.

The back yard was soon filled with home-grown vegetables, but Anne never had enough left over to store in the barn. The children tended to gobble them up the moment they were ripe for the picking.

Mel was happy as a sandboy when he joined sisters Sheila, Mary B, Maura and brother Kevin on the school bus to Laurens School each morning. It wasn't a Catholic school, much to Hutton's disappointment, but it was really the only option in an area with little choice.

Mrs Evelyn Koelliker was Mel's first-grade teacher, followed by Mrs Katherine Sapatek in the second and Mrs Zelma Ainslie (now Shapely) in the third. 'He was a very bright youngster. Actually, all the children were,' said Mrs Shapely.

Sports teacher Pat Grasso held a forty-minute group games session at the school every day when all the youngsters played kickball, relay races and catching. His memories of the little Mel are dim, but Hutton Gibson made a lasting impression on him. 'His father was most concerned about some of the teaching in the school. He seemed to expect there to be more religious instruction. Frankly, he could be quite a pain,' recalled Grasso.

On Sunday, 7 October 1962, just a few weeks after entering his new school, Mel received his first Holy Communion at the small Holy Cross Catholic Church in the nearby community of Morris. Hutton had fastidiously assessed all the Catholic churches in the area before finding one that lived up to his high standards. He was obsessed with making sure they did not encroach on any of the High Mass observations and ritual to which he strictly adhered.

During his reconnaissance mission to locate the finest Catholic church, he became painfully aware that Upstate New

York was overwhelmingly Republican and Protestant. The political part he could easily live with; his own beliefs appear to border on extreme conservatism. But the virulent dislike of the Catholic Church was deeply offensive and very disturbing to Hutton. He had earlier ignored it when overhearing a 'friendly' neighbour in the local store refer to the 'Catholic invasion'. But clear evidence of religious discrimination was everywhere he looked.

The assassination of John F Kennedy on 22 November 1963 shocked the world. Yet in the communities around Mount Vision, some Protestants were actually celebrating the death of a Catholic President. Hutton's disillusionment with the United States was gradually building. When, in 1964, the Warren Commission report concluded that Lee Harvey Oswald had acted alone in killing the President, Hutton was not the only American citizen who began to question the direction his country was taking.

He read with disdain in August that year how Lyndon Johnson had decided to escalate the war in Vietnam after North Vietnamese torpedo boats allegedly attacked the US destroyers *Maddox* and *Turner Joy*. For all Hutton's conservative beliefs, he could not condone war. He had seen the horrors of battle at first hand.

Further, all the Gibsons' close family and friends knew that the family's dream life on the farm was not going according to plan. 'They'd gone to a place where you really couldn't do much. It was very, very hard, with Red working on the railroad down here [in New York City] and Anna and the children being alone during the week up there,' explained Aunt Kathleen.

At 12.30am on the morning of 11 December 1964, Hutton Gibson was going about his work as usual aboard engine No. 8595 as it waited in the Croton-on-Hudson railroad yard. Another arduous week was coming to an end and he was looking forward to returning home to Mount Vision for a welcome sojourn with the family. He did not see the pool of oil on the engine floor until it was too late. He slipped and fell heavily on to the railroad roadbed and lay there unable to move. Spasms of agonising pain were stabbing through his back.

Fellow workers rushed to help him to his feet, but he could not move. Eventually, paramedics arrived and took him to a nearby hospital for overnight observation. There were genuine fears that he might have broken his back in the fall. Hutton Gibson's long ordeal had only just begun.

It wasn't until just before dawn the following day that Anne Gibson got a phone call from a railroad colleague of Hutton's. The news wasn't good at all.

A myelogram – an X-ray procedure in which the outline of the spinal cord and the space surrounding it can be seen – revealed that Hutton had sustained various spinal injuries, including herniated lumbar discs. A series of painful operations followed. A laminectomy was performed to help ease the injury to the spinal cord. This involved an agonising procedure during which the spinal canal is opened by the removal of the posterior wall. Hutton also had to endure the spinal fusion of one of his discs, and this was in addition to the whiplash injury of the cervical spine which resulted in arthritis and degenerative changes.

Much more anguish was to follow. For more than three years, the New York Central Railroad refused to admit responsibility for the accident and fought Hutton's claims for reparation.

Throughout these difficult times, Papa Gibson did not once lose faith in God. If anything, he increased his involvement in the church while accepting that he had to sell the Mount

Vision farmhouse and rent a cheaper place nearer the city. Evidently, difficult times were ahead, but neither Anne nor the children were heartbroken by the move. They were armoured in Hutton's belief that fate had dealt a cruel blow but that everything would be for the best in the end.

They found a huge, ramshackle house across the river from Verplanck in Salisbury Mills at a peppercorn rent. It was in a decrepit state, but its lakeside site made up for that in many ways. The children spent untold hours swimming in the lake, and their landlords, the Seamans, let them take boats out on it for fishing. The lake froze in winter and child skaters congregated from a five-mile radius. Hutton Gibson might have lost his job, but still he gave his brood a lifestyle fit to make many wealthier youngsters envious. Most importantly, they were still one happy family.

Rugged, hilly Salisbury Mills lies between two hulking mountain ranges and local weather had a nasty habit of scourging the area with violent, tree-shedding thunderstorms. But climatic tantrums were the least of the Gibsons' concerns. Somehow, they had to exist on little or no income.

'They were practically starving. Whatever we could do, we did, but we could do very little,' explained Aunt Kathleen.

Ed Stinson affirms, 'They were almost destitute during that time in Salisbury Mills.'

Not only was Hutton's spine seriously injured, so was his pride and self-image as a hard worker capable of any hardship or sacrifice in the campaign to provide for his family. Now he was disabled, possibly permanently, and unable to function as breadwinner and staunch guardian.

Mel's two elder sisters, having finished high school, found jobs to help the family survive. One became a library assistant and the other worked in a newspaper office at nearby Newburgh. Anne longed to venture out and get a job, but caring for ten children was a full-time occupation. In any case, Hutton would never dream of allowing his wife to work. The other youngsters – including Mel – attended school in Washingtonville, where Hutton again managed to find a Catholic church called St Mary's that conformed to his high standards. There, on 22 May 1965, Mel was confirmed.

Witnessing the service were Mel's older sister Patricia and brother Kevin. They had just announced to a delighted mother and father that they were entering strict religious orders. Kevin was to go to a seminary near Newburgh and Patricia to become a novice at a convent near Albany. Already, the teachings of Papa Hutton had obviously had a profound effect on two of his children.

Meanwhile, with his wife and children's encouragement, he sent off a letter to *Jeopardy*, the high-stakes quiz show in New York City. The whole family had never forgotten how, some years earlier, Hutton had won a few hundred dollars on another local quiz programme.

A few weeks later, Hutton swept the board on *Jeopardy*, answering a barrage of questions thrown at him by host Art Fleming, and walked off with winnings of several thousand dollars. The family had by this time got one tiny black-and-white TV set, which they crowded around and cheered each time their father came on the small screen. At the *Jeopardy* championship final some time later, Hutton went all the way and won $21,000. It could not have come at a better time for the Gibsons as they were on the verge of being evicted from their home for non-payment of the minimal rent.

But Hutton was a realistic type of fellow. Despite his family's joy, he knew he could not feed and clothe them for ever on quiz show winnings and he was well aware that his battle with the railroad would end with a settlement or the sack (most likely both). So, shortly after marching victoriously off the set of *Jeopardy*, he visited the New York Rehabilitation Center in Newburgh to be assessed for a new career. The results of an IQ test were astounding. He was pronounced a genius and encouraged to enrol in the then new and arcane field of computer programming.

Computer school on Fourteenth Street in Manhattan was a breath of fresh air for Hutton. He had begun a new career in his mid-forties and with it came a new lease of life. But there was still one cloud looming – the court case about the accident.

After three years and two months of struggling to support his family, the case of *Hutton P Gibson v The New York Central* finally came to trial at the Westchester County Court House in White Plains. Presiding was Judge John J Dillon and representing Hutton was Anthony Ferraro, of the law firm Ferraro, Lombardi and Decaro. Hutton's Catholic tastes even stretched as far as his choice of lawyer.

Figures approaching $2 million were mentioned initially, as Ferraro revealed there had been a recent flare-up of his client's injuries. But when the trial ended after seven days, on Valentine's Day 1968, the jury awarded Hutton $145,000. Even after paying a big chunk for attorney's fees, there was enough for them to settle their debts and make the biggest decision of their life – to emigrate to Australia.

Hutton, as usual, had thought long and hard about this move to his mother's homeland. But it wasn't just family ties that were luring him away from the United States; the Vietnam War was being fought out in horrifying conditions and Hutton's experiences in the last war had left him with a lasting obsession – to avoid sending his own children off to die in battle.

Years later, Mel – who has played more than his share of war heroes in his time – was candid in revealing the motivation behind his father's decision. 'My older brother was about to get drafted and my father didn't want to send his sons out to get jungle rot and worse. He didn't want to have to send us off one by one to get chopped up.'

Intriguingly, Patricia and Kevin immediately withdrew from their religious orders and insisted on travelling with the rest of the clan to Australia. Not even their vocations could snap the extraordinary bond uniting the Gibsons.

The family's final Stateside day was, by all accounts, a solemn occasion. Gibson relatives and friends gathered for a picnic lunch at Aunt Kathleen's house outside New York. This was no vacation, but emigration and a parting of unknown duration, which accounted for the low-key partying. Hutton, Anne and their brood were in great shape, however; wherever they wandered, they were secure in each other.

Instead of flying direct to Australia, Hutton organised stopovers, turning the life-changing journey into a virtual world tour. He was frugal but never cheap, so this was a startling but not uncharacteristic move. Severing his roots and taking ten children across the globe did not daunt him in the slightest. They were Good People, after all, so what could go wrong?

THREE

WHENEVER THEY USED TO HAVE RAFFLES AT HOME,
I WAS THE GUY WHO WON THE TURTLE. AND WHEN
MY PARENTS TOOK US TO IRELAND FOR A FAMILY
VACATION, WALKING DOWN THE STREETS OF BRAY,
I USED TO FIND POUND NOTES AND STUFF. I WAS
ALWAYS FINDING MONEY.

In her capacity as mother, Anne Gibson had always been of warm heart and easygoing disposition, but amid the customary chaos at Rome's busy Leonardo da Vinci Airport, she was close to panic stations.

Nowadays, Anne might be castigated in the papers for neglecting her son. At the time, the child in question was Mel Gibson. All 12 in the family were about to board a plane for Australia, the final destination of their world tour and the place they intended to settle in – when it became clear that 12-year-old Mel was not among them. A frantic search eventually discovered a smiling Mel in the men's restroom.

'I knew you'd find me so I stayed put,' Mel said.

Even the friendly airline clerk looked shocked as she flicked through the tickets presented at the check-in gate by Hutton Gibson that sunny day in late October 1968.

'Ten children? Mamma mia!'

Papa Gibson beamed. He had grown increasingly proud of his clan during their three-month world trip on the way to Australia. Their first port of call after leaving New York on (aptly) American Independence Day, 4 July, had been Ireland.

Where else? For this trip was as much a pilgrimage to Catholicism as it was an adventurous trek to far-off places. In Ireland and Scotland, the Gibsons visited the birthplaces of both Anne and Hutton's relatives. They were understandably proud of their Gaelic heritage and they wanted the children to understand precisely where they came from.

The family spent a few days in England, but it was not the highlight of their world tour. Anne Gibson felt uncomfortable among a nation whose citizens had broken down front doors in her home village of Marley, County Longford, more than 40 years earlier.

All the Gibsons agreed that the highlight of the trip was the visit to the Vatican, world capital of the Roman Catholic Church. To Hutton and Anne, this was the ultimate pilgrimage. They and the children spent many days praying and attending daily masses. To the older Gibson children, like Patricia, then 23, Sheila, 21, Mary, 20, Kevin, 18, and Maura, 14, Rome was a real eye-opener. Cheeky Italian waiters would constantly be trying to chat up the girls and Kevin had never seen such beautiful women in his life.

Stuck in the middle were Mel and the twins Daniel and Christopher. The terrible threesome played countless pranks on their brothers and sisters, but they must have wished they had been just a few years older, fully to appreciate the sights and sounds of a city that never sleeps.

'MEET THE GIBSONS – ALL 12 OF THEM' was the headline accompanying a king-size photo of Hutton and his clan in the Melbourne *Herald* on 4 November 1968. The family had been talked into posing for an airport press photographer who could see that their pilgrimage across the globe was worthy of a piece in the local newspaper.

'So you think YOU have trouble keeping your children within spanking distance ...', read the article. It went on to describe Hutton as an 'American computer programmer' and quoted him as saying, 'I thought Australia offered pretty good opportunities for me and my children.'

After visiting all of Australia's main cities, Hutton decided that Sydney was the best place to set up home. This thriving metropolis still has a fairly relaxed atmosphere, with its abundance of clean, sandy beaches north and south of the city. The Gibsons fell in love with Sydney's beautiful harbour, complete with spotless hydrofoils and regular commuter ferries chugging across the calm waters of the bay. They were mesmerised by the beautiful tropical plants and red-tiled roofs of the rows of Victorian terraced houses often overshadowed by brilliantly coloured, purplish-blue jacaranda trees.

It all seemed a million miles away from those long cold winters in Upstate New York. Here, the climate was warm for most of the year and gardens often housed parakeets and other exotic birds.

Hutton swiftly found a property in the Mount Kuring-gai area just north of the city and set about finding schools for his younger children. For Mel Gibson, one of the most miserable periods in his life was about to begin.

As an American in Australia, Mel was something of an oddity and he hated the fact that many people could not understand a word he said. But, worse than that, his father had found a good, old-fashioned Catholic boys' school – run more along the lines of a prisoner of war camp than an educational establishment.

St Leo's College was located in the quiet, leafy suburb of

Wahroonga and run by a group of Catholic priests known as the Christian Brothers. Outside the school gates were pleasant detached homes occupied by bankers, doctors and lawyers. But inside St Leo's, a spirit-crushing regime ruled, and Mel, used to the more gentle school system in Upstate New York, was having a very rough time.

To start with, he felt a complete idiot dressed up in the school uniform of straw boater and blazer with grey flannel trousers. St Leo's prided itself on being run on the same lines as the fee-paying British public school system. It should also be stated quite clearly now that St Leo's links with the Christian Brothers were broken some years ago and it is now a standard – and respected – private school for boys and girls.

Then there was the constant teasing by the other boys, anxious to assert their superiority over the 'Yank'. Within days, Mel was getting into regular scraps with his classmates, leading to horrendous beatings from teachers that have emotionally scarred him to this day. 'I got picked on because of my accent. I hated that school,' said Mel many years later, but still with a trace of bitterness.

As with many unhappy children, Mel soon shed his shyness and became a troublemaker in the eyes of his teachers – all of whom were allowed to use the strap on students whenever necessary.

Classmate Mark McGinnity says that Mel was so unhappy at St Leo's that he would deliberately seek to antagonise the teachers. Three boys, including himself and Mel, even devised a bizarre competition to see who could get the most strappings in one day from a maths teacher who bore the brunt of much of Mel's outrageous behaviour.

'Mel won easily. He annoyed this teacher so much by copying his mannerisms and mimicking his voice that he ended up being strapped 27 times. Mel was crazy.'

Mel later admitted to a friend, Deborah Foreman, that he was very deeply affected by his experiences at St Leo's. 'Mel said the priests were very mean,' she remembers. 'He thought they were wrong in their teachings and he said they were very brutal and the teachers were not properly trained.'

Aged just 13, Mel's misery at school soon manifested itself when he took up smoking and drinking beer. During one memorable week, Mel was caught smoking in the school toilets every single day and was duly strapped on the bottom on each occasion. Mel even started to think seriously about becoming a priest and entering a seminary. Anything had to be better than than the hell he was suffering at St Leo's.

But, throughout all this pain and anguish, Mel still managed to come out smiling. He showed grim determination not to be beaten by the system. And through all the beatings and teasing, Mel continued his pranks. They were a release from all the inner tension of life at St Leo's. 'I used to spend my time trying to get one over on the teachers, pulling pranks. I would walk along normally one moment, the next falling down pretending I was dead,' he says.

Sometimes, Mel would pretend he'd lost an arm, walking around the school all day with it tucked up the back of his school blazer. Other days, he would adopt a Scottish accent and talk loudly all day. Years later, he admitted, 'I wasn't bright at school but I'm no fool – I just didn't like it.'

And neither did Hutton Gibson. But his dislike of St Leo's had nothing to do with his son's unhappiness. Papa Gibson was most concerned by the fact that the Christian Brothers were not a particularly vigorous religious order. The priests who ran the school may have sanctioned the use of non-stop corporal punishment, but they did fail to make the boys attend mass every day and that bothered Hutton Gibson immensely.

'He came to the school one day in a real mood. He was most unhappy about the way his son was being taught religion,' explained Eileen Leiden, St Leo's school secretary at the time.

Hutton Gibson had taken the law into his own hands. That black-or-white philosophy he has preached throughout his life was being demonstrated yet again. But then Mel was hardly complaining about his father's intervention. He was delighted to be getting away from the straw boaters, strappings and sinister teachers of St Leo's.

And once Hutton resolved that Mel would be better off at the local state school and being taught religion at home, the teenager reckoned that perhaps Australia wasn't such a bad place after all. At the Asquith High School, Mel encountered the same sort of 'Yank' taunts, but this time he decided to retort with his fists and it soon gained him wary respect.

'He threw a few real punches and scruffed a few of the boys who had given him a verbal bashing. We had to pull him into line several times a week,' says Ken Coleby, a senior prefect at Asquith during Mel's early days there.

'Mel had a controllable energy, was stocky and not easily intimidated. A couple of meeker teachers were horrified and thought Mel was too outrageous for his boots.'

And the star himself has agreed. 'I was considered a bit of a larrikin, and a bad influence.'

Mel was soon performing his stunts. This time, the model for his pratfalls was the late, great Peter Sellers. 'He could move very quickly towards a door and seemingly collide with it with a head-splitting sound, a crunch, and fall prostrate to the floor or ground,' says Ken Coleby. 'He was as good as Peter Sellers. Incredibly co-ordinated.'

Another, slightly more disturbing habit was Mel's very convincing impersonation of a head-butt. It enhanced his reputation as 'a bit of a devil'.

But there were no overtly or offensively effeminate teachers at Asquith. It was every boy for himself and Mel soon adapted his accent to Australian, buckled down to work (sort of) and immediately began to find life much easier. He even acquired a prophetic nickname – 'Mad Mel' – after an American disc jockey on Sydney Radio, who for reasons known only to himself and the station management always appeared with a hood over his head.

But Ken Coleby says that Mel 'showed he could mix it with the best and his schoolwork improved, too. I guess he was a rebel in most ways but also did his work at the desk.'

Anne, meanwhile, was getting broody again. Intensely maternal, she was now too old to have children, and 30 years of meal-making and nappy-changing were about to become history. The kids were either grown up or away at school each day, and she had no career to revive.

Her sadness and sense of imminent loss may have been sharpened by Hutton's renaissance. Fully recovered from his catastrophic accident, he was making a living in a good job and even managed to get on to some Australian TV quiz shows.

His wife realised that only one thing would make her happy again – another child. Anne had made a secret vow to St Gerard, motherhood's patron saint, that, if they arrived safely in Australia, she would adopt an infant. So, little more than a year after settling in Sydney, nine-month-old Andrew became the eleventh junior member of the Gibson household. Anne was fulfilled once more.

Recalls one of Mel's friends, 'He told me his mother simply could not understand how people could *not* love children. They meant so much to her.'

Anne became wrapped up with the new arrival, and Hutton Gibson found an equally absorbing, fulfilling pursuit – he went to war against the Holy See. As a die-hard Roman

Catholic traditionalist, he detonated fiery debate among Australia's Catholic clergy.

During the late 1960s, Hutton was shocked by the introduction and spread of the so-called 'new order' mass. Implacably opposed to compromise, fudging (and, perhaps, progress in most forms), he was certain that the new style of service was 'neo-Protestant' and of dubious validity. Hutton Gibson therefore began writing campaigning, temperature-raising letters to fellow traditionalists throughout the world, and considered heading an Australian branch of 'old-school' Catholicism.

He was driven by a burning conviction that the mass should always be in Latin, not the vernacular, as was then becoming more commonly the case. Within two years of arriving in Australia, Hutton was secretary of the Latin Mass Society, and Hutton's growing involvement with the society disturbed some of his friends, particularly the fact that Hutton expected all his children to support his views. Mel, even in his middle teens, seemed to be completely spellbound by his father's ideals. Even today, he does nothing to distance himself from what his father has been fighting for.

'Mel is highly respectful of his parents. He really looks up to his father. He felt that Hutton was a very godly father and he respects that deeply. Really, he has modelled himself on his father. Mel can even recite prayers in Latin like his father. He was always saying how wonderful his dad was and how he was taking on the Catholic Church and would challenge people,' recalled one of Mel's former girlfriends.

Hutton's opinions on Communists and Zionists are extreme. They include an open reference to the then Pope's 'Jewish connections'– based solely on the fact that he was occasionally photographed wearing the *ephod*, the robes and vestments symbolising Jewish high priesthood. Often, Mel's father would refer his children to these pictures of the Pope as positive evidence that the Pontiff was in league with the 'dangerous' Jews. Such attitudes would surface strongly again in Mel's film released in 2004, *The Passion of the Christ*, in which the involvement of the Jews in the build-up to the crucifixion formed a significant part of the action.

Hutton's most extreme action against the 'degradation' of the Catholic Church, as he saw it, was launched in 1975 when, as the head of a 1,000-strong group, Hutton broke away from the main Catholic body to celebrate their cherished 'outlawed' mass in secret locations around the city. These included Papa Gibson's living room. He gave his children specially recorded tapes as a basis for their religious observances. Thus they could be taught the essentials of Catholicism without crossing the threshold of any recognised church.

Within months, he added 'author' to his list of accomplishments, though the book Hutton wrote was not designed for bestsellerdom. *Paul's Legacy: Catholicism?* is a long rant about his traditionalist movement. In a single sentence, Hutton crystallises his stance towards life in general: 'How do you know you're right when so many in authority disagree with you?' By implication, if you are Hutton Gibson, supremely confident in the justice of your cause, faith is impervious to disagreement.

Throughout the theological jousting, with its faint overtone of a Resistance movement, Anne and the rest of the family gave the patriarch their full support. In turn, he expected them to read every word of the regular newsletters he was composing for his splinter group, the Australian Alliance for Catholic Tradition, which he formed after being axed as Secretary of the Latin Mass Society.

Ed Stinson received one from Hutton dated December 1990, entitled 'Our Greatest Crime is Silence'. It is headlined

'THE WAR IS *NOW*!' and has Hutton's name and address printed on the cover. In it, he talks in conspiratorial terms about Spaniards and Catholics who were secret Jews and claims that Jews have infiltrated almost every religion in the world. He claims that Jews have tried to destroy the Catholic Church.

At home, the 14-year-old Mel adored and worshipped the ground that his parents walked on and knelt in prayer at least three times a day with the rest of his family. He knew the Bible backwards and he passionately backed his father's obsessive beliefs about the Catholic Church. But, away from the house, he had become a regular tearaway – smoking, drinking and beginning to think about women, of whom there was no shortage in Sydney. However, Mel's shyness, which he disguised by being aggressive at school, came back to haunt him whenever he was in the presence of females other than his mother and sisters.

He also kept up his friendship with Jeremy Connolly, a staunch ally and fellow sufferer from St Leo's PoW Camp. Both youths were painfully timid in many ways and would haunt snooker halls and milk bars in the Bondi Beach area, a haven for teenagers from all over Sydney.

Jeremy – taller and the more macho-looking of the two – would buy the beers in local pubs, then sneak outside with a pint mug for his pal. The two would then watch a procession of bikini-clad blondes strolling by seductively from the beach.

In those days on Bondi (and still, to a lesser extent, today), the girls went for the surfers. Unfortunately, Hollywood hero Mel was not a great surfer. Instead, the short and stocky teenager became more and more dependent on booze to fuel his social courage.

It wasn't until a few months after his fifteenth birthday, in the early part of 1971, that Mel actually plucked up the nerve to date a girl he met while out drinking with his pals.

'Wanna come to the flicks?' Mel mumbled the words as quickly as possible in the hope the girl in question would say yes immediately and then he could get back to his beer. The next day, shaking like a leaf, he just managed a lingering French kiss in the back row of his local cinema. Typically of Mel, though, he tried to play down the adolescent rite of passage, years later. 'It was not that exciting. I wondered what all the fuss was about. I was a really shy lad. It was hard asking girls out.'

In fact, Mel decided after that first date that it was much easier just to stick to hanging out with a group of mates all the time. That way he could avoid having to make conversation with girls on their own. It was the part he found hardest. A constant flow of wisecracks was not enough to keep a teenage girl content. She wanted warm, romantic conversation – something that Mel did not know anything about. Or want to know, one gathers.

'I was never a womaniser. I didn't have the right chat. I'd go all tongue-tied or say something embarrassing if a girl came near me,' says Mel now. But he certainly left a trail of broken hearts behind him.

Back home as a reserved, still highly religious teenager, Mel faced a grilling from Hutton about what career he would like to take up after school. Mel's initial thoughts of joining the priesthood had disappeared along with his taste for lemonade. Journalism had a vague appeal but Mel did not feel particularly keen on exposing other people's lives – something to which he would fall victim, a long way down the road.

Sitting in the living room with Mel and his father was older sister Sheila. Mel had always been her favourite and she was especially concerned about his future, even though she had by now married an Australian and had her own young family to worry about. She decided there and then that she would influence Mel's career decision, and filled in an application form for him, including his photo and $5 admission fee, then sent it off to Sydney's most prestigious school of dramatic art.

She had witnessed enough of her kid brother's pranks over the years to be convinced that he could one day make a wonderful actor. Sheila also knew that if she even bothered to mention it to Mel he would never get around to filling out an application form.

The Australian film industry was in the process of rising from the grave of obscurity where it had been for more than 40 years. Mel was about to ride to fame on the crest of its exuberant revival.

FOUR

YOU HAVE TO LEARN TO PLAY THE GAME – NOT BECAUSE
YOU WANT TO PLAY THE GAME, BUT BECAUSE YOU WANT
TO KNOW HOW TO BEAT IT.

M el was a tad irritated when he got a letter from the
National Institute of Dramatic Art, Sydney, telling
him that if he cared to go along for an audition, he would be
considered for a three-year acting course. After all, his sister
Sheila had not even bothered to tell him she was sending off
an application and acting was something he had never even
considered as a career.

But a gruelling three-month stint in an orange juice bottling
factory on the outskirts of Sydney convinced him that he had
to do something worthwhile, more interesting, so he
wandered along to NIDA for the audition. With his shoulder-
length hair and beard, Mel looked more like a juvenile hippy
than a would-be matinée idol. Appearances meant little to
him in those days. His attitude towards life was relaxed to the
extreme. He had been protected by a strong-willed father, a
warm and loving mother and five bossy older brothers and

sisters, every inch of the way. As a result, you could say that Mel lacked cold ambition. He knew that, if all else failed, he had his family to fall back on.

Ironically, it was this laid-back attitude that probably helped him get a place at NIDA more easily than most of his peers. For many students, this was make-or-break time during which their life's ambition to be a thespian would be realised. Many had pushy parents pressuring them to succeed no matter what. Others took their chosen career so seriously that they spent every waking hour reading plays and books and rehearsing for whatever class they had the next day.

Meanwhile, there was Mel – shy, vulnerable but completely unconcerned about whether he made it or not. That helped him immensely with the audition.

'They made us do all these silly things – improvise, sing, dance. I know I was terrible, but it seemed good then. I guess they saw something raw in me. I didn't really give a hoot. I thought, What's the rush? you know. Over the years, I'd got so good at pretending, convincing people I'd done my homework, that I already knew how to act,' he said years later and with wry, trademark modesty.

One friend from NIDA days remembers it slightly differently. 'While all the rest of us were taking it deadly seriously, Mel would stroll casually around college as if he did not have a care in the world.'

Another peer from NIDA, Monroe Reimers, described Mel as 'pretty gawky' throughout the first year at acting academy.

But it was attractive 18-year-old student Linda Newton who probably gained the best insight into the then 19-year-old Mel. Every day, she shared a ride in her father's car or a train journey to and from NIDA with Mel.

'We both lived in the upper north shore area so it was natural to share a ride,' says Linda, who became a successful actress, appearing in an Australian sitcom called *My Two Wives*.

But life at NIDA was anything but glamorous. The college consisted of a handful of prefabricated huts wedged between two University of New South Wales buildings on High Street, in the Sydney district of Kensington.

'They were more like accommodation cottages,' explained Linda. 'It was freezing in the winter and boiling in the summer.' Cockroaches and rats shared many classes with Mel and his fellow NIDA students. 'And when it rained, water poured through the leaking roof in our classroom,' Linda adds.

Mel was having real problems settling in. His tutors criticised him for being 'too cerebral', for not 'externalising' and 'keeping too much inside'. Now he admits it did not all come as naturally to him as it did to many of his fellow students. 'I found it difficult to break through the barriers and not feel ridiculous and uncomfortable.' And it took that first year before Mel, as he now says, 'started to like or enjoy acting. Enjoy it. Finally, NIDA was like another little world that I could get lost in.'

One of Mel's fellow students was a thin, pale, very nervy 20-year-old. Judy Davis has gone on to receive many acting awards, as well as Oscar nominations for her roles in *Husbands and Wives* and *A Passage to India*, proving to be one of the most famous acting talents to come out of Australia in recent times. Back in those days, Judy was best known because her lunches usually consisted of liquorice sticks and green apples. 'But Mel would eat anything,' explained Linda Newton. 'He was short, stocky and very good-natured.'

However, he was already using formidable natural acting abilities to hide his true feelings – he was miserable as hell working alongside all these very serious students. He felt inferior and, worst of all, he had so little money he could not even afford to go to the pub each evening and drown his sorrows.

'I didn't really like it to begin with. But I found it was something I couldn't let go of,' admitted Mel just after leaving NIDA.

The truth was that he had no idea why he was there in the first place. When one NIDA teacher went around the entire class asking each student why they wanted to be an actor, Mel stumbled over his reply because he did not know the answer.

To some of his fellow students, this complete lack of ambition was very frustrating, even annoying. And according to Linda Newton, Mel kept pulling regular practical jokes as a way of disguising his true feelings about NIDA. 'That light-hearted attitude did not always meet with the approval of his teachers or students. They saw him as someone who did not take his calling as an actor seriously and some even wondered what on earth he was doing at NIDA, anyway. And he continued hiding his face under a mass of hair.

As the hours in those scruffy prefab sheds accumulated, there developed an experimental element in some of the exercises carried out by the students at NIDA. Both Linda and Mel – by now good friends but 'definitely nothing more' – found themselves frowned upon when it came to taking part in one particular class. Linda explained, 'We had to pretend to be members of different Aboriginal tribes and walk about pretending to make things out of nothing. It was supposed to be creative, good for our imagination. But it was ridiculous!'

Mel would regularly collapse in fits of giggles after such exercises and then he and Linda would have a laugh about them on the way home that evening. Hardly the sort of behaviour one would expect from a budding thespian.

And, as Linda revealed, with the end of the first year rapidly approaching, there were serious doubts about who would actually be invited back to continue the course.

'We all knew they would probably keep Judy Davis and two others, but it was becoming clear that no one else was definitely going to be asked back.'

Mel, Linda and the others were all pulled into NIDA administrator Elizabeth Butcher's office and asked if they really wanted to be actors. Miraculously, both of them just slipped through the net and were offered places the following term.

'About half the students were not asked back. Well, Mel was not on the throwaway list, but I'm pretty sure he was on the "grey list" of those who were on a kind of probation for about the first six months of the second year,' says Linda now. 'I certainly wouldn't have picked Mel as one of the most talented in the class. He looked more like a surfie. Judy Davis, on the other hand, was always focused and determined – it was obvious she was destined for stardom.'

During the summer holidays, Mel plucked up the courage to announce to his closely knit family that he was planning to cut the umbilical cord and find a place to live. During those first few uncomfortable months at NIDA, he had rekindled the friendship with his old pal from those difficult days at St Leo's – Jeremy Connolly. Jeremy also toyed with the idea of being an actor, but as he recalled, 'It wasn't really for me.' Jeremy told Mel that his father owned an empty apartment in the King's Cross area of Sydney – a cosmopolitan district not dissimilar to New York's Greenwich Village. It sounded like the ideal place for him and Mel to live.

It was a big move for Mel. His mother and father had always prided themselves on keeping the family together and Hutton Gibson was particularly concerned that his son might let his Catholicism lapse under the influence of new-found, free-thinking actor friends.

Then there were all those other 'evil' temptations like drink, smoking and girls. By all accounts, Mel was managing to dabble in all three of these sins but he naturally did not want to confess this to his father.

And his incredible effect on women was about to cause him no end of grief – for the first but certainly not the last time in his life. A pretty young blonde in the year below him at NIDA just would not take 'no' for an answer from Mel.

'She was completely obsessed with him. She was just one of those impressionable type of girls,' recalled Linda Newton.

Why he rejected the girl is unclear but, according to fellow students, the two had a brief fling and she took things rather more seriously than Mel – something that was to happen on a number of future occasions.

'This girl would follow him everywhere,' explained Linda Newton.

Somehow, the woman in question got hold of a copy of the front door key to Mel and Jeremy's apartment in King's Cross. 'And every time Mel got home at night, she would be waiting there in bed for him,' added Linda.

Mel confessed to one friend at the time that he was completely panicked by the situation. 'Instead of sitting down with the girl and trying to work things out, he just ignored her. He just didn't know how to handle it.'

For the following few weeks, the girl continued shadowing Mel's every move. But, says Linda Newton, he claimed he had absolutely no idea why the girl was so besotted with him. 'He was not comfortable being chased by women. I think it must have had something to do with his background, and that situation with the woman letting herself into his flat was a very extreme example.'

None of Mel's classmates seems to know if Mel actually slept with the girl. But they all recalled how he openly joked about the situation. Once again, he was hiding his true feelings behind a mask of good humour. It was already becoming a reflex action.

Eventually, Mel and Jeremy found that life in King's Cross was less than restful. The long-running saga of the female stalker and the wilder aspects of living in such a crowded, colourful (and squalid, in patches) city area spurred them to move to the beach.

Mel asked his NIDA friends Monroe Reimers and Steve Bisley (who later starred with Mel in his first two films) if they wanted to share a flat with him and Jeremy. They jumped at the chance. From being the loner during his early schooldays, Mel now found it much easier to handle life if he surrounded himself with a group of friends.

The quartet soon found a run-down, four-bedroom house in Henderson Street, just a stone's throw from Bondi Beach. Mel was about to embark on a period that he possibly feels was the happiest of his life.

Steve Bisley – who became a close friend – recalled the first day they all went to see the house. 'It was due to be pulled down and looked like it. But the rent was cheap and we were really poor – so poor that we used to have credit running at the pizza place down the road!'

One night, Mel and Steve even staged a mock fight at the Astra pub in Bondi by falling over tables and chairs and then crashing down the stairs into the street. It was a typical bit of Mel Gibson tomfoolery, carried out because he had had a few beers and 'felt a bit bored'.

Bisley went on, 'This huge crowd gathered around and about three other fights started. We stopped ours and hot-footed it out of there just as the police paddy-wagon arrived!'

Linda Newton says the four Bondi flatmates 'were like a little gang of guys. They certainly had a good time and Mel was going out with lots of girls.'

Mel and his new pal Bisley became renowned keep-fit

fanatics at NIDA, despite Mel's later claims that he never went to a gym to keep in shape.

NIDA administrator Elizabeth Butcher recalled, 'I can tell you that Mel was very hard-working. He and Steve Bisley would come in at eight every morning and work out in the gym so they'd be warmed up to start class at nine!'

For the first time, Mel encountered drugs in large quantities. The beachside community of Bondi was and still is a haven for young people doing everything from smoking pot to shooting heroin. In the mid-1970s, the drug culture was at its peak. A trip to nearby taverns, like their favourite Limerick Castle, at weekends, would invariably involve being offered speed, cocaine or grass, and many of Mel's friends at the time were heavily involved.

When the four friends decided to hold a party at the flat in Bondi, there naturally had to be a supply of drugs on offer. 'We did drink and smoked cannabis at those parties and there were flagons of red and white wine and beers. It was right in the middle of the drug culture,' explained Linda Newton. 'People would sit around drinking and smoking and getting bad hangovers the next day. There would be smooching on the dance floor.'

One of those girls who was smooching and taking more than just cannabis at one of Mel's parties in Bondi was a young brunette actress called Debbie Foreman. Stoned on amphetamines, she watched as the handsome host went outside to deal with police sent by angry neighbours fed up with the noise blasting out across the street. Mel never noticed Debbie on that occasion. Less than a year later, their paths crossed in a much more dramatic fashion and almost cost her her life.

Best friend Jeremy Connolly – who eventually became a taxi driver in Sydney – claims he could make 'a lot of fucking money' out of revealing some of the wilder secrets of Mel's young life. But he still holds the star in great regard, despite a major run-in with him and wife Robyn some years ago, according to Monroe Reimers, Mel's former flatmate. 'Mel got Jeremy to look after his farm when he had to rush out to Hollywood and offered him the measly sum of $5 an hour to look after it while he was away. Jeremy went over there and stayed on his own and rang up all his friends because he was lonely. But when Mel and Robyn got back, she left a message on Jeremy's answering machine threatening to sue him over a $25 parking fine he incurred, and a $400 phone bill.'

Monroe Reimers is still bitter about the incident. 'They were just awful. I could not fathom why they behaved like that. I look at all the hype about Mel and think, Fuck, he is not like that!'

Jeremy refuses to get drawn into discussing the incident but Monroe Reimers believes it is an incisive example of how much Mel has changed in recent years – and also of the total control Robyn exerts over all domestic matters. Jeremy has not spoken to Mel directly since, although he is still in touch with his brother, Donal Gibson.

Back in Bondi nearly thirty years ago, and barely surviving on a peppercorn grant, Mel and his flatmates devised a special way of eating out for nothing. They would all crowd around one of the hamburger stalls littered throughout the Bondi Beach area, order their food and then run off without paying. None of them saw it as dishonesty in the normally accepted sense. Mel rationalised that it was 'all a matter of survival'.

But one thing Jeremy Connolly happily admits to was that the communal flat was 'a fucking mess'. There was no phone and they only got a fridge by stealing one from a low-budget film Mel and Steve Bisley appeared in at the end of their course at NIDA. As the only non-drama student in the apartment, Jeremy sometimes felt a little left out, but Mel always went to great lengths to involve him in everything they did outside of NIDA.

The four friends had a run-down Australian Holden station wagon between them. 'It was a very old car and Steve and I used to repair it for Mel to drive,' recalled Monroe Reimers, now a scriptwriter living in Sydney. 'Mel was the worst driver in the world and I don't think he has improved much.'

Interestingly, Mel was not in the least bit ashamed of his parents. Most people around his age would go out of their way to avoid introducing their family to their friends. But Mel did the opposite. He still worshipped the ground his father walked on. He seemed positively proud of his folks and often took his friends home to sample one of Anne's delicious pies. But the day he allowed Monroe Reimers – a plain-speaking character by anyone's standards – to get into a 'heavy' discussion with Hutton Gibson seems to have scarred the ex-NIDA student's opinions of Mel.

'His father is a complete bastard. I just happened to mention something about abortion and the father blew up and threw me out of the house. He branded me a heathen and Mel sided totally with his father – I was banned. You cannot disagree with. Mel's father. He just goes on about how fantastic God is all the time.'

Mel's biggest struggle at the time was a financial one. Friends remember him as being constantly broke and he seems to have borrowed relatively small amounts of cash from a number of them and sometimes 'forgotten' to pay them back. The four flatmates were supposed to share all household bills but there were frequent occasions when Mel just did not have the money. And Monroe Reimers maintains that Mel – now a multi-million-dollar celebrity – had a car crash but managed to get out of paying for the damage to the other person's car.

'It was Mel's fault, but he couldn't afford to pay for the damage, so he went to the guy and said he would give him $2 a week, and pay the rest when he was rich and famous. I don't know what happened with that.'

But what most of his NIDA friends conveniently forget is that the traditional source of subsistence – one's own family – did not exist for Mel as his father had so many other children to support; and he was self-confessedly stingy, even when he had the money to spare.

At NIDA, Mel was becoming the most talked-about student at school. 'You could never give him a small part, because he'd take over the play' recalled Keith Bain, Mel's movement coach at NIDA. 'He was once given a very small role as a very dumb soldier. When I look back on that production, it is Mel's performance that I remember more than any others.'

Mel's first encounter with overt homosexuality occurred towards the end of his three-year stay at NIDA. One drama teacher deliberately placed Mel in the centre of every scene in an end-of-term play because he was so besotted by the young student's good looks. 'I think this man fell in love with Mel,' says Linda Newton, who is sure that Mel often had no idea of the sexual impact he had on both men and women. 'Mel just did not realise it a lot of the time but he definitely had this effect on people.'

When rumours started flying around NIDA that Mel had a male admirer, he was the last one to find out and, says Linda Newton, he did not appreciate it. 'Mel was not very good at dealing with that kind of stuff.'

Linda also remembers going out with Mel and a group of NIDA pals to a notorious gay nightclub called Patches in Oxford Street, in the centre of Sydney. For probably one of the few times in his life, Mel definitely did not want to be in a nightclub. Instead of relaxing with his friends, he tensed up and became very anxious that 'something awful' might happen to him. Linda Newton remembers, 'Mel would not let go of my hand. He just hung on to me. He did not want to be in that nightclub.'

Mel clung to Linda for dear life in the hope that none of the men throwing admiring glances his way would try to follow through with actual approaches. 'He was not comfortable to be amongst gay people.'

For once, Mel's famous ability to laugh his way out of a sticky situation completely failed him.

According to Linda Newton he was 'terrified' and even refused to go to the lavatory all that night because 'he was convinced he would be raped on sight'.

Linda Newton remembers another occasion when Mel found himself the highly embarrassed object of a famous gay singer's desires when he was appearing in a theatre in South Australia. 'Mel did not cope very well at all. He used to make jokes about it, but he did not like it.'

This particular singing star – who was touring Australia from his native Europe at the time – spotted the young actor when he attended the play that Mel was appearing in. That very same evening the overweight recording artist made his first move – by turning up at the stage door in a Rolls-Royce with a bottle of champagne to 'entice' the attractive thespian into his arms. But the actor rejected the singer's attempts at seduction by completely ignoring him and looking the other way before heading at high speed down the street in the opposite direction from the waiting limousine.

According to Linda Newton, the pop star returned on at least three evenings to try and persuade Mel to change his mind. By the fourth night, Mel was completely panicked by the attentions of his famous admirer and, according to Linda, got very 'pissed off'. 'He did not like men or women chasing him. I think that is probably why he wanted to share a house with so many people – then girls like that earlier one in King's Cross could not throw themselves at him so easily.'

Back at NIDA, Mel's acting abilities were being noticed by more and more people. To some fellow students, Mel had transformed into an ambitious, ingenious player, while others say he had a natural talent that just took time to emerge from within his shy persona.

'In the third year, he underwent a change ... a kind of crazy ambition came over him. He began to play on his image as the leading man – he was always groomed at NIDA for that and it changed him. A part of his personality came out that was quite ambitious and ruthless,' says Monroe Reimers with a hint of disapproval.

But fellow student Peter Kingston says the opposite. 'He was a very unpretentious guy, unaware of his own talents and charisma. Over the three years, he just kept on blooming and showing new dimensions of himself. He didn't seem to be overly ambitious. I just remember a really unassuming bloke, a pretty ordinary kind of bloke really, who just happened to be really talented.'

But all Mel's fellow students and staff at NIDA agree that it was not until he finally agreed to shave off his beard and cut his hair for a role in a 1940s period play that his now famous matinée idol powers were unveiled.

'We were all shocked because suddenly we all saw this wonderful face. It was as if Mel had evolved before our very eyes,' says Peter Kingston. 'Until then, he had a mane of hair down to his shoulders and looked like a lion.'

And Linda Newton concurs, 'Once he cut off that long hair and beard, I looked at him in a different light.'

As if in response, Mel began to excel, although he still plays down his stardom at NIDA by claiming that his favourite classes at the school were fencing. 'I loved plotting out the duels – figuring out the dirtiest, most violent ways of stabbing people.'

By all accounts, Mel's sweetheart, a girl called Julie from a good, middle-class home near him in Bondi, was having real problems coming to terms with his career as an actor – and her parents certainly did not approve of their daughter going out with someone in such an insecure profession.

'Once you go through drama school and do all these strange things, it becomes very hard for anyone who is not a part of it. It takes up so much of your time,' explained Linda.

For some months, Mel desperately held on to his relationship with Julie and she, in turn, became increasingly anxious to marry the 20-year-old would-be actor. The situation provoked some intense discussions between Mel and Linda.

'Julie wanted to marry Mel and my boyfriend wanted to marry me and if we had not gone to NIDA then we might well have. But we were completely immersed in drama school and neither of our partners could come to terms with that.'

Mel's romance with Julie eventually came to an end, but not until after at least half-a-dozen on-off, off-on interludes between the couple. As one friend argues, 'Mel had a real soft spot for Julie but he was also very ambitious and he knew that marriage at that time would more or less destroy his career.'

Eventually, Julie went off and married a plumber, with her parents' whole-hearted approval. Meanwhile, Mel got back to the task in question – building his career. He went out on dates with a number of actresses like Zoe Bertram and Debra Lawrence, more recently a star of the television soap *Home and Away*. But actresses did not really click with Mel. The last thing he wanted from a relationship was intense discussions about the stage. His own wisecracking approach was intended to lighten proceedings and many serious-minded young actresses did not find that attitude to their liking.

Mel now looks back on his NIDA grounding with great fondness, and has always been most generous about how much he owes staff and students for his success. In 1991, he even donated the proceedings from the gala openings of *Hamlet* in Sydney, Brisbane and Melbourne (plus, apparently, a percentage of the box-office takings) to help set up a scholarship for actors at NIDA. He was persuaded, after genuine reluctance, to let it be named after him. But Mel's main intention was to encourage more raw talent to take the plunge and go to drama school in just the same way as he had done.

FIVE

THE WORST THING THAT CAN HAPPEN IS YOU CAN
SCREW UP. I'VE DONE THAT BEFORE AND IT'S NOT TOO
DAMNING. I'VE DONE SOME REAL STINKERS. LUCKILY
MOST WERE EARLY ON.

By November 1976, Mel had become much more settled at
NIDA. His earlier doubts about pursuing a career as an
actor had completely disappeared and he was fast gaining a
reputation as a real talent.

This new-found confidence was partly due to the fact that
Mel had spent the previous year living out of the shadow of
his revered father, Hutton. While there is absolutely no doubt
that Mel worships his father, Papa Gibson expected those
living under his roof to adhere to his strict code of ethics. Life
at that house on Bondi Beach was gloriously laid-back in
comparison. Mel had started learning to fend for himself, to
cope with life away from the protection of his family.
Admittedly, he still regularly popped back to the Gibson
household for a plateful of his mother's finest homemade
meat pie.

Flatmate Steve Bisley became an especially close friend

during this period. The two young thespians literally ate, breathed and talked acting. They encouraged each other to push performances to the limit – and they both knew how to sink a few pints of beer.

In the middle of November, Australian producer Phil Avalon contacted Mel and Steve at NIDA and asked if they would be interested in appearing in a little beach movie he was planning. Mel's sheer good fortune at being in the right place at the right time imposed itself again.

Steve and Mel were delighted. The fact that the movie in question, *Summer City*, was being made for a minuscule budget of less than $100,000 and producer/actor/screenwriter Avalon intended to offer them the union minimum of $400 (which Mel later claimed he never even received) did not deter them in the slightest. Here they were, still students, yet about to star in a movie.

Neither boy noticed glaring holes in the script or wondered how on earth a film could be produced on such a small budget. They were swept along by the glamour associated with any movie project, however cut-price. Mel learned a lot of lessons during the making of *Summer City*; many have helped turn him into a shrewd, adept Hollywood player. He has also been highly critical of the project, in hindsight.

'It was an abomination, a cheap, nasty flick that was cranked out in three weeks on a tiny budget. My character was a 19-year-old surfer who simply surfed and acted dumb, which was all I could possibly handle at that time. The movie actually got a release but, fortunately, only in Australia,' Mel snapped at one interviewer who dared ask about his début movie.

Summer City really isn't that bad, considering the shoestring budget and its shoot-from-the-hip style. And producer/actor/screenwriter Phil Avalon is still hurt about Mel's attempts to disown the picture, and his taunt that he never got paid for the film.

'This story keeps being run by Mel but it is not true. I personally sent him the cheque and it was definitely cashed. I think it's just become a bit of a publicity stunt to keep claiming he wasn't paid for his first film role,' recalled Avalon.

'Of course, now he is regarded as something like Jesus Christ within the movie industry, it must be very hard for him to remember that time. I look back fondly on those days and I'm really disappointed to hear that some people don't.'

Avalon says he even wrote Mel a letter to try and end malicious gossip. 'It's more of a mate's note and said the no-pay story was old hat. I don't think it has been mentioned since.'

Mel only got the part of a surfer called 'Scollop' after Phil Avalon failed to recruit another actor, Nick Papadopoulous. And *Summer City* was, as Avalon points out, really Steve Bisley's film. 'Boo', the character that Bisley played, was 'an outrageous, self-opinionated mongrel and he enjoyed the part and played it brilliantly'.

Avalon is less laudatory about Mel, and revealed that he had to use a stand-in surfer for some scenes because Mel was so bad 'on the boards'.

Mel's first-ever appearance on screen is fascinating in that he is recognisable from the moment he steps in front of the camera – despite having his hair dyed a dreadful blond and looking at least ten kilos heavier than he does these days. In that initial scene, he used the same swagger that he has deployed to such great effect in recent years and which tells an audience instantly who they are watching.

Years later, a Hollywood executive stated that the difference between Mel and several other young actors pushing for stardom was like comparing a still photograph with film. Even in those novice days during the making of *Summer City*, he was having the desired effect.

Considering Mel's attitude towards homosexuality, it does seem rather ironic that Mel's very first screen kiss was with a man – Steve Bisley! It occurs about one-third of the way through *Summer City* and, for some reason, has never been stressed in subsequent publicity surrounding the film and Mel's part in it.

'It does seem hilarious that macho Mel, the guy all the girls love and adore, only got to kiss a *man* in his first movie,' comments one Hollywood producer.

The joke is obviously not appreciated by Mel, who has never been asked to kiss a man since. Neither has he ever mentioned this scene in since *Summer City* was made. It has to be said that the scene involves Mel kissing co-star Bisley firmly on the lips as a 'gesture of friendship and nothing more', according to Phil Avalon. 'Neither cared about kissing each other. It was just done in jest. It was a bonding thing. They were close friends on and off the screen.'

Summer City also marks the first recorded baring of the Gibson backside. Its only real significance in Mel's career is that, for the following couple of years, he consistently refused to go naked in movies and even claimed it was something he would never consider. He first went bare for *Gallipoli* and subsequently appeared unclothed in virtually all his following films – which Hollywood producers now reckon adds at least $20 million at the box office. Wistfully lusting cinema-goers are said to shout, 'Turn around! Turn around!' every time Mel's bare bottom appears on screen.

The off-screen mooning episode was more disturbing entirely, and nearly ended violently, as Phil Avalon remembers. They had all been forced to vacate their accommodation for one day to make way for a wedding reception. So the cast and crew had, naturally, ended up at the pub.

In the tavern, the Catherine Hill Bay Hotel, Mel and Steve Bisley decided to get smashed and proceeded to down beers at an alarming rate before struggling across the road to the RSL Hall, where they were staying, to see if the wedding reception was over, so they could bed down for the night in the sleeping bags they had been using all week.

When the two drunken pals found the wedding reception was still raging, it seems they took umbrage and, inspired by that scene they had just shot for *Summer City*, dropped their pants in front of a group of giggly girls standing at the entrance to the hall. Then they disappeared in the direction of the pub across the street. Within minutes, a lynch mob gathered around Phil Avalon, who was huddled, terrified, in his car. They began pounding on the car bonnet and roof, smashing fists up against the windows.

'Dirty bastards,' hollered one man.

'Flashers. Bloody flashers,' yelled another.

'I thought I was going to be in serious trouble. I even got my .22 rifle from the back of the car because there were so many people surrounding me,' recalled Phil Avalon. 'They were out for blood. They had gone from a happy, celebrating group to one that seemed hell-bent on revenge. But I didn't even know what they wanted revenge for. All I knew was they wanted to bash my head in. I played it cool because I had to find out what was happening.'

After a few minutes of terror, Avalon managed to persuade the mob to let him go and retrieve his two stars from the pub, where Mel and Bisley sheepishly admitted what they had done.

'My problem was that I was laughing so much I had difficulty finding the right words to apologise. I mean, it was funny. But not to the family folk at the wedding. We got back in the hall the next morning more by luck and guile than approval.'

Despite Mel's reluctance even to acknowledge the existence of *Summer City*, it undoubtedly taught him a great deal about movie-making. Towards the end of the shoot, he began studying the rushes closely, sometimes wincing and agonising as he saw his image flicker across the screen.

'Hell, is that me?' he would mutter. 'Ooh ... the eyes are wandering ... aah, I'm nodding too much ... I didn't know you would be that close.'

The final weeks of the shoot were completed in very trying circumstances, with Avalon virtually broke and unable to advance even a few dollars for expenses. 'I had to borrow from friends, anywhere I could. I'd go out and buy a lot of mincemeat, chop some onions and carrots into it, cook it myself, and that was lunch.'

A few years later, Mel reflected on his role in *Summer City* by saying, 'It was a case of wondering day and night if you ate, slept, got paid or what. There was this madness as we went from day to day, a kind of excitement.'

There was another, far more significant reason why Mel has tried to bury the memories of *Summer City* for ever. 'One of the actresses was very keen on Mel. She has married now but she was carrying a torch for Mel and it all ended in a very unfortunate incident. But they were very young at the time,' says Phil Avalon.

The actress's name was Deborah Foreman and, for almost 20 years, she kept silent about her relationship with Mel Gibson. Now happily married and the proud mother of two, Deborah – an attractive, 36-year-old brunette – lives in a modest beachside house 32km north of Sydney. Her account of her relationship with Mel provides the first-ever glimpse of Mel the lover.

At times during this interview, Deborah was close to tears; she still holds the movie star in very high regard. 'We were just a bunch of kids having a good time, I guess. Mel had a crush on me and I had a big crush on him. We went out together for about two months. I was crazy in love with him. He was great. We had such fun times together. He was so warm, shy and vulnerable. A very decent chap. A funny, loving character. I really enjoyed that feeling of having someone fall madly in love with me. He was completely different from anyone else. I have never met anyone like that, apart from my husband.'

According to Deborah, when she met Mel he was still 'very keen' on Julie, that previous girlfriend who eventually walked out on him to marry a plumber.

'He was still a bit in love with Julie at the time I met him. A lot of people on *Summer City* were matchmaking us. They wanted him to get his mind off Julie!'

Interestingly, Mel – the man so adored by millions of women throughout the world – certainly was not a born romantic. Deborah explained, 'He never once got me any flowers. He was just not that type and he never even opened doors for me either. Basically, he did not like taking girls on dates. You just tended to hang around with him and his mates. There were no candlelit dinners. He is a very Australian man.

'I used to have to buy all his drinks because he had no money. I even drove him around in Steve Bisley's car a lot of the time. Mel was more like a romance you would have when you are about 15.

'We went to pubs, and played pool across the road from where we were staying during some of the filming of *Summer City*. Mel had this habit of telling long-winded stories that hit you like a shaggy dog story at the end!

About two weeks into the filming, Mel and Deborah took off with Steve Bisley, John Jarratt, another actor and a technician for a week-long holiday in a caravan further north along the coast. They weren't playing truant – Avalon was away, too, raising more cash to continue the movie.

She says they stayed together in an annex to the caravan. Sharing a bed with Deborah did not stop young Mel holding forth on morality and marriage. It was a dire display of double standards, the stud lecturing his highly strung mistress on why a girl like her was unacceptable when he came to seek a wife.

As the twig is bent, so grows the tree ... Mel was no wimp but he could be warm, compassionate, understanding and giving, especially around kids. Yet the same person was crassly insensitive – as good as telling Deborah he was there for the companionship and the sex, forget anything deeper. One need not be fanciful to discern Hutton Gibson's uncompromising script being spoken by his raffish son.

Deborah struggled to control her emotions when recalling this side of their relationship. 'Mel had very definite ideas about what women should be and how they should behave. He was very old-fashioned and said that women should be virgins. They should be "nice", he said things like that.

'He had quite a conscience about morals, immorality. It was to do with do way he had been raised. He tried to cover up when he did sleep with someone. He wanted to stay very clean. I think he belonged to my parents' generation. He was more like my dad. He got around a bit but ...' her tone is regretful, 'he wanted to marry a virgin.'

And Mel made no secret that he intended to have a large family. 'He always said he would marry and have lots of children. He definitely believed in that sort of thing.'

In a controversial interview with the Spanish magazine *El Pais*, Mel affirmed his detestation of abortion – a stand he had hinted at during his relationship with Deborah. 'God is the only one who knows how many children we should have,' he declared, 'and we should be ready to accept them.'

About midway through their relationship, Deborah stayed the night with Mel and his parents at the ultra-religious sanctum of the Gibson family home. He hadn't taken her there in the courtship ritual of 'Meet my folks', though. The senior Gibsons took pity on her when chauffeuse Deborah drove him there one night.

As she explains, 'It was so late, so they asked me if I wanted to stay the night. The house was built of double brick and had a very long table in the kitchen. It was like a rabbit warren of beds and rooms. But his parents weren't very interested in me because I was an actress. I remember Mel's mum had an incredibly strong American accent.'

There is absolutely no suggestion that Deborah slept with Mel at the family home. It is just surprising that she was even offered a bed for the night.

On at least three other occasions, Deborah says she went to the home Mel shared with his pals in Bondi. But they could only snatch brief kisses and cuddles, more often than not because Bisley, Monroe Reimers and Jeremy Connolly were always around.

'The flat was very sparse. Nobody ever cleared out of there when we arrived. I would have liked a few more private moments with Mel.'

But she says that, during one evening out together, Mel told her, 'I am really starting to fall for you in a big way.'

Deborah recalled that his enthusiasm worried her. 'I was afraid I wouldn't like him any more if he got too close. I was really enjoying feeling in love with him but ... He could have very solemn moods and be very miserable, then he would be up again. I remember discussing the fact of there being no middle ground with him. He said he was on an even keel, but the truth was that one moment he was funny, the next he was quiet and introverted.'

One particular incident is still painful for her to talk about. Deborah will only say, 'There was one thing he did to me I would rather not mention. He was pretty mean to me. It was something which a well-brought-up person would not do.'

Deborah insists that Mel will know exactly what she is referring to and she would rather keep it between themselves. Tantalisingly, she insists it was the reason they broke up. 'I dropped him because of what he did. It was obvious that he still loved Julie. He hurt my feelings very deeply. I was messed up for a long time afterwards.'

Deborah says that, for two weeks after their break-up, she 'went through a pretty painful time. I hardly ate, I drank a lot and took drugs.' Then she bumped into Mel at a party at a friend's house. She was with a friend and he was with a girl. 'I was still very miffed at him. I was drunk and I was stoned and I had dropped a few pills. I was out of my mind. I got really mad at him and then I threw a glass of wine all over him and kicked him. This other girl took me aside and told me that what I had done was atrocious.'

Throughout all this, according to Deborah, Mel remained passive, visibly stunned by her onslaught. She went outside, into the garden, and burst into tears. Then she took a decision she has regretted ever since. 'I was so out of it on drink and drugs, I slashed one of my wrists. I had considered suicide several times before and struggled with depression. Now I have a scar on my wrists I never want my kids ever to see.'

Deborah says that bumping into Mel at that party 'was the trigger for what happened. It wasn't so much him. In fact, it was more me than him. Now I wish I hadn't done what I did. It was very embarrassing.'

In an extraordinary scene, Mel – who had been told what

had happened by the other girl – rushed into the garden and tried to restrain Deborah as her wrist bled. But, instead of hugging the man she loved, Deborah started punching him. 'I fought him off. Blood was oozing slowly from my wrist. There was nothing he could do to stop it.'

Deborah says Mel was shocked and upset by what had happened and then became especially hurt when she brushed off his efforts to help. 'He was very concerned. I feel such hurt inside my heart about what happened. I was an idiot. I had cut myself extremely deeply but the blood wasn't gushing out. I looked down and thought, I don't think God wants me to die yet.'

Moments later, Deborah was driven to a nearby hospital by a girlfriend, where she underwent microsurgery. She spoke to Mel just once again, many months later, seeking advice about whether to take a part in a play. 'I got through to him at his parents' house. He was very nice to me considering what had happened and he told me I was a natural actor and should do very well.'

Besides seeing him across a crowded cinema during a glitzy Sydney film première some years later, Deborah confirms that she has never seen or heard from Mel since their affair. But she says that her relationship with the world's so-called sexiest man did help her in many ways. 'What happened with Mel did bring things to a head with me. I changed after that.'

Deborah's never fully recovered from the emotional turmoil caused by her relationship with Mel. And she was not the last actress to suffer that fate after a liaison with the star.

Summer City eventually opened in Sydney in December 1977 and was billed as 'The one you have been waiting for! Funnier than *American Graffiti*. Heavier than *Easy Rider*.'

It did reasonable business, mainly through being one of the first movies of its genre to come out of Australia. Years later, it gained a cult following on video and made a small profit for then 28-year-old producer Avalon, who went on to make more than half-a-dozen Aussie movies, including *The Sher Mountain Killing Mystery*, starring former world heavyweight boxing contender Joe Bugner, plus *Fatal Bond* with Linda Blair and Donal Gibson, Mel's younger brother.

Stephen Marston, writing in the prestigious Australian magazine *Cinema Papers*, believed that *Summer City* had been 'directed in a scrappy, disjointed fashion and the camera bumps in and out of the action in a style better suited to gritty documentary or home movie.

'None of the performances is weak, they are just rarely given a chance to be strong. We are only allowed a very limited understanding of Boo and Sandy; just Abigail (as a downtrodden pub wife) and Mel Gibson (Scollop) emerge as real people.'

Mel and his good friend Steve Bisley returned, battle-scarred, to the realities of NIDA and their final year of drama school. Both felt disillusioned by the kick and scramble side of film-making, as they considered it left them little time to fine-tune their performances.

But Mel – whose name was now being mentioned throughout the Australian showbusiness community – was soon approached by Sydney agents Faith Martin and Bill Shanahan. They suspected he had what it took, and they managed to elicit offers of work while he was still at NIDA. On paper, some of these openings looked promising. He happily accepted a two-week stint on the Australian soap opera *The Sullivans*, reckoning that a mainstream television project had to be more professional than a low-budget surf movie.

Mel lived to regret making his hasty decision to take the

job, rather than toil away at college. Eventually, he rued it as a bigger mistake than *Summer City*. 'It was a shocking experience – terrible scripts, no rehearsals, just knock it over in a day. I did two weeks' work and I was on screen every night for three weeks. I played a naval officer – I inspected navels.'

Yet again, Mel felt cheated out of his rights as an actor by not being given sufficient rehearsal time before working under directors who rarely did more than three takes on any set-up. But he was absorbing all these experiences to throw back at directors and producers when he had gained some power.

As he cruised through those last months at NIDA, he decided that his career needed a return to the theatre. He had jumped at two very poor film and television roles and it just did not make sense to him to continue along that path. In any case, his experiences at NIDA made him hunger for the stage.

A job touring with the South Australian Theatre Company seemed a golden opportunity to get back to what he liked doing best. Mel was soon getting rave reviews for his performance in Beckett's *Waiting for Godot*, which inspired his great friend actor Sam Neill's shrewd comment, 'Mel Gibson is a character actor trapped inside a leading man's body.'

In Adelaide, Mel went flat-hunting – and met the girl who would become his wife. Robyn Moore was one of the people sharing an apartment he was interested in.

For the first few months they did little but exchange the odd casual glance. NIDA classmate Tony Prehn – who appeared with Mel in *Waiting for Godot* – remembers, 'She was a dental nurse and he met her when he was looking for a room to rent.'

One of Robyn's classmates at the Woodlands Church of England Grammar School in Adelaide explained that the neatly-presented brunette was 'so quiet, she was more like a dormouse. She was very skinny and very shy, but she excelled in sports like hockey and softball.'

More than ten years later, Mel himself recounted that first meeting with Robyn. 'I woke up one morning and went into the kitchen and there she was making breakfast. She was my new flatmate. We shared the rent on the house. It wasn't a huge romance straight away. We became great friends first and used to do things like go shopping together.'

One of Mel's NIDA classmates said that, at first, Robyn did not consider Mel as anything more than a good friend 'because she had heard stories about what actors are like. Robyn came from a quiet, secure background and she wanted to give any suggestion of a real romance with Mel some very careful consideration before she took the plunge.'

There was a practical reason why the two did not 'connect' instantly. Robyn already had a boyfriend and he was much larger than Mel, who jokingly admits, 'I sort of waited until he fell by the wayside.'

While Mel and Robyn played a waiting game, agents Shanahan and Martin were busy spreading the word about their exciting new discovery. This time, when Mel heard that doctor-turned-director George Miller wanted to discuss the possibility of his playing the lead role in the good doctor's low-budget, futuristic action movie, he was much more cautious.

SIX

PEOPLE WHO ACHIEVE MINOR SUCCESS WHEN THEY'RE
SO YOUNG SHOULD HAVE A TRAINING SCHOOL
TO GO TO. SOMEONE OUGHT TO TEACH YOU HOW
TO HANDLE IT.

In September 1977, just before graduating from NIDA,
Mel went to Sydney casting agent Mitch Matthews's
office to try out for a role in a movie called *Mad Max*. Mitch
– a well-liked and respected figure in the Australian film
industry – had been given Mel's name by Betty Williams, a
voice teacher at NIDA.

'I had asked Betty if she knew any spunky young guys to
put in the movie. She immediately suggested Mel Gibson and
a few other raw youngsters,' recalled Mitch.

Those 'youngsters' included Mel's classmate Steve Bisley
and shy, sensitive NIDA student Judy Davis, who went on to
gain an international reputation.

The legend of the casting session at Mitch Matthews's tiny
studio in North Sydney has been repeated many times and
spawned headlines like 'MEL'S PUNCH-UP', as well as articles
that begin, 'A wild punch-up in the pub put Mel Gibson on

71

the road to stardom ...' But as with all good yarns, the truth was a little more mundane.

Mel claimed in many a subsequent interview that, when he went along to that fateful gathering, he 'looked a mess' after being 'really worked over' by three men at a party.

'I ended up with masses of cuts, broken bones, black eyes and a flattened nose. The casting director took one look at my mug, then she nodded and muttered, "Yeah, yeah, you look fine." I ended up playing the lead in the first *Mad Max* movie.'

That casting director was Mitch Matthews and she insists that Mel's claims are 'absolute, total nonsense'. Speaking at the same little studio where she tested Mel all those years earlier, Mitch bursts the fantasy by saying, 'There is no way Mel was in a fight. I have seen these stories and I know they are not true.'

What's more, Mitch's daughter Celia – who has worked with her mother for almost 20 years – was also present when Mel showed up. She said, 'He never came in here with all those fight injuries. It had absolutely nothing to do with why he was cast. He certainly did not have a black eye when we tested him.'

Even *Mad Max* co-creator and director Dr George Miller has never referred to this so-called fight in numerous accounts of how he came to cast Mel in the movie that did more than any other project to make him into a star.

Neither Mitch nor Celia was the least surprised by the fight fable. It is common practice in the movie business to spin legends out of nothing. Their only reason for pointing out the true situation is that Mel did not need a gimmick to help him get the part of Max. Mitch says he got it the moment he appeared before her video camera for the test.

'I got shivers up and down my spine when I saw Mel

through the eyepiece. He was just magic. He had great depth and sensitivity.'

George Miller says, 'I still remember the moment I saw the TV monitor with Mel reading this monologue. Suddenly I thought, God, there is something special there. I replayed the screen test and the feeling was still there. I forgot I was a director trying to cast his first movie. I sat and watched and got transported by the moment.'

In fact, the only comparatively well-known actor in the film was Australian Roger Ward. But Miller made him shave his head for an unrecognisable appearance.

'I was unimpressed by the rather small, spindly youngster who would play Max. But the kid spoke with authority and didn't seem intimidated or frightened to work out various methods and interpretations of certain scenes,' Ward concedes.

Steve Bisley – who had 'stolen' *Summer City* the previous year – was this time chosen to play a secondary role to his old friend and flatmate. But Judy Davis was deemed to be 'too strong' by Mitch Matthews for the role she tried out for, and was rejected.

But there was one big problem about casting Mel as Max – his tutors would not let him leave drama school until he had graduated in October. So the movie's eccentric director, Dr George Miller, held back production until Mel got on a plane for Melbourne, the same day he left NIDA. An official, trained actor at last.

A few hours later, Mel was knocking at the front door of a tatty Victorian house in the Melbourne suburbs. A man who looked as if he had just walked out of a hospital casualty ward answered.

'Ah ... sorry,' said the 21-year-old Mel, thinking he had arrived at the wrong address. 'I'm looking for George Miller's place, the film people ...'

The hospital patient looked amused. 'This is the right place. Come on in.'

'I'm Mel.'

Extending a bandaged hand and grimacing as Mel shook it, the 'patient' explained that he was Grant Page, stunt co-ordinator for *Mad Max*.

Mel must have felt a little suspicious. He had already experienced the trial-and-error school of film-making on *Summer City*. This operation had that familiar, low-budget feel to it, but then Mel met Dr George Miller and realised that this could well turn into something much bigger and more exciting than 100 movies like *Summer City*.

The Melbourne home housed all the cast and many of the crew for the film. It was a definite improvement on the wooden floors of that hall Mel had slept on during the making of *Summer City*, but it was pretty basic all the same. Each room slept six or seven people on a variety of 'beds' made out of such things as camp stretchers, beanbags and even mattresses.

Mad Max was set in a distant future in an urban society suffering from terminal decay. Inner-city highways became white-line nightmares where nomad bikers and young cops in souped-up pursuit vehicles had created an arena for a weird apocalyptic death game.

'They say we haven't got any heroes any more. Well, damn them. You and me, Max, we're gonna give 'em back their heroes,' says the police chief character in the movie.

The basic premise behind *Mad Max* was, director George Miller admits, to create a futuristic Western. The film used the same type of plot and characters.

Miller saw it as a way to counter some of the gloomy portraits of life Down Under, given worldwide critical acclaim during the preceding five years, but which had limited appeal.

He could see that they had little chance in the lucrative international marketplace.

Filmgoers were already tiring of artistically valid yet downbeat fare, and Miller knew that what audiences really wanted was escapism. And he was the man to provide it. 'It is a Western in new clothes. Each country has its own frame of reference. In Japan, they liken it to Samurai pictures. In Scandinavia, they say it is a Viking picture. All are basically Westerns,' explained Miller.

Miller and his producer Byron Kennedy (who later died tragically at the age of 33 in a helicopter crash) had lovingly developed the *Mad Max* script (with journalist James McCausland) for at least three years before getting the project off the ground.

After years of struggle, Kennedy and Miller managed to raise $250,000 to make the film. It was a minuscule budget for an action film involving numerous stunts. But the moment Mel met Kennedy and Miller, he was infected by their enormous enthusiasm. He even – a significant concession for an actor – ignored the fact there were only 14 lines of dialogue for the main character.

The two young film-makers had agreed before casting the movie that they would use unknown actors so that the characters would be 100 per cent convincing. First choice to play Max was Irish-born actor James Healy, then living in Melbourne. The young actor was desperate for any acting job, as he was 'resting' between work by hauling carcasses at a local abattoir. But, after reading the script, Healy declined the lead role – Max had such meagre, terse dialogue.

Miller tried desperately to convince Healy but he would not budge. In later years, he turned up in Hollywood to star as Joan Collins's manipulative lover Sean Rowan in *Dynasty* and then as a scheming romeo in America's daytime soap *Santa*

Barbara. In 1993, Healy was arrested by Los Angeles police after allegedly shooting a relative – quite a Max-like act.

According to Dowding, the *Mad Max* shoot, mainly at a desolate area just outside Melbourne, was a 'very rock 'n' roll' scene. The location consisted of flat plains, an expanse of Australian desert as far as Perth to the west, and an abandoned industrial park with just a handful of horses grazing, and little else. To the east, a vast range of mountains marked a snaking coastline.

Everyone put in gruelling 18-hour days and, as is common on film shoots, drugs were available to those wanting to buy.

There is no suggestion that Mel took any illegal substances but, by all accounts, many of the cast and crew took amphetamines and cocaine, if only to keep going during those long hours.

'The whole film was achieved on the smell of an oily rag and generated by a lot of mind-altering substances, spur-of-the-moment decisions,' according to Dowding. 'We were like a guerrilla unit. There were some appalling days and a lot of close shaves with the stunts. We were all naïve and some stupid risks were taken.'

Filming had a chaotic start. Mel and Steve Bisley nearly got themselves arrested as they drove to the *Mad Max* location in the souped-up Interceptor car, specially adapted for the movie. The two actors – kitted out in their black leather uniforms complete with fake guns – were stopped by a curious policeman in a Melbourne street.

'They almost freaked out when they saw the guns,' said Mel. The actors avoided instant arrest by showing the officer official documents proving that they had permission to film.

And four days after the start of shooting, leading lady Rosie Bailey was involved in a head-on car crash, broke her leg and had to be replaced by Australian soap star Joanne Samuel.

But, despite these setbacks, *Mad Max* was made, and proved an instant box-office hit. Most critics were full of praise for it, particularly the stunt work, all the more creditable because of the tiny budget. But within Australia there was an element of snobbery about the subject matter. Some of the industry's self-appointed elder statesmen felt that Miller and Kennedy had sacrificed artistic integrity to make an unashamed 'smash it and grab 'em' film.

Phillip Adams, later to become chairman of the Australian Film Commission, assailed *Mad Max* for having 'the moral uplift of *Mein Kampf*', and suggested that it could foster violence. Adams later described Australia's other huge international movie hit *Crocodile Dundee* as 'listless' and star Paul Hogan's performance as 'lacklustre', so his judgement calls are not exactly impressive.

Mel's aunt, Kathleen Lyons, described *Mad Max* perfectly when she said, 'All that noise and car wrecks and people getting murdered. I thought Mel was terrific but the movie was something I just didn't expect. Even with all that dirt, blood and make-up and the passing of the years, it was little Mel up there, the kid who always wanted to play games and have fun. Now he was being paid to do it and everything was like a dream. I had to sit in my seat at the cinema for several minutes before staggering to my feet and going outside.'

Mel later admitted sneaking into a cinema in Sydney finally to see the film for himself – and getting quite a shock. First, he found the theatre full of the very type of bikers portrayed in *Mad Max*. Life, rather worryingly, imitating art. Then he noticed that the movie had a very real effect on the crowd. 'I must admit I didn't like what it seemed to do to them. A lot of them seemed to take it a little too seriously. But I suppose there'll always be those sort of people. I'm just glad a couple of the bikers didn't bother to look at who was sitting next to them.' He also insisted that he 'cringed' whenever he saw himself on the big screen.

Miller and Kennedy were infuriated when *Mad Max* was released in the US with Mel's voice redubbed because the movie's American distributors claimed that American audiences would not understand the Aussie dialogue. Not surprisingly, the film bombed in the US but its worldwide success forced Hollywood to sit up and take notice of star and creators.

And Jon Dowding – who helped design many of the bizarre futuristic vehicles used in the movie – said, '*Mad Max* represents the Australian film industry's renaissance. It was a captivating piece of writing. It was quite brilliant.'

Mel himself varies enormously when asked his feelings about the original *Mad Max*, but his usual verdict is that it was 'probably the classiest B-grade trash ever made'. Then he often backtracks a bit by adding, 'It's actually a fairly good film in a trashy, badly scarred kind of way. It's a cartoon. You have to remember that.'

The movie won six Australian Film Institute awards, including the Jury Prize and Best Actor for Mel. It also received top honours at Avoriaz, in France, where the world's most prestigious fantasy and science-fiction film festival is held each year.

In Sydney, *Mad Max*'s extraordinary success was having a knock-on effect on Mel Gibson's career. Agents Faith Martin and Bill Shanahan were swamped with enquiries about his availability. Numerous offers of work came in from home and abroad, and renowned Hollywood agent Ed Limato was pressing Mel to appoint him as his Los Angeles agent.

Mel admitted wonderingly that fate played a vital role in his progress. 'It's all been accidental. There wasn't any plan. It wasn't a considered move until well after I was into it. Fate has a funny way of tipping you into things.'

Three years later, Mel was persuaded to put his Max leathers back on and reprise his most successful role thus far.

He had been in a number of much gentler movies in the meantime, but none of them had the same box-office clout. With a budget of $4 million and an allegedly less violent script by George Miller and his writing partners Terry Hayes and Brian Hannant, Mel accepted a surprisingly modest fee of $100,00 for *Mad Max 2* and didn't object when he discovered even fewer lines of dialogue than the first time around.

Taking up where *Mad Max* left off, the movie opens with a much more battered-looking Max, complete with leg brace, at the wheel of his V8 Interceptor in an eerie, ravaged landscape, travelling at hurricane speed on a long, lonely road towards an ominous horizon.

Miller gave Max a dog and a heroic child, and transformed the gang members into homosexuals, much to Mel's amusement. The result is 94 minutes of non-stop action, backed by superb Dolby sound-effects as Max becomes the reluctant champion of a band of idealistic but bewildered survivors. It climaxes when they find themselves defending their makeshift oil refinery from the marauding gay bikers and their cronies. After fleeing the compound, Max leads them to survival in a remarkable chase sequence.

Mel was, once again, surprised by the terror instilled in many people watching Max in action again. 'I thought it was funny. It was a comedy almost. A very black comedy. Even the violence in it wasn't that brutal sort of violence. It was just thrill, thrill, thrill.'

And Mel was still full of praise for George Miller. 'He is a true film-maker, with a completely unique way of going about it, of using film and its techniques to tell a story. It takes somebody pretty talented to actually get that simplicity on film.'

One of Mel's co-stars was eight-year-old Emil Minty, who played the Feral Kid. Although only just out of his teens himself, Mel befriended Emil, showing that special Gibson charm when it came to handling children.

Minty recalls that Mel taught him how 'to throw a boomerang and head-butt people without hurting them', something that Mel had used to great effect during his own boyhood at St Leo's College.

Minty also remembered how Mel took him out to see *Mad Max* at a drive-in cinema with wife Robyn and his three children, who were staying with the star on location.

'My mum made me promise I wouldn't actually watch it, but Mel did not seem too worried about allowing his own children to see it,' says Minty, who still lives in Sydney. Mel disputes this version and insists that *Mad Max 2* is the only one of those movies that he had allowed his kids to see.

Mad Max 2 broke all Australian box-office records in its first five days of screening, grossing A$802,000 in just 58 cinemas. In Britain, it was much the same story. And at the US box office, it took a healthy $24 million and eventually outstripped *Mad Max*'s international revenue of $100 million. Critic Meaghan Morris enthused, 'There isn't really much to say about *Mad Max 2*, except that it is one of the best action spectacles ever filmed.'

But other film critics acclaimed little eight-year-old Emil Minty's performance. Fran Hernon, in the Sydney *Sun*, wrote, 'Mel Gibson walks away with the throbbing hearts, Emil Minty walks away with the acting honours ...'

But, despite being allegedly overshadowed by his young friend, the movie established Mel as a potential Hollywood star. What set it apart from many other similar action movies was that women were dragging husbands and boyfriends to see it, rather than the other way around. A US fan club was set up around this time and one member proudly announced she had been to see *Mad Max 2* 123 times. Released on video, *Mad Max 2* sold more than 50,000 cassette units, making it eligible for platinum certification. It also became a firm favourite at Saturday-night late shows in cinemas across the States, running for years.

Attending a première of *Mad Max 2* in Perth, Western Australia, Mel walked through the crowds outside the Paris Theatre, whereupon 500 screaming, ecstatic women pounced on their idol. 'Mel-mania' had been born. Completely trapped, Mel looked daunted and tried to find a route through the lusting females. Then he realised that the only way to calm the crowd was to start signing autographs and, after completing around 400, he escaped unhurt. Our hero called this incident 'one of the most frightening experiences of my life. I found myself horribly trapped. I was petrified. I thought I was going to be ripped to pieces.'

Mad Max mania was not restricted to Australia, America and Europe. In Japan, Mel was known as the 'samurai on wheels' and was obliged to do a whistle-stop promotional tour of the country. During ten exhausting days, he gave interviews to thirteen newspapers, two movie magazines, four weekly papers, five monthlies, seven television and nine radio programmes. The Japanese even compared him to Steve McQueen and Paul Newman.

During a 24-hour flying visit to Melbourne, promoting *Mad Max 2*, Mel confided to journalist Kim Trengove that he 'expected to be washed up in a year'. This was a remarkable confession from a young actor on the crest of a wave at the time. But Mel was feeling gutted by the non-stop publicity work on *Mad Max 2*, he was hating every minute of it and, like any freelance worker, he feared that the work might dry up at any moment.

'It's good to be in demand now but the offers could stop tomorrow. There are high times and there are low times – you have to take insurance out on yourself.'

In an interview with *Cinema Papers*, Mel was asked how he would manage to stay realistic amid success. He replied, 'It depends on your upbringing and whether you hang on to what you were taught. It is good to have little reminders along the way – things that put you back in touch with what you have learned. There is nothing like a good stretch of not working to do that to you, or somebody whom you know very well being brutally truthful in their criticisms.'

That 'somebody' was Robyn and Mel's parents and brothers and sisters. Unlike traditional Hollywood players, he still remained close to his family and relied on their truthful opinions. His main priority was to keep both feet firmly on the ground.

After the release of *Mad Max 2*, George Miller announced that Max was dead and buried for ever; there would be no more sequels. Mel approved, saying he was 'not particularly keen on the idea'.

But few in Tinseltown believed either of them and, in June 1983, Miller and his producer Byron Kennedy caused no ripple of surprise when *Variety* announced that Max was on the road again.

The budget this time would be $8 million – double the cost of the second *Max* and 20 times the budget of the first. In key with that, Mel's new Hollywood agent Ed Limato held out for $1 million for his client. Miller and Kennedy felt it was money well spent and, when they agreed to Mel's fee, he became the first Australian-based star to receive $1 million for a picture. This time around, Miller brought in stage director George Ogilvie, who had worked in the theatre with Mel, to take charge of the acting, while he concentrated on the stunts that had to surpass the last *Max* movie. Miller kept details of the plot top-secret and would only disclose, 'When we came up with the story, it was something festering deep down in our dreams and unconsciousness.' Miller insisted he was making a third movie because Max had 'become a personal obsession'.

But tragedy struck *Mad Max 3* (later changed to *Mad Max Beyond Thunderdome)* just one month after that initial announcement. Byron Kennedy died when his helicopter crashed into Lake Burragorang, south of Sydney.

Mel was deeply depressed by the news and, at one stage, he and George Miller considered whether *Mad Max Beyond Thunderdome* should even go ahead. They decided that Kennedy would have definitely wanted them to carry on, so the project continued.

In September 1983, Mel announced the inauguration of the Byron Kennedy Award at the Australian Film Institute awards, as a permanent tribute to his friend. A grant of $10,000 was to be given to a 'young person in the Australian film or TV industry engaged in the same pursuit of excellence that characterised Byron Kennedy's work'.

Mad Max Beyond Thunderdome went before the cameras almost a year later. This time there was no V8 Interceptor, only one death-defying crash and no references to Max's tragic past. Critics said it drew its inspiration from *The Wizard of Oz* ... or *The Thing with Two Heads*. There were 60 children, a headstrong monkey called Sally-Anne, a herd of camels led by an equally headstrong creature named Rodney, and 400 pigs.

Miller's writing partner and *Mad Max*'s co-creator Terry Hayes emphasised that they aimed at giving Max humanity. 'What we want to do is have a lot of fun out there, especially with the kids, and show there's something unquenchable in the human spirit.'

But the most significant change was the creation of Aunty Entity, a powerful, exotic black woman with a dark blonde head of hair and a magnificent body, who could be played by only one person – American rock 'n' roll diva Tina Turner. When George Miller summoned her to Australia to play Aunty Entity, it was an offer the multi-Grammy award-winning singer could not refuse – although she confessed, 'I only wish I could tell you what this role is all about.'

Despite the press's desire for an explosive off-screen romance between the two stars, Tina laid it on the line: 'Mel's beautiful and handsome, but he's a boy and I like a man. I like strength in a man; a man also has to like me. But he must have that masculinity about him – and a few other things besides ... I'm sorry, I can't tell the girls he's a great lover.'

It was becoming clear around this time that Mel was tending to launch every morning with a can of beer, and he was once again putting his foot in it, helped by a *People* magazine reporter sent to do a piece from the set of *Beyond Thunderdome.*

'I don't even want to be making this film ... Don't print that,' rasped the allegedly sneering, surly Mel. Naturally, the reporter printed every spit, comma and euphemistic asterisk.

But it was his comments about that recurring, haunting theme of fame and how to handle it that conveyed his true feelings at the time. 'It's all happening too fast. I've got to put some brakes on or I'll smack into something. It's hard to keep your head above water when the flood-tide of Hollywood hype hits. My brain keeps me sane and my wife and family, who have no illusions about me.'

In a classic 'Mel-ism', he described being a star as 'having your pants down around the ankles and your hands tied around your back, so it's a good opportunity for some parasite to come up and throw darts in your chest'.

Mad Max Beyond Thunderdome got good reviews on its release in July 1985. The *New York Times* said Mel has 'that stately world-weariness that makes him irresistible', while the *New York Post* suggested, 'In the end, the crazy images and unthinkable brutality creates and communicates a unique crude poetry that is both primitive and beautiful. Acting is the last thing on anybody's mind, but Mel Gibson gets through it without smiling and Tina Turner, as the barbaric queen of Bartertown, is Grace Jones with soul food.'

Even the normally staid *Los Angeles Times* critic Michael Wilmington saluted the movie as 'outrageously entertaining … It's a hideous world, but it has a hideous energy. It pulses with furious life.'

Mel read the reviews with bemusement. He had tried to break away from the *Mad Max* mould by starring in numerous other, completely different types of movies. But the character of Max remained the one his adoring public liked best.

Wanting to experience all types of roles, he was starting to learn that he could use his stardom to find new projects that might really test him. The hazard was that many of those scripts did not contain the right ingredients for his fans.

In January 1987, Mel turned down an extraordinary $22 million offer to play Max one more time. Having already filmed the first in the *Lethal Weapon* series, Mel knew that it was best if Max remained dead and buried. Although he did not disclose it at the time, his desperate search for a potential series of movies had ended with *Lethal Weapon*.

One of his associates states flatly, 'No amount of money will lure him back to play Mad Max again.'

The *Mad Max* films appeared when the Australian film industry was in the midst of a boom, and Australians were beginning to believe in their own, home-grown talents. Yet, until *Max*, they tended to churn out nostalgic accounts of the past rather than tackle livelier issues. The *Max* movies did not take safe, soft options. Boldly, they confronted the public with a hero who would be equally at home in Dodge City or Ancient Rome. The films were brave, innovative and accomplished, with an energy unique at the time.

Long afterwards, George Miller told the *Los Angeles Times* that Mel was and still is the only Australian-based actor capable of making it really big in Hollywood. 'I would have been surprised if you'd told me that any Australian actor would become a mainstream star but, having said that, I'm not surprised it is Mel. Mel is a greater actor than we've seen on the screen.'

SEVEN

I DON'T GO FOR THAT FREUD STUFF.
IT'S A LOAD OF CRAP.

When filming on the original *Mad Max* came to an exhausting end, Mel took off for Adelaide to join the State Theatre Company of South Australia for a stint on the stage, where he genuinely believed he belonged. He still considered himself to be learning his craft and paying his dues, as he later put it, 'Doing Greek tragedy and Shakespeare, and carrying spears and saying, "I take my leave, my liege."'

He appeared in a number of mainly secondary roles in such plays as *Oedipus Rex*, *Henry IV*, *The Les Darcy Show* and *Cedona*. But almost 1,500 km away in Sydney, his hard-working agents Faith Martin and Bill Shanahan were discovering that Mel's performance in the still unreleased *Mad Max* had created quite a stir. George Miller was raving about the young actor to anyone who would listen, including one of Australia's best-known film industry figures, Michael Pate.

e returned to his homeland after finding fame and fortune in Hollywood as an actor. Since returning to Australia, Pate had become a highly respected producer and director.

On hearing about Mel, Pate immediately contacted Faith Martin and Bill Shanahan to ask if the young actor would be interested in the title role of a film he was slated to direct, titled *Tim*. Based on a novel by Colleen McCullough, writer of *The Thorn Birds*, it was a sensitive story of a sweetly innocent, mentally retarded young handyman who became the object of desire of a spinster old enough to be his mother. The agents immediately sent Pate the video of a screen test Mel had made. Hooked the moment he saw it, he booked the next flight to Adelaide and met young Mel, despite having earmarked his own son Christopher for the role.

Pate remembers his first meeting with then 22-year-old Mel as notably unimpressive. 'I found him ingenuous, naïve, charming in a sort of primitive way and I was beginning to think I had really been too optimistic. I had seen him in *Summer City* without realising it at the time. He had his hair dyed.'

The veteran movie-maker was studying the scruffy young man in faded Levis and a denim jacket, tumbling over his coffee and chain-smoking, and wondering if he had been expecting too much. 'Then I had the idea that perhaps this kind of "face-to-face", casual as I was keeping it, might be too much for him.' So Pate suggested they go to a hotel run by some friends in North Adelaide. Mel insisted he drive.

'You should have seen the inside of that car! It really looked as if he was living in it – which he well could have been.'

Even Mel has cheerfully confessed over the years, 'I am a bit of a slob. I live in my own squalor. Dirty socks ... pants hanging off the light-bulb.'

Pate learned that, after a few drinks, Mel relaxed more and

started to chat away merrily, 'generally being the sweet, open boy he was then'.

That was enough for Pate. He resolved there and then to take a chance on Mel. It turned out to be an interesting experience for all involved. It was also the first time Mel had been properly directed for a movie role.

Tim was essentially the story of Mary Horton (Piper Laurie), an attractive woman in her mid-40s, who meets Tim (Mel Gibson) when, as a building labourer working next door, he is asked to hose dust from her garden. Gradually, a friendship develops, during which Mary helps him to read, to paint and to understand a little more of things he never had the chance to learn. Without Mary realising it, Tim is also helping her, teaching her, by example, to enjoy simple pleasures, bringing warmth into her life.

The script was essentially a two-hander for Tim and Mary – which presented some testing scenes for writers, directors and actors. Like all simple movie stories, it had to be very real and identifiable to work.

Up-front as ever, Mel told Pate, during the first few days of filming, that he had 'never been directed' before, that all he could remember about *Mad Max* – true or false – was being told to stand here, look there, walk here.

'He really had very little film technique in those early days on *Tim*. But he absorbed direction like a great big sponge; he learned very quickly and, I considered, very well. After all, the cast around him were all very experienced and competent film and TV performers,' recalled Pate.

Among those performers was twice-Oscar-nominated actress Piper Laurie, playing the older woman who seduces Tim. She and Mel hit it off from the moment they met.

'It's incredible when you realise it was only Mel's second feature film. It's not an easy role, yet he brings a warmth and presence you expect only from an actor who has been around for a long time,' says Laurie.

It's interesting to note the reference to his 'second film'. Already, Mel was avoiding any mention of *Summer City*. Studio publicity hand-outs fail to mention his real début movie.

Shooting of *Tim* was carried out mainly around the picturesque peninsula area, about 60km north of Sydney. Mel, used to the kick-and-scramble school of movie-making, nonplussed the production co-ordinator when he announced the day before filming started that he would be staying at various addresses around the area. It was a situation that every line producer dreads – nightmare scenarios of him not showing up on the set were rushing through the executives' minds.

Initially, Mel suggested he would travel back to his parents' home in Mount Kuring-gai each night, and get up at dawn to make the 7.30am call-time. But then came his alternative plan – which threw the whole production into chaos. Production manager Betty Barnard remembers, 'We were about to start the shoot and there was this awful problem of getting Mel to the location, after he decided to stay with friends. Either there was something of the nomad in his blood or he had friends everywhere, because we'd get a series of telephone numbers to follow his wanderings.'

Even Mel apologised obliquely, in an interview flanked by his mother, after the film had wrapped. 'I guess I've been a bit nomadic these past months. But I always come home … don't I, Mum?'

Anne Gibson just nodded her head in bewilderment.

Back on the set of *Tim*, Mel's lack of a home base did nothing to stop it being by far his most enjoyable movie-making experience to date. He praised Michael Pate as 'an actor's actor and an actor's director. He really knows what it is all about and what to ask for at exactly the right time.' Even Piper commented on this. She said it was something that eluded many directors.

And after making two films where money was so tight that most scenes were shot at breakneck speed, Mel found himself admired for his extraordinary ability to get it right on the first take.

'One-take Mel, we called him,' said Betty Barnard. 'It was marvellous to see a new face with loads of talent to match.'

But what the production team did not realise was that Mel was angry with himself every time he got it right so quickly – because he wanted to develop the character of Tim and try different approaches to each scene. But once Pate and his crew had a good take in the can, they simply moved on to the next set-up.

Those two previous films had made Mel, in his own eyes, much too sloppy. He wanted to slow down. He believed that the key to success in his acting was to do every scene to perfection, but until he actually managed to land a role in a big-budget feature film that opportunity always eluded him.

Author Colleen McCullough – one of Australia's most celebrated writers – was full of praise for Mel, whom she saw as the perfect Tim. 'He was absolutely right for the part. Michael Pate is a shrewd judge of talent. *Tim* worked wonderfully and I must admit that Mel Gibson was one of the prime reasons.'

Mel himself tried very hard to mould the character of Tim into something that he thought would appeal to everyone. He made a special point of observing the behaviour of one of his young nephews and made low-key visits to mental institutions to help him understand the role more clearly. He refuses to share the impression left on him by those visits, but they seemed to bring out yet another side of his character. Those

91

close to him say that he became a more sensitive person during the filming of *Tim*. Many believe that having to play someone with learning difficulties made Mel examine his own role in life. He explained during filming, 'I'd read the book and knew how I was going to attack it. It had to be pretty low-key. You can't have a spastic-looking guy. It was more like childlike innocence and obedience ... It wasn't all that difficult – I'm quite simple myself really.'

The truth was that, despite the happy atmosphere and Michael Pate's gushing enthusiasm, *Tim* was a fairly amateurish-looking movie that did reasonable business in Australia but totally failed at the all-important US box office. As is sometimes the case in inferior productions, Mel's performance in *Tim* seems all the more impressive because the movie is mediocre.

'It's difficult not to shine when you are in a film like *Tim*,' commented one film critic. But the *New York Post* perceived Mel's performance as 'a thing of beauty, in its subtle shading of an adult with a very young mind'.

Mel has been relatively non-committal about *Tim* in recent years, although it did him more good than harm and earned him an Australian Film Institute Best Actor award in 1979. It was a remarkable achievement for someone who had made only three films.

Making *Tim* also thrust Mel much more into the public eye. *Mad Max* had not yet been released in cinemas and there was little hint of the incredible success that film would attain.

Many critics so far had been relatively non-committal about Mel's attributes. Not so Liz Porter, who, writing in Australia's *Cleo* magazine in December 1979, was one of the few writers at the time to appreciate what made Mel tick. 'For Mel Gibson to be identified with the role of strong, silent Max would be particularly unjust. Mel is anything but sullen ... or silent. He's a natural clown and a hilarious comic. Not a show-off, clowning just appears to be part of his nature, which makes him a most delightful and entertaining victim for an interviewer,' she stated in an article aptly headlined 'MAD ABOUT MEL'.

Met returned to his NIDA lead role in *Romeo and Juliet* at Sydney's Nimrod Theatre around the time that *Mad Max* was finally premièred in January of 1979. With crowds of movie-goers flocking to see him ripping people's arms out of their sockets, and shooting villains galore, it did not go unnoticed that the talented young star was playing exactly the opposite role on the stage.

As Mel put it in deadpan style, 'Romeo is a young guy who is just dying to be loved – in fact, he does die for it ... I love the words and the scope of Shakespeare. His words are full of possibilities for interpretation, for nuances in delivery.'

His co-star in *Romeo and Juliet* was Angela Punch McGregor, a well-known Australian stage and television actress. She was stunned when young women in the audience started throwing bouquets at the stage. At first, she assumed they were for her, then it dawned on her that the avid stares of lusting young ladies were exclusively for her young co-star.

At that time, shy dental nurse Robyn Moore was not even engaged to Mel Gibson, far less wed to him. Yet while staying behind the scenes, she was a major if gentle influence. Robyn had crossed an important personal threshold and had made an implicit statement by following him out to Sydney just before shooting started on *Tim*.

But only to personal friends did Mel so much as mention his Robyn. It was as if he was treating her as somebody too special for small-talk with people who didn't matter. Not for nothing has he called her 'my Rock of Gibraltar, only more beautiful'.

He had picked, in psychological terms, a highly significant and potent symbol. Surely Robyn Moore represented sanity and reality to somebody fighting for recognition in an environment where those qualities are as rare as endangered species.

Despite his intensely private wooing of Robyn, the press and many of his colleagues preferred to think of the Hot Young Actor as a carefree, girl-crazy Lothario who regularly played the field. It made sense – he had ample opportunity.

A brace of strong stage performances followed *Romeo and Juliet*. Mel appeared in *No Names, No Pack Drill*, playing Rebel, a US marine who shuns the Halls of Montezuma to go AWOL in Sydney in 1942 and have an affair with an Australian nightclub singer. Then came Samuel Beckett's gnomic masterpiece *Waiting for Godot*.

Rave reviews rewarded Mel's portrayal of Estragon, lost soul and probably the most famous waiter never to see the inside of a restaurant. Yes, it has been a long and winding – and surprisingly cultured – road to reach Martin Riggs, the living Lethal Weapon.

Mel gave a characteristically straightforward appraisal of his performance. 'Now that was something. Strange casting, do you think? I thought so, too. I'm 60 years too young for that role. But we used that. It was a very stylised production. We were clowns more than bums. That part required probably the most physical strength I ever had to produce for a role.

'We did vaudeville and we did things that seemed to defy physics and gravity. I had to make myself short without appearing to be stooping or something. Plus stand on tiptoe on one leg with my other stretched out at a forty-five-degree angle for like minutes on end. It was discipline. It was fantastic.

'I lost about ten pounds every night. From sweat. By the end of the show, we'd look shithouse. We'd go out there with sort of tramp make-up on – sort of white but with five o'clock shadows – and we'd end up being just mud. Everything running down our faces.'

What Mel did not tell the world was that, during his stint on *Waiting for Godot*, he developed alarming breathing problems, made worse by his 30–40-cigarettes-a-day habit. Fellow actors recall him having five-minute-long coughing fits backstage which left him gasping, eyes streaming.

He found himself literally struggling to breathe on stage one night. Lying down supposedly asleep while his co-star Geoffrey Rush as Vladimir was in the middle of a long soliloquy, Mel lay there for minutes in absolute agony, praying that he could resist the oncoming coughing fit. Every now and then, his body would twitch as he went rigid to try and avoid the inevitable. Gradually, tears of pain started rolling down his cheeks but he did not flinch and managed to survive without any embarrassing moments.

Years later, as his smoking habit worsened, he must have wondered if it would have been better if his coughing fit had occurred that night, then it might have made him stop immediately. As it was, he used the dreaded weed more and more, finding it impossible even to rehearse his lines without a cigarette between his lips. Significantly, he still *never* smoked in Hutton Gibson's household.

Mel would opine about his passion for the theatre with the same level of energy that he put into his performances each evening. He adored the atmosphere, the crowd and the no-safety net nature of it. He maintains that, if he could have supported a family purely on his theatrical earnings, he would have been the happiest guy on the street.

But the Australian film industry was re-emerging from decades of inactivity at that time and Hollywood became aware that interesting talent could be found Down Under.

Admittedly, some not so desirable film projects managed to thumb a ride on the back of the good name of the rapidly expanding Australian film industry. One such movie was *Attack Force Z*, and it would plunge Mel Gibson into an artistic abyss and, to his mind, put his career into a steep decline.

When Mel and co-stars John Phillip Law, who had made a name for himself in *Barbarella*, the New Zealand-born Sam Neill (later to star in films like *The Hunt for Red October*) and two talented Aussies, Chris Haywood and John Waters, signed up for *Attack Force Z*, they had no idea of the problems they would encounter or the sexual adventures ahead.

The story sounded, and read initially, like a good, old-fashioned World War II adventure: a bunch of undercover Aussie soldiers, led by a Dutch commando, land on a Japanese-held island in the Pacific and, aided by loyal Chinese, bring back a defecting Japanese scientist.

Mel did not hesitate to sign up for the movie when he met highly regarded Australian director Phillip Noyce, who had won international acclaim for his newsreel nostalgia drama *Newsfront*. Noyce's own father had been a member of the real-life squad of commandos upon which the story was based, so Mel felt he had a superb grasp of the subject.

The other 'bonus' was that *Attack Force Z* was going to be filmed entirely in exotic locations in Taiwan, partly because it looked right but also because it was a cheap place to hire labour and the film was being partly backed by an Asian company, the Central Motion Pictures Corporation of Taiwan. The project's other partner was the successful Australian company John McCallum Productions, makers of the television series.

But even before filming began, director Noyce clashed with *Skippy* producer Lee Robinson over changes he had made in the script. It was that old familiar story of an artist (the director) being forced to compromise the quality of a movie, thanks to a producer trying to make sure it did not go over budget. The day before shooting was scheduled to commence, Noyce – who went on to direct *Patriot Games*, *Dead Calm* (with Sam Neill) and *Conundrum* with Sally Field – departed. His replacement was Tim Burstall, an experienced Melbourne-based director with some highly-praised Aussie films such as *Alvin Purple* and *The Last of the Knucklemen* to his credit. Unfortunately, Mel and the other actors, excluding American star John Phillip Law, feared that this change in leader would be a complete disaster. Law was deemed the star because of his work on a string of Hollywood films. He also happened to be a box-office attraction in Asia.

Tim Burstall had never spoken about working with Mel on *Attack Force Z*, but in a series of talks he revealed the full story of what really happened during that six-week shoot in Taiwan.

'It was a crazy situation. Chaos. I certainly did not get what I wanted. The film suffered from so many problems.'

Within hours of arriving at their base in the capital city of Taipei, Burstall was facing a deputation of actors led by Mel and Sam Neill, who made it perfectly clear that, if they could wriggle out of their contracts, they would desert the film immediately.

'I took them aside and said, "You make me ashamed to be an Australian. What the *fuck* are you doing?" It was the most disgusting example of Aussie unionism. I was pretty angry. I felt like taking them outside and kicking their fucking heads in. I wanted to shame them into doing something.'

That night, Sam Neill visited Burstall in his hotel and told the director that he had talked to Mel and 'we have no choice but to work together'.

The director is painfully candid. 'The person least happy was

Mel. He disgusted me the most. He placed me in a continually difficult position.' He even suggested that Mel distrusted him partly because of the rivalry that exists between Aussies from Sydney and those from Melbourne. The truth was far more complex – Mel felt he had yet again been betrayed by the broken promises of cheapskate film producers. Here he was on his fourth movie, with second billing to a major star like Law, yet the problems haunting *Summer City* and *Mad Max* and, to a lesser extent, *Tim* had returned.

Law – who today, ironically, lives only a few miles from Mel Gibson's home in Malibu – also broke a long silence to talk about the film. He accepts that 'the movie was blown apart by Phillip Noyce's departure. It was a terrible situation for the actors. They felt double-crossed by the producers.'

But Law sided entirely with new director Burstall because he knew they had to get the film shot. And Mel and the other Aussies were further needled by the fact that Law was staying in a grand hotel overlooking their smaller accommodation in Taipei, and he was supplied with a car and driver for the entire shoot. The rest of the actors were given rides in a scruffy old van to and from the location, and had to fend for themselves the rest of the time.

In later years, Mel laughed off his experiences in Taiwan, claiming that his skill at miming springs from trying to communicate with the Chinese on the set. 'Up there in Taiwan, we were all good mimers. As we didn't speak the same language, we used signal language. In the end, we found there wasn't any barrier in communicating.'

The truth was that barriers were being set up daily as problem after problem plagued the production. There were local gang members to be accommodated, Burstall was rewriting the script as they went along – a disastrous method when you are shooting to a tight schedule – and then there was the cinematography of local cameraman Lin Hung-Chung. It could be best described as 'choppy', but the biggest omission was that those famous azure-blue eyes of Mel's were never even passingly exploited.

Tim Burstall believes that Mel 'had some personal troubles at the time' and cites one flare-up with the young actor that shows just how on edge he was feeling. 'There was a fight sequence and I remember explaining something to Mel and halfway through he just threw his gun down and said, "You're fucking taking away my responsibilities as a hero." He had failed to grasp the whole point of the fight sequence. He did not realise I was trying to help him. Mel just would not accept what I was saying.'

Intriguingly, Burstall also says that Mel had trouble acting out the emotional scenes in the film. 'I was unhappy with his approach when he had to show emotion. These were moments that required his internalisation: He just did not give it enough.'

Attack Force Z also marked the first time that Mel had cause to regret his lack of height. Co-star John Phillip Law towered over him at 6ft 5in. In publicity hand-outs, Mel is said to be somewhere between 5ft 9in and 5ft 10in. But, like one of his biggest movie heroes, Gary Cooper, Mel is actually often much shorter than many actors around him. Law thinks he is about 5ft 6in, but it would probably be more realistic to estimate his height at around 5ft 8in. During shooting of *Attack Force Z*, they devised all sorts of tricks to make him appear to be a similar height to Law.

'I am very used to doing that equaliser thing, but I was very taken aback by his size,' Law says. 'I had to regularly kneel down and have him alongside me, standing. That way, we could do things together. Often, he would stand and I'd duck around the set. There was a lot of effort made to make him look the same height. It was perfectly understandable. A lot of actors are sensitive about it ... I did all my close-ups with my legs spread apart so both our heads could be in the camera frame.'

And during filming of *The Year of Living Dangerously* with 6ft 1in Sigourney Weaver towering over him, Mel's shoes were secretly given a built-up instep so that he would look taller.

Halfway through the troublesome and unhappy *Attack Force Z* shoot, Chinese star Mr Koo took it upon himself to improve communications by inviting Mel, Law, Burstall, Sam Neill and another Aussie actor on a getaway weekend to Kaohsiung, Taiwan's second biggest city, where Mr Koo was an uncrowned king. The five men gladly accepted Mr Koo's offer, especially when he insisted on paying for the entire trip.

On the first evening of that trip, Mr Koo actually took the *Attack Force Z* party to a brothel. He believed that, by indulging his round-eyed colleagues sexually, it might help them all to 'bond' better.

'Koo called it a restaurant but it was basically a brothel, serving Japanese food,' recalls Tim Burstall. 'It turned out to be an absolute feast. A new girl would come round every second course. All they had on were little towels around their necks and they would pull a chair up and sit next to us. Mr Koo would then say something like, "Touch them, Mr Tim." We were made to feel like royalty.

'Koo wanted to make us all get along better. He was forcing drinks down us and all these women were made available. This was hospitality Chinese-style. The tradition in China is to fix up Westerners with women and then find out exactly what they like.'

John Phillip Law has an even more vivid recollection of the experience. 'At first, we all sat there shit-faced and didn't know how to act. We were so worried about offending anyone. We had a hell of a time. It was such a bizarre evening. Mr Koo just wanted to do his thing for us, and this was it … boy!'

At first, disclosed Law, none of the party realised where Mr Koo had taken them. Initially, they settled down in. a huge room with a big round table and waited to be served.

'We were totally unaware of what was to come. I remember there was a bed in the corner with a lamp. It became a topic of conversation between us.'

As the night wore on, a girl walked into the room.

'She sat on one of the guys' laps and then the parade started. Koo paid for everything. He was the host and would have resented us offering to pay. Koo would orchestrate a little and say: "Which one do you like?" and "Take your pick". It was like a sample situation. He said have as many as you want. It says a lot about the film that this was the most memorable thing about it.'

Law, remarkably, argues 'there was nothing sordid' about what happened in that bordello.

'It was an ice-breaker. When in Rome do as the Romans do. There is not the stigma attached to their occupation as there is in other countries. If a girl is from a poor family and she is a knock out then she can better herself. It was just doing a service. It was very refreshing to see it. It was very amusing. It is hard to be judgemental about situations like that.'

Two years later, Mel slammed *Attack Force Z* in a bad-tempered outburst, saying he had only taken the role 'for the money'. 'It was just a vulgar attempt at a war/action movie with Aussie WASPs [White Anglo-Saxon Protestants] shooting Chinese dressed up in Japanese uniforms. I don't like to talk about or even remember that film. You do that kind of film because you are starving to death.'

In Australia, *Attack Force Z* was released in a cinema in Melbourne in June 1982. It was never released in American cinemas and ended up being shown on US cable television, but many believe that Mel's criticisms of the movie are based as much on his real-life experiences during the shoot as they are on the quality of the end-product.

One review in *Variety* concluded that it was 'a good example of a well-paced, finely-acted war film, not much short of super ... ahead of many more-vaunted Aussie productions'. The same reviewer heaped praise on much-maligned director Burstall, writing that 'he got to grips with essentials of structure and plotting, and developed the characters firmly and economically'.

Scott Murray, of *Cinema Papers,* concedes, 'It's not as bad as it's made out. It is an OK picture of its kind.'

The *Attack Force Z* shoot ended around January 1980. Tim Burstall was pleasantly surprised when embittered Mel turned up one evening in the cramped editing room in King's Cross, Sydney, where Burstall was trying to knit together the film, some months afterwards. 'We had a drink and he told me he was getting married. He was rather sheepish about it and most of his friends thought it was Disasterville – that the girl was trying to get him and he was just a poor demented Catholic kid.'

One of Mel's best friends at the time said there was talk of Robyn being pregnant; it might explain the eventual birth of their eldest child Hannah later that same year.

To most people these days, marrying after conception of a child is hardly a shocking situation. But, for Mel, it would present a few problems at home – where Hutton Gibson was still passionately fighting the Roman Catholic hierarchy. Now his own flesh and blood was about to undergo a shotgun wedding to a Church of England girl.

EIGHT

I GET MY EARS BOXED IF I'M NOT HOME BY MIDNIGHT.
MARRIAGE IS HARD WORK.

Mel could not wait to get back to the sanity of Sydney
after the madness and mayhem in Taiwan. In many
ways, his lengthy stay in that tiny country had taught him
more lessons about life than he cared to admit. He'd escaped
from those unhappy work conditions in bottle after bottle of
the local beer. Mel felt overwhelmed with guilt, the sort
you can only really suffer if you have been brought up a
strict Catholic.

People who encountered Mel in the early months of 1980
report that he was more moody. The cocky self-confidence
that had seemed so much a part of his character was replaced
by something quieter, more thoughtful. But then 1980
threatened to be among the most significant years in his life.

First, there was Robyn. She was content to remain firmly in
the background, but Mel's experiences in Asia made him
realise how much he needed her calming influence. Back in
Sydney, Mel was suffering from that classic actor's problem –

103

lack of work. His $6,000 fee for *Attack Force Z* was disappearing fast and he was finding himself more and more reliant on Robyn's hard-earned wage as a nurse. She, in turn, was more than happy to go out and earn the money while Mel waited for a good, quality job to come up. His experiences in Taiwan had taught him never to accept acting work simply for the money; there had to be some quality to the projects. He was better off starving than damaging his career.

And to her immense credit, Robyn, still no more than his girlfriend at the start of 1980, was prepared to support Mel all the way. He was amazed by her generosity and deeply touched by her loyalty. Mel also loved the fact that, after three years of talking, eating and breathing acting with friends like Steve Bisley and Monroe Reimers, as well as a procession of acting girlfriends, here was someone who neither knew nor cared much about the art of being dramatic. In fact, Robyn could not have been less similar to some of the actresses Mel had encountered during his late teens and early twenties.

It also says much about his interest in her that he waited at least a year while Robyn went through that other relationship with a boyfriend before the two even began to consider actually dating.

As the boredom of being unemployed set in, Mel grew even surer that Robyn Denise Moore was just the sort of girl his father Hutton had always advised him to look out for. The little matter of her being brought up in the Church of England was the only minor obstacle. Marriage was being talked about between Mel and Robyn when he bumped into *Attack Force Z* director Tim Burstall in April, during the middle of one of his 'lean spells' of unemployment.

There was gossip among his closest friends and stage acquaintances that Robyn was pregnant and a wedding was imminent. Mel, for his part, volunteered little. After all, he had spent many years preaching the importance of marrying a virgin, even to girlfriends like Deborah Foreman. And his opinions on abortion were absolutely crystal-clear, as he stated very bluntly in an interview with *Cosmopolitan* less than three years later, 'Abortion? It's inhuman because it destroys life. Who presumes to know where life starts? I'll tell you one thing – the foetus grows, its heart beats. It's like when you strike a match ... is there a flame, or do we just imagine it?' Asked if he would ever force a woman to have an abortion he replied, 'Well, I wouldn't get one!'

The irony of the situation was that no one, apart from Mel and his family, was that bothered about the fact that Robyn was pregnant. The most important thing was that he truly loved Robyn and wanted to spend the rest of his life with her – and there was absolutely no doubting that. Mel found her to be a rare, stable, down-to-earth person, and his is a business where personal relationships crumble with alarming regularity.

When Mel got a call from agent Bill Shanahan to say that an offer of a meaty role in a new Australian television series called *Punishment* was on the cards, he decided that, pregnancy or no pregnancy, he should marry Robyn as soon as possible.

The wedding on 7 June 1980 was a restrained affair and no one present has ever provided an account of what actually happened. All that is known is that it took place in a church in the community of Forestville, New South Wales, and the priest who officiated was the Reverend Clement Gailey. Most families would have proudly announced such a wedding in the local press and Mel, by then the veteran of three films, might well have attracted the attention of the media. It was even claimed by one newspaper that the marriage was carried out in such secrecy because Mel did not want to ruin his image as a sex-symbol. The truth seems more likely to be that religious differences, and the possibility of a baby being on the way, made for a hastily arranged ceremony.

Whatever the circumstances, Mel felt hugely relieved to be married, though he and his bride were still relatively young at 24. He had been brought up to believe in the sanctity of marriage and he genuinely believed that having a partner like Robyn would stabilise his life. Above all, they truly loved each other.

His mother Anne recalled how Mel broached the subject of marriage in a very roundabout way with his parents, shortly before the wedding.

'He was talking about marriage and families in a general way and asked us for advice. Hutton, who's always been Mel's hero, said he should never marry a dumb woman, and pick someone who can be your friend for life. I added the reasoning of a mum, telling Mel he should always be kind to his wife.'

In fairness to religious fanatic Hutton, he does not seem to have been as upset by the circumstances surrounding the marriage as some of Mel's friends expected. Both parents had warmly emphasised to their son that true love and happiness in a marriage had little to do with religion, and more with respect and friendship.

Mel and Robyn spent their honeymoon at a friend's beach house up the coast from Sydney. For the first time since leaving home in his second year at NIDA, Mel felt that he was getting his life under control once more. He was more settled and hoped that his acting career would start moving in the right direction.

Unfortunately, that direction did not lead to the Channel Ten prison drama *Punishment*. Mel regretted accepting the role of an inmate of fictitious Longridge Prison the moment he walked on to the set at the East Sydney Technical College. He had accepted the part after a long stint of unemployment but his heart wasn't in it. The relentless six-day-a-week shooting schedule evoked the worst aspects of his experiences on *The Sullivans* a few years previously. Television's churn-it-out ethic was not something that Mel could warm to, let alone welcome, and he showed that by turning up late on one occasion when many of Sydney's press were present on set. It didn't go unnoticed.

While *Mad Max* might have bombed in the United States, agents Bill Shanahan and Faith Martin knew that Mel was now hot property. Throughout the rest of the world the film had been a huge commercial success and Shanahan was particularly adept at exploiting the explosion of interest in his young client. The agent became a showbusiness father figure to Mel as he nurtured and humoured him. Shanahan was not a stock type, get-rich-quick agent. He was a patient, caring man with Mel's best interests at heart. Mel, in turn, greatly respected the opinion of Shanahan. So both men were delighted when director Peter Weir made an approach to cast Mel in one of the lead roles in his movie *Gallipoli*.

Weir – who had made his reputation with the wonderfully haunting *Picnic at Hanging Rock* – spent four years honing and moulding the perfect script in conjunction with Australian writer David Williamson. Then he had carted the project around from company to company in a desperate effort to get it financed at a level that would enable him to film a true, authentic version of one of the most tragic events in Australian history.

Peter Weir wanted to bring all the horror, futility and madness of Gallipoli to the screen through the eyes of two young Australian soldiers who set out to war thinking of it as an adventure only to discover a nightmare.

Weir and Williamson's script floated around Sydney for

years until theatrical entrepreneur and record producer Robert Stigwood showed it to his new business partner Rupert Murdoch, the most famous Australian publisher in the world. Stigwood – master of groups like the Bee Gees and backer of *Saturday Night Fever* – and Murdoch were an unlikely partnership but their R and R Films claimed to be committed to backing Australian movies to the tune of $50 million.

Murdoch – owner of the very same tabloid newspapers that would come to stalk and pillory Mel in later years – had another, very deep-set interest in *Gallipoli*, beyond being a patriotic Australian. His own father, the great Australian journalist Keith Murdoch, had covered the battle, landed with the ANZAC troops in Turkey and sent back dispatches that helped expose the tragedy caused by inept generals and Winston Churchill himself.

Murdoch – who later went on to purchase 20th Century Fox – and Stigwood were so taken by the *Gallipoli* script that they immediately contacted Peter Weir and struck a deal. Stigwood told the rather overawed director, 'This is the film we want to make.'

Weir then made his approach to Mel, who was instantly captivated by the subject matter, especially since it cast the British in a poor light. Mel was particularly moved by one scene in the film when the Aussies are ordered by their British superiors to advance into battle, bayonets drawn but rifles unloaded, in spite of the Turks having dug in. Mel saw it as a typical example of the stupidity and cowardice of the British.

The director had always wanted Mel for the key part of Frank, and Mel saw *Gallipoli* as an opportunity to play a role with real depth and compassion – something that had so far eluded him as a film performer.

But Mel did make one stipulation to director Weir before agreeing to the $35,000 fee on offer for *Gallipoli*. He steadfastly refused to do any explicit sex scenes, although he did bare his torso for a nude bathing sequence.

In an interview with respected movie journalist Dan Yakir, Mel provided a unique insight into, perhaps, his true feelings about sex when he said, 'I might do a love scene, but nothing too explicit – no close-ups or noises because it would be an obstacle in my way. It would kill something I want to preserve. I don't want to give too much to the viewers – mystery is important, because the moment they think they know you too well ...'

On signing up for *Gallipoli*, Mel plunged into weeks of research, reading books by historian CEW Bean, diaries and letters written by soldiers and tracking down and chatting to old soldiers. Mel knew he had to gain a sense of history about Gallipoli, otherwise he could not truly honour the emotions felt by all Australians about this national disaster. And Mel saw Frank as a knight in shining armour fighting a battle in which men's lives were sacrificed as if they were nothing more than pieces of meat.

The part of the other soldier, Archie, was to be played by blond, blue-eyed Mark Lee. His character – although working-class, like Frank – believed all that propaganda about the rightness of fighting the Germans and their allies. Mark had never before acted in a feature film and admitted that he was 'terrified' at the prospect.

For the first few weeks of filming, he found it virtually impossible to relax, on or off the set, and even out-puffed Mel in the chain-smoking department. Lee – a softly spoken, all-Australian character – never really emerged from beneath Mel's shadow in *Gallipoli*, although the other man tried hard to make their relationship work.

Lee sounded completely in awe of his co-star when he said, 'Mel has it – he is wonderful in *Mad Max* ... he adds a human dimension to a comic strip character.'

In Hollywood, stars often go out of their way to overshadow newcomers. But Mel – as the veteran of the pair – did not react that way at all. He recognised that it was completely in his interests to elicit a good performance from Lee, and so did Peter Weir.

The director at one stage slapped and shook Lee to snap him out of his fear-riddled paralysis. 'Then he would make me laugh by making faces at me and taking his shirt off. He took me by surprise and kept the energy going,' said Lee.

'I was going about it all wrong. I would smoke a dozen cigarettes between takes and shake as though I had a fever. I was lost.'

Gradually, Lee gained sufficient confidence at least to make the relationship between the two characters believable. Mel took pains to win the younger actor's friendship. They grew to like each other and the most moving scenes were shot after they had 'connected'.

Throughout the shoot, it sometimes seemed as if Weir deliberately put his stars through the mill to make sure they felt the full horrors of war every time they stepped before the cameras.

The first location was near the outback settlement of Beltana in the lower Flinders Ranges in South Australia. Temperatures were consistently above 40°C and regular dust storms added to everyone's anguish. There were no hotels for hundreds of kilometres and home for a few weeks was a shearing shed with the occasional sand-gritted meal supplied from the bed of a pick-up truck. Mel had started in films under the impression that it was a glamorous business, but here he was on his fourth movie and, so far, he had only stayed in a hotel during the making of *Attack Force Z* – and that had been a dump.

In Beltana, the crew were relegated to a nearby woolshed,

although there was serious debate over which building was more smelly. However, all complaints soon subsided when the *Gallipoli* cast and crew got to their next location, Lake Torrens, an ancient, dry salt plain on the edge of the desert. This time, it was bitterly cold and infested with poisonous funnel web spiders capable of killing a human.

'They're the most vicious spiders in the world,' Mel expounded with relish. 'If they bite you, you're a goner. Deadliest things around – big, black, hairy and very aggressive.' Luckily, no one got bitten.

Next stop was Port Lincoln where, much to their relief, the cast and crew found pubs complete with cold beer and welcoming locals. 'We embraced the town – and they embraced us,' said actor Bill Hunter, who won the Australian Film Institute's award for Best Supporting Actor for his *Gallipoli* performance.

But filming in Port Lincoln was no easier; everyone worked horrendously long hours, from dusk to dawn, complete with high temperatures, constant swarms of flies and yet more sandstorms.

However, none of this seemed to bother Mel in the slightest. He felt as if he truly belonged in *Gallipoli*. When he wasn't needed in front of the cameras, he would help prop men load and unload equipment. He enjoyed being one of the boys and the crew warmed to him as 'being one of us'. But Mel kept one thing very much to himself – Robyn's pregnancy. As the weeks on *Gallipoli* passed, Mel began hoping and praying that filming would end on schedule so that he could get back to Adelaide, where Robyn had gone to be with her family before the birth of their first child.

The last two weeks of filming were a race against time for the producers, rapidly running out of funds, and for Mel, who was running out of days before Robyn had that baby.

Unfortunately, as Mel later joked, the movie's location scouts had decided that the last sequences to be filmed would be in Egypt, which took him well beyond reach of Robyn if that baby appeared.

Weir wanted to show Frank and Archie enjoying the sights and sounds of Cairo's *souks* and then marvelling at the pyramids, before leaving for Gallipoli.

Mel joked with producer Pat Lovell that he would walk off the set if Robyn's baby turned up early. As with many of Mel's wisecracks, there was a serious undertone.

At the end of November, Mel put one of his daily calls in to Robyn at her family's home in Adelaide. The baby was already on the way and Robyn's sister suggested Mel call back later.

'No way,' came the reply. He was seething because he could not be there. Now, at least, he had a chance to hear the birth, if nothing else. The phone was rested on a bedside table and he sat down on his hotel bed and listened.

So, with an Egyptian hotel telephone operator regularly interrupting to ask if the actor had finished his long-distance call, Mel monitored as a midwife, doctor and close family gathered in that tiny bedroom in Adelaide and Robyn gave birth to a healthy little girl called Hannah.

Mel exulted, 'I got through just as the baby's head was appearing. I could hear every sigh and cry. I heard everything – and I mean everything – not just somebody telling me.'

But the line kept cutting out and the anxious expectant father admitted later it was 'touch and go'.

Once the baby was born, Mel heard the midwife and Robyn's sister saying, 'Oh it's beautiful ... Oh-oh ... Hell, it's a girl.'

'It was a wonderful experience,' exclaimed Mel.

Predictably, the reviews of *Gallipoli* were superb, except in Britain where the *Sunday Times* described it as 'a curious piece of work ... by turn sanguine and tragic, schoolboyish and disillusioned, artless and arty'. The normally stuffier *Sunday Telegraph* admitted, 'to a large extent, it succeeded', and described the final shot of the movie as an 'image of considerable poetic resonance'.

In Australia, the highly regarded *Australian Film Review* magazine acclaimed *Gallipoli* as 'a symbolic focus for the industry's aspirations – a key event in Australia's history, rich with accumulated mythical force, brought to the screen in irreducibly Australian language by leading talents backed up with enough money to give them range and flexibility'.

In the United States, critics described Mel as 'excellent' and *Newsweek* called his role 'most enjoyable'.

Surprisingly, the film was labelled 'predictably anti-British' by film-maker and movie writer Scott Murray, editor of Australia's *Cinema Papers* magazine. 'It was definitely let down by the Pommy bashing and it is like a celebration of failure, and I felt there was no spark between Mel and Mark Lee.'

But Richard Wherrett, who directed Mel in *Romeo and Juliet* in his second year at NIDA, has no doubt that his performance in *Gallipoli* was a turning-point for the young actor. 'It is his physical participation, a sensuality that marks his acting. He is mettlesome, unflappable without being complacent, enormously demanding of his fellow actors and the director. Then there are those intelligent, sensitive eyes. It's simple really – he has a head, a body and a heart.'

Unlike the disastrous camerawork in *Attack Force Z*, director of photography Russell Boyd managed to light Mel's azure-blue eyes to perfection and it was in *Gallipoli* more than any of his earlier efforts that they became his trademark.

Mel offered his own verdict by saying, 'I'm pretty sure it will succeed. It's a very complete movie and, while it doesn't have a happy ending, it's emotionally satisfying.'

Three months before its release, Robert Stigwood pronounced himself so pleased with the just-edited version of *Gallipoli* that he was signing Mel to an exclusive three-picture deal. The Sydney *Sun-Herald* announced an 'unprecedented deal' with Stigwood and Murdoch.

It was reported that Mel and Bill had been flown specially to New York by Stigwood to sign on the dotted line for one Aussie project and two films to be made in the US. Within a short time, the deal faded into oblivion. But it did Mel some good, sparking strong interest from Hollywood.

Three months later, in Australia, the *Gallipoli* première in Sydney was the biggest event in the country's cinematic history. 'OVATION FOR GALLIPOLI' read a headline in the Sydney *Daily Telegraph* on 8 August 1981. Underneath it was a photo of Mel, Robyn and co-star Mark Lee, still looking painfully uncomfortable, just as he had through much of the shooting of the movie.

Gallipoli picked up many awards, including nine from the Australian Film Institute. Mel won yet another Best Actor award. The film also did well at the box office considering its $2 million budget, very modest for the epic nature of the movie. In London, it even beat opposition from the latest James Bond movie, while in the US it grossed $4 million, at that time the best figure for any Australian film.

Yet for some reason, soon after the movie's release, the two Rs – Robert Stigwood and Rupert Murdoch – abandoned their well-publicised plans to inject tens of millions of dollars into the Australian film industry. There was talk of inferior projects being offered to the two tycoons, though there is absolutely no doubt they were delighted with *Gallipoli*. Many inside the Australian film industry believe that, if Murdoch and Stigwood's plans had gone ahead, Mel might well have resisted the temptation to go to Hollywood.

Meanwhile, after *Gallipoli*, Mel was facing a resurgence of interest from the press. Adjectives like 'rebel' and 'temperamental' were being used, projecting Mel as Australia's answer to James Dean.

'A lot of people think I am a rebel. I get a lot of beat-up articles written about me. It's probably because I don't follow any code, any behavioural pattern. I freak people a bit because they don't know what to think about me but there's nothing I can do about that,' he told one interviewer, with brazen unconcern.

Mel was really much more intent on mapping out his career. He told his Sydney agent, Bill Shanahan, that he desperately needed a comic role to play. Shanahan – a wily old hand – agreed with his star that it would be great, but he knew that Mel could fade into oblivion if he stretched himself too far too soon.

Shanahan, in his fatherly way, was more interested in making sure that Mel got his act together now that he had a family to look after. He was worried over Mel's complete inability to turn up on time for appointments – even missing vital casting sessions because he had not noted their time and place. There were also the literally hundreds of fines that he incurred by dumping his old car in restricted parking areas. Shanahan gave his client a diary and told him not to lose it, otherwise his career would be over before it had begun. Bill had seen too many promising careers go down the pan and he truly believed that, in Mel, he had found someone very special indeed.

With his fee from *Gallipoli* still virtually intact, Mel bought a family home in the pleasant Sydney beachside suburb of Coogee and tried to get away from the spotlight, and get used to being a father.

He turned down an offer to play a drug addict in *Monkey*

Grip, produced by Pat Lovell, whom he had met during the making of *Gallipoli*. Mel insisted he could not play someone whose life revolved around something as immoral as drugs. An interesting decision, because eight years later he agreed to play a similar role for a multimillion-dollar fee.

NINE

WHEN I WAS A LITTLE KID, MY OLD MAN TAUGHT ME
THE TEN COMMANDMENTS. THEN HE SAID, 'NOW I'M
GOING TO TELL YOU THE ELEVENTH.' I SAID WHAT WAS
THAT? 'THOU SHALT NOT KID THYSELF, THAT'S ALL.' I
KNEW WHAT HE MEANT. HE LIVES BY IT.

'Are you feeling brave?' the voice growled.
'What do you want to know that for?'
'Get out or we will kill you!'

Mel slammed the phone down in his Manila hotel suite, wondering if his decision to accept his biggest-ever fee of $150,000 for the lead role in his friend Peter Weir's new film was really worth it. For the first time in his career, he was staying in civilised accommodation, only to face death threats from Muslim fanatics determined to disrupt a movie titled, aptly, *The Year of Living Dangerously*. He and the rest of the cast and crew had been assigned bodyguards on arrival in Manila – a safety precaution following the previous year's death threats to foreign celebrities attending the Manila Film Festival.

Mel found himself shadowed by a huge 1.9m Filipino minder toting a .38 in a holster under his shirt. But no one had anticipated that the film unit would be threatened by a group of Muslims who presumed that *The Year of Living Dangerously*, based on a novel by CJ Koch, would be insulting to Allah. Protesters started besieging the set. When that failed to persuade the producers to pack up and go home, fanatics made death threats towards the director and stars of the $6 million movie.

'The threats were real,' recalled Mel later. 'They'd come in like clockwork and the phone would be snatched off me by the bodyguard, who would start jabbering down the line in Tagalog, the native tongue. Then he would slam the phone down and tell me not to worry.'

But director Peter Weir – reunited with Mel after the success of *Gallipoli* – could not just pack up and relocate. He had spent months scouting the area for perfect locations; no amount of threats were going to influence him. The movie's Hollywood backers, MGM, were so concerned they contacted the CIA, the Philippines Intelligence Agency, the police and the Army in an effort to find out who was behind the activity.

Mel, for his part, tried to remain calm amid all the tension. He mused over having accepted the role of an ambitious journalist because it was a challenging part that would help him get away from the stereotypical tough guy image of *Mad Max*, just enjoying its second dose of international success thanks to *Mad Max 2*. He had also been gratified by Weir's offer of a percentage in the film – something which actors at early stages in their careers are usually not offered. It was only half a per cent, but it made Mel feel as if he had broken through. Unfortunately, the movie never made enough money to pay Mel as much as one dollar in royalties.

He'd read the script of *The Year of Living Dangerously* a few months earlier, between rehearsals of the most controversial project he had ever undertaken – a two-handed play called *Porn No Rape Trigger*. Mel and co-star Sandy

Gore played a couple falling out of love and resorting to sexual games and fantasies in an effort to revive their passion. It was a brave choice by Mel; against the odds, he was never taken to task about it. He believed the play – written by Australian David Knight – was artistically valid, worthwhile and well crafted. Theatre critics agreed.

Just a few days after impressing audiences in that play, Mel made his first public appearance at a political rally. Although not eligible to vote in Australia, he had strong views on the Fraser Government's decision to slash Arts subsidies.

Floats, giant puppets, impromptu bands and 3,000 weirdly dressed thespians lined the streets of Sydney on Thursday, 19 November 1981, to protest at the cuts. They had real fears that the Australian theatre might die if the grants did not continue. And Mel, banner in hand, was in no mood for compromise.

'The Fraser Government must be forced to accept that the theatre is the very lifeblood of Australia's cultural health,' he asserted. For the first – but by no means last – time, Mel was flexing his political muscles.

Having read the script of *The Year of Living Dangerously*, Mel became convinced that it had the same sort of romantic drama undertones as the classic movie *Casablanca*, one of his all-time favourites, with his boyhood hero Humphrey Bogart.

The Year of Living Dangerously is set in Indonesia during the downfall of dictator Sukarno, 17 years earlier. Weir and his production team chose Manila because its vast crowds would give the project a more realistic feel.

Mel portrayed Australian Broadcasting Service reporter Guy Hamilton, arriving in Djakarta in 1965, ready at all costs to make a name for himself on his first overseas assignment. Indonesia at the time was a tinderbox threatening to ignite into a bloody civil war.

Hamilton meets elegant British embassy attaché Jill Bryant,

played by American actress Sigourney Weaver. The two fall in love but Hamilton must choose between swashbuckling journalistic adventures and his passionate relationship with Jill.

The third major character in the film is a diminutive Indonesian photographer, Billy Kwan, who provides Guy with many local contacts, helping him scoop the opposition. Kwan was played by tiny American actress Linda Hunt (just 1.4m tall), who went on to win an Academy Award for Best Supporting Actress in the part. It was the first time a 'crossover' performer had won an Oscar.

Mel has always been warm in his praise of Linda Hunt and Sigourney Weaver – though not of the film in general. It was a classy picture in Hollywood terms, but made little money at the all-important box office.

To Gibson, Hamilton is 'a hybrid like me, belonging to two cultures but really belonging to none. He's the sort of fellow who goes in boots and all. He takes chances. He gets off living dangerously.'

But Mel's respect for the character diminished somewhat after the event. 'Dimension-wise, Guy Hamilton provided a very limited framework for an actor. He really was just a puppet … He seldom initiated anything. For an actor, it was a question of filling up the role as much as possible to make it interesting.'

Mel found himself working with three American performers who did not come from the same school of acting – Sigourney Weaver, fresh from spectacular success in *Alien*; Linda Hunt, giving a *tour de force* performance; and lesser known but equally adept Michael Murphy. Mel admitted he was put on his mettle by the talent surrounding him.

'I did stand off and watch, and I found that each of the American actors had their own, totally different way of getting into what they did. One thing all three of them had was this greater degree of energy. They had tons of energy. It was as if they got charged up a bit more than I'd ever seen somebody do in Australia. That's the American way of doing things.'

Mel knew that Linda Hunt, although delivering an extraordinary performance, was nervy about the effect playing a man was having on her. She reported being 'freaked out' when a waiter at their hotel kept calling her 'sir' and she frequently doubted the validity of what she was doing.

But Mel was full of admiration for Linda and, as in his previous movies, made absolutely no attempt to grab the limelight from his co-star. *The Year of Living Dangerously* was the first Mel Gibson movie in which his performance did not dominate. But he never objected.

'Most Hollywood stars are so insecure they would have tried to instigate script changes to ensure that Linda's role was not too dominant,' explained one Los Angeles producer. That was not Mel's way. He regarded the role of Billy Kwan as the toughest in the film and would happily tell everyone on the set what great work Linda Hunt was doing.

On the set, Weir ordered cast and crew to call Linda by her middle name, Phipps, because he felt this would cause the other actors less confusion in scenes with a woman who was supposed to be a man.

Linda analysed Mel as 'the type of actor who's not there before a scene. His attention is somewhere else. He's deliberately uninvolved, absent. It's a macho thing – "Movies aren't work". But when he gets in front of the camera, his attention is forceful and total. He controls the camera. It's how they say the early Brando acted – saving himself, marshalling his energy for the performance. Watch Mel on screen; it shows. There's absolutely no waste.'

It was Mel's eyes that, according to Linda, said it all about the man behind the mask. 'Those great blue eyes take you in but erect a barrier and push you away.'

But the on-screen relationship expected to cause a spark was between Mel and Sigourney Weaver. She was the tall (over 1.8m), red-haired actress, five years Mel's senior, who – physically at least – dominated her handsome co-star.

Again, Mel's overt lack of vanity is worth examining. He did not seem to give two hoots about looking like a midget alongside the New York actress. When the producers insisted he wear built-up shoes, he obliged them, and has laughed about it ever since. Even at a première for the film more than a year later, Sigourney Weaver was amazed that Mel did not mind wandering around the party afterwards alongside her as she wore high heels that boosted her height to colossal proportions.

Mel took Sigourney's credentials – she had a bachelor's degree from Stanford and a master's from Yale, as well as wowing audiences in *Alien* and *Eyewitness* – in his stride, although he did feel a trifle wary, especially since she was only his second leading lady. For whatever reason, it was onscreen love scenes that he found difficult to handle.

'That kind of thing is always a touchy area with actors. It requires a lot more simplicity than anything else. Man ... woman ... attraction ... it's animal stuff, an instinctive type of behaviour,' he recalled later.

Weir helped him overcome shyness by going to a film library and picking out some movies with the most famous kisses of all time. Then he showed Mel the scenes and they both picked out Ingrid Bergman and Cary Grant's lingering embrace in the Hitchcock classic *Notorious*. Seeing it inspired Mel and gave him the courage to start approaching his role from a romantic standpoint.

Gradually, the leading man and leading lady became closer

and began to feel confident in each other's company. It led to inevitable gossip over a romance but, in fact, Mel and his attractive co-star simply respected each other as actors.

Sigourney was full of praise for her co-star. 'The most gorgeous man I have ever seen. But people focus too much on his looks. He's also shy, and a very devoted family man. And as an actor, he is extraordinarily good.'

As the shoot drew to a close in Sydney, Mel had other things on his mind. Robyn was days from giving birth to their second child and he was stressed by the impending birth and that age-old actor's problem – where would he get his next job once *The Year of Living Dangerously* wrapped?

On 2 June 1982, Robyn gave birth to twins at the Women's Hospital in Crown Street, Sydney, and this time Mel was there to see the whole proceedings.

Mel treasures witnessing the birth of twins Christian and Edward as 'one of the happiest days of my life. I was right there with her through the entire delivery and it just knocked the stuffing out of me. I wouldn't have missed that experience for anything.'

Sigourney Weaver was full of praise for Mel's professionalism. He had been up all night with Robyn as she gave birth to the twins. 'Yet he turned up right on time early next morning.'

All three of his children so far had been born while he was making movies for Peter Weir. Robyn joked just after the birth that he had better not work for Weir any more.

Reviews of *The Year of Living Dangerously* were good, but Mel was clearly no happier having to court the press and publicise the movie. 'The very fact I'm doing this interview is killing my credibility as an actor,' and to another journalist he remarked, 'I don't like doing interviews because they reduce my potential to surprise an audience ... but I've got pretty good defences. When this interview is finished, you won't know much more about the personal side of my life than you do now.'

Producer Jim McElroy was not best pleased by the way Mel handled press conferences after the release of *The Year of Living Dangerously*. 'Mel is two different people, you see. He's Mel the confident and articulate actor. Then he's Mel, the ordinary guy.'

Within weeks of finishing *The Year of Living Dangerously*, Mel was breathing down Bill Shanahan's neck for a theatre role. He was determined not to be another jobbing movie star. He wanted to refresh his instinct by treading the boards. Shanahan could have tried to dissuade Mel; scripts from Hollywood were literally piling up in his office. And there was a huge offer to play a Prince Charles-type character in an American film entitled *Myerson and the Prince of Wales* about a Jewish girl from the Bronx who falls for a British royal. Mel never seriously contemplated the role. Playing a member of the British Royal Family was not his lifetime's ambition.

Shanahan felt sure that the only way to keep Mel safe was to keep him in Australia. He was also well aware that Hollywood sharks were circling, looking for a piece of Mel to take home to Tinseltown. William Morris Agency top gun Ed Limato had already signed Mel as his Hollywood client and he would be putting Mel under pressure to accept fat pay checks.

Limato was as stunned as Mel was delighted when the actor landed the $250-a-week role of Biff, disaffected son of Willy Loman, in a two-month run of *Death of a Salesman* at Sydney's Nimrod Theatre. Director George Ogilvie, who would go on to co-direct *Mad Max Beyond Thunderdome* with George Miller, was in no doubt that if the young actor had been around in the Thirties 'he would have been a Cary Grant – although underneath it he is really a character actor'.

And Mel must have further infuriated Hollywood by claiming that 'Sometimes, it's a lot better to do a little stage play somewhere than a big-budget movie – you can get an excellent chance to polish up your craft.' This did not fit with Ed Limato's grand plans for Hollywood domination.

Mel enjoyed every minute grappling with the complexities of playing the son of Willy Loman (an acclaimed performance by Warren Mitchell) on stage and did not regret turning down a lucrative offer to star in a US film called *The Lords of Discipline*. Shanahan was taken aback when Mel also rejected *Once Upon a Time in America*, with Robert De Niro, after much procrastination. Mel admits that his biggest professional fault is taking too long to make up his mind about movie offers. But his decision turned out to be a wise one – the $38 million film was dismissed as twaddle by many critics and failed miserably at the box office.

Mel believed that, for the time being, he could continue to combine stage and film work. The fact that one day he would be staying in a luxurious hotel suite and the next, rehearsing in a cold, damp hall for a stage run did not bother him. He prided himself on the fact that he brought homemade fruit and date loaf, complete with two apples in his lunchbox, from home every day during theatrical appearances.

'I started in theatre and it gives me a lot. I like it,' Mel mused. 'There is nothing that replaces that kind of empty feeling you can get in films. You really have to trust the director. He is your audience.

'What I plan to do is find a happy mix of both, to intersperse my stage work with films. But for me stage work is far more exhilarating than any other form of acting. It just doesn't pay as well.

'I've been very lucky in working with good people on stage, like Warren Mitchell. He is a bloody good actor and he draws a lot of his acting just from having been around so long. As an actor, the older you get, the better you get, just through having lived more.'

Much of Mel's appeal as an actor at this time had to do with the fact that he was the man from Down Under who was starting to make it in Hollywood.

Mel had never concealed the first 12 years of his life in the United States, but then some Sydney newspapers decided to reveal his 'shocking secret'.

The *Australian* announced with horror, 'MAD MAX STAR NOT AUSSIE AFTER ALL' and went on to tell its readers, 'Australia might have claimed actor Mel Gibson as its own, but Gibson sees himself as an American ...'

Mel was stunned. Bill Shanahan had always advised him, with great foresight, not to take out Australian citizenship because it would make working in Hollywood all the more difficult. Mel's outlook is more 'Aussie' than 'Yank' but there is no getting away from the fact that he is American by birth.

A slightly defensive Mel told New York's *Interview* magazine, 'American citizenship ... despite all the cynicism in the world today, I'm proud of it. You have to be. The United States is not a bad place, they're great people.'

The harder-hitting Sydney *Sun* took the would-be controversy a stage further by grilling Mel to explain his love of Australia even though he might always be officially American.

'It's not that I don't love Australia and Australians. I do. I married one and I've fathered three ... I regard Australia as my home. My work may take me around the world, but when I'm not working, this is where I want to be,' he added. And he knew full well that his career could depend on his ability to make an accent switch back and forth. 'It's not hard to turn it on and turn it off again,' he pointed out.

Director Peter Weir confirmed that Mel was 'unpigeonholeable'. 'When I was working with him in Australia, I sometimes thought of Mel as an American, but when we were in New York, he seemed totally Australian. This gives him an extra cutting edge as an actor. An interesting tension is set up – a sort of who-am-I-where-do-I-belong? dilemma, a push-pull energy he can draw on.'

Mel believes, 'I'm in tune with this place. It's not a question of Australian loyalty. I just want to do interesting work.'

In November 1982, just a few weeks after finishing his highly acclaimed run in *Death of a Salesman*, Mel got his first real taste of what it is to be a film star.

MGM chief Freddie Fields hosted an informal gathering at Elaine's restaurant in New York. It was billed as a getting-to-know-Mel-Gibson event. But Mel found it a terrible strain. 'I start a conversation with one person and, just when it gets interesting, someone else nudges in and I have to turn away and begin a new conversation,' he moaned.

When a tall woman swooned over Mel, waving a book of matches and trying to get him to light her cigarette, he casually took the matches and lit his own.

Everyone was now wondering where his allegiance lay, and one question would come back to haunt him in the following years: Would you consider living in California? 'Never. I have to return to Australia to clear my head and think things out, like this party.'

Months later, Mel summed up a difference between the Australian and Hollywood film industries when he said, 'In Australian film-making, everybody sort of pitches in. There are no unions. I carried camera gear up the pyramids in *Gallipoli*. On American film sets, someone runs to get you a drink and shoves a chair under your backside every five minutes – that can get on your nerves. I like to be comfortable ... but you can go too far.'

Although he did not realise it, he had already waved goodbye to those relaxed times and was about to embark on a trip to megastardom ... and the ticket was a major movie.

The first of those was to be *The Running Man*. But Mel pulled out as it started pre-production, to go for a movie that Ed Limato promised would make him a truly international star – *The Bounty*.

TEN

I'D GO INTO A BAR, PULL UP A FEW BEERS
AND PUT SOME SCOTCH IN LIKE A DEPTH CHARGE ...

The sweet and troublesome smell of success hung like a huge fluffy cloud waiting to turn black and rain on everyone's parade ...' So read a quotation in an American magazine and, contrived though it was, it reflected perfectly what was going on in Mel Gibson's life in 1983. He was already being hailed as the latest contemporary film hero, and the attendant circus had him in a state of almost constant bewilderment.

He had been to war epically in *Gallipoli*; behaved with care and courtesy in *The Year of Living Dangerously*; fought futuristic villains in *Mad Max* and *Mad Max 2*; and his latest mission was to portray the clean-cut and caring super-hero Fletcher Christian in *The Bounty*.

A nine-week shoot on the island of Moorea, near Tahiti, sounded idyllic with its lagoons, coral sand beaches, lush green vegetation and palm trees. In reality, it turned into a painful experience that put Mel off location filming for many years to come and probably marks the period when his drinking and unpredictable behaviour reached an all-time low.

Even his co-star, Sir Anthony Hopkins, grumbled, 'Paradise can wear a bit thin after a while. If you're on Moorea for more than two weeks you can go stark raving crazy. There's a feeling of confinement on the island. There's also heat – terribly enervating. After a while, you see the same faces at breakfast and it starts to get to you …'

Mel and many of the cast and crew of *The Bounty* got through the experience by embarking on massive drinking bouts and, inevitably, bar-room battles. 'Mel liked to drink the whole time,' alleges Hare Salmon, a costume designer who became a drinking pal of Mel's throughout his stay on Moorea. Hare broke a ten-year silence to speak about his friend. He said that the actor's behaviour in the bars on the island endeared him to the locals if not *The Bounty*'s producers. And he chuckled over the night that Mel got knocked to the ground after interrupting two Tahitians arguing during a mammoth liquor session at the Tattoo nightclub.

'I was with him. I told him to keep out of it. The Tahitians were fighting over a girl. He said to me, "I am Mel Gibson, I will go over there and stop them. They will respect my work, you watch." But the two locals took absolutely no notice of Mel, beyond smashing him to the ground.

'They hit him in the head with a Coke bottle. Mel just loves to brawl.'

Staggering to his feet, Mel was taken back to his hotel where a very worried unit production manager quickly contacted a hospital in the capital city of Papeete, five minutes' flight from Moorea. The whole of one side of Mel's face was cut and bruised. The filming schedule was hastily juggled so that scenes without him could be shot while he spent a day in the hospital having his face fixed.

A shame-faced Mel admitted to friends that he had gone 'stir crazy'. 'Those Tahitians are big – 6ft across. I tried to get our guys out of there but suddenly this huge gorilla hit me on the side of the head. When one of them hits you, you stay down. Let's just say there was a serious lack of communication for a while.'

Even some of Mel's closest pals were astonished by his bravado. 'He seemed to be so proud of what had happened,' said one old friend.

Once again, Mel's drinking had got out of control because Robyn and the children were not staying with him on the island. It was as if their presence was needed to remind him of his responsibilities as father and husband. It was a recurring problem through many of the films he made during this period.

Bar-room brawls were simply Mel's reaction to a very difficult series of circumstances on the set of *The Bounty*. He had taken to the bottle in an effort to forget that the film was feeling like an unmitigated disaster. Showings of the rushes each evening gave the distinct impression of an episode of *The Onedin Line* rather than a $20 million Hollywood movie.

The producer on *The Bounty* was Dino de Laurentiis, after Warner Brothers had pulled out, and he immediately authorised a $2.5 million payment to a New Zealand company, Whangerei Engineering, to build an exact replica of the *Bounty* from original plans held at the Maritime Museum in Greenwich, London. This 'little shitpot', as Mel later described it, was a 380-ton vessel built of steel then planked with wood, her ropes and sails virtually identical to those of the original ship. Above deck she was a copy of the *Bounty*. Below, she was a modern cruiser with luxury cabins, microwave ovens, automatic pilot, satellite navigation and twin 400hp engines giving a range of 8,000 kilometres.

The original director on the project, David Lean, who had long harboured dreams of telling the story of the *Bounty*, approached *Superman* star Christopher Reeve to play Fletcher Christian. Later, Lean referred to the project as 'the saddest dead duck in my career'. His dream project had become far too expensive, and he eventually abandoned *The Bounty*.

For a while it floundered around as a possible TV mini series, then Orion Pictures in Hollywood agreed to finance it and recruited young New Zealand director Roger Donaldson to the project. Reeve, upset by all the changes, pulled out of the film just six weeks before shooting was scheduled to commence.

Anthony Hopkins had already been signed up to play Bligh, but actors in line for Fletcher Christian ranged from Jeremy Irons and Anthony Andrews to rock star Sting. For various reasons, they all passed on the project. Mel Gibson was approached almost as an afterthought.

At first, he was not at all keen. 'I thought Christian was made to look too weak. Besides, he was hardly in the picture. And I didn't want to get involved in the remake of a film which had been done a couple of times before.'

But agent Ed Limato assured him it was a good project. He reminded Mel that he had by now turned down *An Officer and a Gentleman* – a role that helped elevate Richard Gere to international stardom. Roger Donaldson, who had made just two films – *Sleeping Logs* and *Smash Palace* – also appealed to Mel to consider the 'richness' of Bolt's script and, the more Mel researched the subject, the more he was intrigued. As an oftenmisunderstood maverick himself, he liked the fact that Captain Bligh was not being made out to be such a monster as he had been in previous versions.

Mel signed on and, cleverly, asked a London psychiatrist to assess different aspects of Christian's life. Then he made a pilgrimage to the house in the Lake District of Cumbria where Christian was born.

'I discovered he had left his footprint in the lead guttering on the roof and scratched his initials in metal. I put my foot inside his imprint and discovered it fitted perfectly.' Mel thought that alone was worth the journey.

But, when cast and crew arrived in Tahiti, they discovered that producer de Laurentiis had taken it upon himself to cast a Tahitian first-time actress as Princess Mauatua, with whom Fletcher Christian falls in love. Beautiful 18-year-old Tevaite Vemette had been plucked out of a local high school and made to feel she was on the verge of international stardom. At first, there was talk that Tevaite might have broken strict local employment laws by leaving school to make the movie. Shooting was eventually rearranged to make sure she was free to study – while taking a role that would make her the envy of women around the world.

She would get Mel. As his romantic interest, the script called for some very passionate scenes between the actor and Tevaite. It was a lot for a young girl to cope with, and Tevaite admitted she did not want to do the film. 'I was a law student, not an aspiring actress. All I really wanted to do was continue my studies – they were much more important to me.'

Director Donaldson and co-producer Bernard Williams were at first astounded by the girl's reluctance to be turned into an overnight star. Back in Hollywood, thousands of actresses would have killed to get a role opposite Mel Gibson.

Then there were the topless scenes involving her and Mel in the lagoon. Local women claimed they degraded the good name of Tahitian women but it turned out to be little more than a storm in a B-cup. However, Tevaite – essentially a shy girl – dreaded stripping, mainly because she had developed a schoolgirl crush on her handsome co-star. 'I liked kissing him. It was very easy!'

Ten years later, she recalled, 'It was funny to kiss him. It was funny for him, too. It was embarrassing. We were both shy. When we were swimming naked, it was very difficult. He told jokes to relax me.'

But one of her oldest friends on Tahiti recently explained why the young actress found the entire shoot so stressful. 'Tevaite just couldn't cope with her emotions. One minute she was expected to be kissing Mel passionately, and the next he would walk past her without so much as a glance.'

Yet another of Mel's screen partners who left acting, Tevaite eventually worked as a nurse in post-operative care at the same hospital where Mel was taken after his drunken brawl on Moorea. She said, 'I do not want to act ever again because I did not find it enjoyable. The other actors did not really help me much. Acting was very difficult and that movie was emotionally draining. I was just a child. It seems like a dream now. It was all so unreal.'

Tevaite was offered millions of dollars' worth of work after her début with Mel but says now, 'I decided I did not want to carry on acting. There is more to life than just being in films.'

When asked if she had felt just a little in love with Mel, as some of her friends claimed, Tevaite blushed.

'I do not want to answer that question. I find it embarrassing. I do not know how to respond.' She did add that it was 'a shame that Mel was married. But that's the way it goes, I guess.'

She also said of Mel, 'He helped me relax. He was very Tahitian in his outlook. He liked to have fun and some of the other actresses did seem a little jealous of me.'

Did he break her heart? Tevaite looked embarrassed and refused to answer.

Mel stayed at a luxury hotel near the island's tiny airport while Tevaite and most of the other Tahitian women employed in the movie lived in rented bungalows overlooking the Pacific near Cook's Bay.

But at one stage, Tevaite 'ran away' from the movie location and a producer had to be dispatched to the main island to persuade her to return to the set.

'She did not want to come back. She just could not cope with it. Maybe it was because she did fall in love with Mel,' said Maimiti Kinnander, who appeared in the movie as a topless Tahitian dancer and became close friends with Tevaite during the shoot. 'Tevaite did not do well because of Mel.'

Tevaite now says that working as a nurse is far more satisfying than acting. 'I am happiest here in Tahiti being a nurse. It is much more fulfilling. Much more satisfying.'

In addition to Mel's penchant for getting regularly slammed – both by the drink and the rough weather they experienced during the shoot – producers and director also had to contend with Mel's habit of improvising all the time. He loved to find a hole in a script and 'improve' it himself, often arriving on the set having decided completely to rewrite a few lines of dialogue.

One of the most important scenes in the film was where Christian tells Bligh he is taking over the ship. Mel felt, as actors will, that his role needed a little 'spicing up'. Neither Donaldson nor Hopkins had any idea what the star had in store for them.

'I only wrote the scene that morning ... the character was lacking and the only place to do something was in the mutiny scene when he flips out. I thought the only way he can do it is by being like a loyal office boy, which is what he was – a loyal public servant. He knew what job he had to do and got fed up with it one day. The only real threat he could make, as I saw it, was to knock himself off and leave them without a navigator. If they knocked Bligh off then he'd threaten to kill himself. It was in the nature of the Christian character. He went schizophrenic one day. Wacko!'

Donaldson and Hopkins were, well ... astonished by Mel's interpretation.

'It was totally unpredictable. Mel just exploded and it caught everyone off guard. It was brilliant,' said Hopkins tactfully. Mel took heart from the crew bursting into applause after his improvisation.

Of Anthony Hopkins, Mel said, 'He was terrific. He was good to work with because he was open and he was willing to give. He's a moral man and you could see this. I think we had the same attitudes.'

The Bounty was given a lavish royal première in London where Mel and his co-stars were presented to the Duke and Duchess of Kent for a fund-raising gala that helped add $30,000 to the coffers of the Variety Club, which helps handicapped and deprived youngsters. Mel may have been unaware that the rest of the proceeds from the event went to the Press Fund, founded in 1864, to assist families of needy journalists!

The movie, however, did not live up to its hype. In a seven-week run in the US, it took just $3.5 million, a pathetic showing considering final estimates of the cost were in the region of $40 million. Meanwhile, *Ghostbusters*, starring Dan Aykroyd, Bill Murray and Mel's one-time leading lady Sigourney Weaver, became that year's highest earner with takings of $127 million.

Unfortunately, the finger was pointed fairly and squarely at Mel as the actor most to blame for the film's disastrous performance. The Sydney *Sunday Telegraph* wrote, 'The only problem with an otherwise fine movie is the casting of Gibson as Fletcher Christian. He is lost at sea. It is not so much that he's outclassed by Hopkins, it's that he's in a different league. It's a large weakness.'

Philippa Hawker, writing in Australia's *Cinema Papers* magazine, accused him of giving one of his 'least convincing performances'. She went on, 'Just before Mel puts Bligh into the lifeboat, he erupts into a raving frenzy, an outpouring of hysteria that breaks his voice and gives us precisely – nothing.'

Hollywood columnist Frank Osbourne was a little less blunt. 'There's hope for Gibson but, if he is to go the distance, he'll need not only to be talented and lucky … he will need to be attracted to the idea of stardom and, frankly, I don't think he is.'

Mel Gibson's assessment was characteristically pithy: 'I liked the film, but it had its flaws. It was a difficult film to make. It took a long time, and the weather was terrible.'

ELEVEN

I AM BEING PACKAGED HERE AS IF I WERE A
HAMBURGER – FAT AND TASTY. THE NEW SEX SYMBOL.

Before sailing off to Tahiti on *The Bounty*, Mel met leading Hollywood director Mark Rydell to discuss the possibility of him casting the young actor in the lead role of a movie that Mel envisaged as his biggest breakthrough in Hollywood. Rydell's reputation was riding high on the back of the multi-Oscar-nominated *On Golden Pond* starring Henry Fonda, his daughter Jane and Katharine Hepburn. So Mel implored his Los Angeles agent Ed Limato to put him up for the lead role of a farmer in *The River*, which Rydell planned to shoot in the mountains of Tennessee the following year.

At first, Rydell was reluctant to consider him seriously, mainly because he believed that an Australian background would make it difficult for Mel to convince, in the role of a hardworking, God-fearing Tennessee farmer trying to stop the government taking his land. Mel – whose happiest childhood years were spent in those country houses in Upstate New York – felt differently. And he was absolutely determined to get the role.

'All I ask is that you wait until I get back from *The Bounty* before casting anyone else,' he implored Rydell.

Within hours of reaching London to start shooting some of *The Bounty*'s interior scenes, Mel was hard at work on his Tennessee accent with dialogue director Julie Harris. She discovered that he had a truly amazing ear for accents, no doubt helped by those early days in Australia as a 'Yank' when he learned to adjust to the local sound or face non-stop ribbing in the classroom.

Three months later, Mel turned up at Rydell's house in Los Angeles. The director was flabbergasted. 'He started reading the script, talking, reading the newspaper, in this perfect Tennessee accent. I was really impressed.'

Then Rydell introduced Mel to actress Sissy Spacek, already cast as the farmer's wife in *The River*. And she was just as impressed. 'When he stood next to Sissy, who's like a tuning fork when it comes to accents, I knew he had damn well done it.'

As Mae and Tom Garvey, parents of a young boy and girl, Mel and Sissy Spacek played small-time farmers struggling desperately to hold on to their farm despite economic depression, mounting debts at the bank, and ravages of nature – the worst being heavy rains making the river near their home flood their crop fields, often wiping out livestock as well as threatening the family's lives.

For Mel, *The River* was a vitally important stepping stone into Hollywood acceptability. It was the first time he would play an American, his first experience under an American director and the first time he had acted on American soil.

Soon, the beautiful mountains of eastern Tennessee were

providing the backdrop for a movie that was probably his most enjoyable experience on location, until then. For much of the gruelling nine-week shoot, Mel had Robyn and Hannah and the twins with him at a picturesque farmhouse rented for the duration of the film, in Kingsport. He had seen at first hand the temptations that can weaken cast and crew members through the long months of a difficult shoot and. he was determined to have his family as near to him as possible. They were a calming influence. They provided him with that little piece of sanity to return home to each evening, and represented a sheet-anchor while he was at work.

As a child, Mel had never travelled outside New York State, so his stay in Tennessee also provided him with an insight into one of the most rural areas of the United States. It was to have a lasting effect, and ultimately convince him to enter the world of livestock farming – and another, albeit part-time, career. In September 1983, shortly after beginning filming on *The River*, newspaper headlines around the world reported that Mel Gibson had died in a plane crash. Sydney agent Bill Shanahan found himself being woken in the middle of the night by an anxious journalist asking him to contribute to an obituary of the star 'who had died at the tragically young age of 27'.

The veteran agent, who had nursed Mel's career so carefully in Australia, was close to tears as he put the phone down. He could not believe that Mel was gone. For an hour, he paced the floor of his bedroom, unsure how to deal with the tragedy. Finally, he rang Mel's house on location in Tennessee and breathed a huge sigh of relief when the star answered, sounding perfectly healthy.

Even with Sissy, Mel was reluctant to talk about himself or his career, preferring to hide behind a stream of wisecracks and innocuous pleasantries, but the actress grew accustomed to his ways and told friends that it was part of Mel's charm.

141

'There's not a lot of bullshit about Mel. He's kinda shy and has a certain reserve that I think is nice.'

Mark Rydell intended *The River* to be 'a tribute to a vanishing America, the America of the independent farm family'. In other words, it was to be about the American Dream. And in Vilmos Zsigmond, he also had one of the world's finest directors of photography on board to evoke it.

But this was an expensive dream; production estimates put it in the $20 million range. Another first in his career: Mel was the star of a movie in which everyone around treated him as such. It was a strange experience; someone was at his beck and call the whole time. If he so much as attempted to help a camera assistant with his gear, that crew member would be severely reprimanded by superiors. Lines had been drawn long before between cast and crew, and they were not to be crossed – although Mel, to his credit, would continue breaking those rules right throughout his career.

He brought his own stamp to the production by encouraging his children to accompany him to the set, where they played with Sissy Spacek's 16-month-old daughter Schuyler as well as co-star Scott Glenn's young daughters Dakota and Rio.

Director Rydell's patience was severely tested when the children started demanding non-stop attention from their parents. Sissy Spacek explained, 'Both of us found our children were just so noisy and demanding that everything was taking twice as long as it should. Mel's little ones and my daughter were all great pals but were too young to understand the word "silence". So we had to keep doing retakes.'

Rydell later conceded that Mel was not an easy person to get to know. 'He's very careful about offering friendship. It takes a long time for him to allow you into his world. He doesn't make friends easily, but when he does, it's an honour.'

Above: Mel (top row, middle), aged 13 at St Leo's College.

Below left: Mel aged 14.

Below right: St. Leo's today.

An article that appeared in the *Melbourne Herald* after Mel and his family arrived in Australia.

Above: A poster for *Summer City*, Mel's first film – one that he's keen to forget.

Below: Deborah Foreman (right) on the set of *Summer City*, a few weeks before she attempted suicide, having fallen for Mel. *Inset:* A more recent picture of Deborah Foreman, taken 20 years after her affair with Mel.

Above: Mel with Joanne Samuel in *Mad Max*, the film that set him on the path to stardom.

Below left: Learning his craft: a scene from *Tim*.

Below right: Gallipoli presented Mel with the opportunity to play a role with depth and compassion.

Above: Tevaite Vernette was Mel's beautiful co-star in *Bounty*. She gave up acting after developing a crush on him during filming in Tahiti.

Below: Sigourney Weaver with Mel at the Cannes Film Festival, around the time of the release of *The Year of Living Dangerously*. The film reunited Mel with director Peter Weir.

Diane Keaton and Mel in a scene from *Mrs Soffel*. The time spent away from his family while on location took its toll on Mel.

Above: The River, in which Mel starred alongside Sissy Spacek. It was a vital role, as it was the first time he played an American and acted on American soil.

Below: Tequila Sunrise. The part was a controversial choice for Mel as the character was an ex-drug dealer.

Mel in his most famous action role – as tough LA cop Martin Riggs and, *below*, sharing a laugh on set with co-star Danny Glover.

The same might be said of Robyn. Concerned by those long, enforced separations, she had already suffered during just a couple of years of marriage, she was happy to stay on location with Mel. But there was an inevitable shyness on her part over getting involved with the actual production. She often stayed back at the house in Kingsport while a nanny accompanied the three children to the set. It surprised some that she did not want to go on the set, but there was little doubting that her husband preferred it that way. As he has said many times since, he never wanted to marry an actress.

Wayne Bailey, local resident and production assistant on the movie, recalled, 'I only saw Mel's wife visiting on the set about three or four times. But his kids were on the set a lot, in Mel's mobile home, with a woman who was there to look after them.'

His thumbnail portrait of Robyn Gibson was, 'My impression of her was that she was kind of backward.'

But Robyn should not take offence at this description, as it is purely a Southern States alternative word for 'shy': backward, she ain't!

Others on the set of *The River* noted that, whenever Robyn did appear there or at the Rydell Sunday lunch parties, she had a strong presence. Her role in Mel's life is pivotal.

'You knew who was in charge when Robyn was around,' said one crew member.

Even when two stunt men were injured in accidents and a union demarcation row led to unpleasant incidents in which cars and film vans were vandalised, Mel remained unruffled. Having his family close to him made it so much easier to handle the glitches and hassles ...

His fee on *The River* was $500,000; director Rydell was convinced he would have been a bargain at twice that price. As the movie-maker edited *The River* back at Universal Studios in Los Angeles, he gloated that Mel had 'the roughness of McQueen, the gentleness of Montgomery Clift and he's going to turn this town upside down'.

Ironically, *The River* was sneak previewed at the first annual benefit of the Lee Strasberg Actor's Studio, the home of Method acting in the United States. Mel – who had already vigorously denied any interest in Method acting – attended the screening and formal dinner at the Pierre Hotel with some of Hollywood's most dedicated Method actors and actresses, including Paul Newman, Joanne Woodward, Ellen Burstyn, Robert De Niro and Shelley Winters. She said after seeing *The River*, 'There was so much water I had to keep going to the john.'

When *The River* opened theatrically in New York, it was to mixed reactions and verdicts. One reviewer described Mel's performance as 'less than convincing, not for lack of trying but because he is just too clean-shaven, too well coiffed and too obviously handsome by half for someone with as hard a row to hoe as farmer Gamey'. And noted Australian critic Scott Murray, of *Cinema Papers*, rated the film as 'only OK. Mel is quite good in it and he puts a lot of energy into his performance.'

Yet it was Sissy Spacek – already an Academy Award winner for her role in *The Coal Miner's Daughter* – who got the most praise, and yet another Oscar nomination.

Almost ten years later, Mel accused himself of doing an inferior job on *The River*, telling one associate, 'I think I did a really bad job on that film. When I look at it, I was young and stupid. And I was trying to phone it in, maybe,' meaning that he had perhaps not tried hard enough on screen.

Even before shooting *The River* – and around the time that his name was being linked with the role of James Bond, a claim that Mel quashed immediately – Mel had committed to another picture to be helmed by Australian director Gillian

Armstrong. He had surprised his Los Angeles agent Ed Limato by continuing to pass on *The Running Man* in order to make this film, entitled *Mrs Soffel*.

'Everyone in town's chasing Mel. You should be grateful. He likes Gillian, he likes the role. Just find a new goddamn title, OK?' Limato told MGM's Freddie Fields when he turned up in his Hollywood office one day.

As a result, Mel, Robyn and the children headed straight for Toronto, Canada, for *Mrs Soffel*. This movie almost killed his enthusiasm for Hollywood and movie-making before his career got into second gear. It also earmarked him unfairly as a 'wild, unpredictable actor' in the eyes of certain strait-laced studio chiefs.

Before shooting got under way, Mel was invited to fly down to Los Angeles to be a presenter at the Academy Awards in April 1984. It was a trip he sensed he should not have made the moment he stepped inside the Dorothy Chandler Pavilion.

Linda Hunt's much-deserved award as Best Supporting Actress was greeted with delight by Mel; his own performance as one of the hosts was widely condemned by the media.

'On the Oscar show, Gibson radiated all the warmth, sincerity and charm of a doorstep, and for good reason ... he was terrified,' sniped one showbusiness reporter the next day.

Mel agreed that he *was* very nervous on the big night. He told a fellow actor, 'Skid marks. It was nerve-wracking. I just can't be relaxed on television, unless I'm playing a role. It's the only way to get through it.'

Mel had taken a few shots of Dutch courage but they had simply accentuated his nervousness. It was an unmitigated disaster and Mel steered clear of the Oscars for many years thereafter.

Mrs Soffel – or 'Mrs Whatchamacallit' as it was known to certain MGM execs who loathed the title – started shooting in

Canada at that time. Mel settled into the cold north with his family and formed a reasonable on-screen relationship with co-star Diane Keaton and director Gillian Armstrong, whose Australian film *My Brilliant Career* had created quite a stir in Hollywood. It did not, unfortunately, turn out to be a prophetic description of the way Ms Armstrong's own Hollywood career proceeded until her 1995 remake of *Little Women* received universal acclaim.

Mel endured sub-zero temperatures and painfully slow set-ups for each scene because he truly believed that this bittersweet Gothic love story about the wife of a prison warder (Diane Keaton) who falls in love with one of the prisoners (played by Mel) was a dark and brooding, non-traditional project that would greatly stretch his acting talents and therefore further his career. He said later he knew it was going to be tough, but he was prepared far all that – and did have his family with him to keep him on the straight and narrow.

However, Robyn and the children soon decided that life at home Down Under was far preferable to winter in Canada. She spent many lonely days in Toronto while Mel was a four-hour drive away in the countryside, returning at weekends. Also, Robyn was expecting the couple's fourth child and wanted to be back at their Coogee beach house with her relatives and friends. Mel was devastated by Robyn's decision. It would be selfish of him to make his family suffer the unfamiliar surroundings a moment longer, but he knew his own weaknesses and feared that Robyn's departure would spark a lot of problems. And he was absolutely right.

'I like Robyn to be there because then I don't forget, we don't all forget, what's reality. It could be so easy. Otherwise, what's the point of getting hitched in the first place?' he said a few months after *Mrs Soffel*.

According to those close to the star, Mel became 'restless' and 'unhappy' both on and off the set as soon as Robyn departed for Australia.

'They've scheduled it so I work only every fifth or sixth day because they think I might run off to Australia and never come back,' he commented, adding, 'You just have to get your mind right. You say to yourself, "Relax, don't be upset by this. Roll with it and see if you can master it." Happiness is a state of being, isn't it? You can be happy with a little or a lot. Mel Gibson can be happy with anything if he gets his mind right.'

Around him raged a feud. Point-scoring MGM bosses started accusing Mel and Diane Keaton of making their lovemaking scenes too sexy, at the insistence of director Armstrong. As so often happens, the actors were getting caught in the crossfire of a boardroom vendetta.

At one stage, both performers virtually collapsed from exhaustion after Armstrong had them kissing non-stop for hours in a scene requiring Mel and Diane Keaton to embrace passionately through prison bars.

The Oscar-winning actress eventually took a breather, sipped tea and applied Blistex to her parched lips, obviously frustrated by her director's obstinacy. Bravely, she continued the scene after whispering to Mel, 'Thank God you're the world's best kisser.' Witnesses say that Mel looked just as demoralised as his co-star.

Ironically, rumours were rife that Mel and Keaton were not enjoying a warm relationship. She was deemed to be slightly aloof because she tended to withdraw into her shell the moment the director shouted 'Cut'. It was her way of intensifying her performance.

'She spent many days between takes listening to her Walkman and saying very, very little,' said one member of the crew.

Mel, frantic to dispel his gloom, made admirable attempts to improve the atmosphere on the set. On one occasion, following the end of a particularly passionate bedroom scene, he suddenly dropped on all fours, crouched like an ape and then chased Diane Keaton, growling ferociously. The actress darted away from Mel squealing; it was a rare moment when she could truly shrug off the intensity of her role.

Mel continued bottling up his frustrations over what was happening on the set, and his loneliness in the evenings since Robyn and the children had left.

A telltale symptom came when, in one scene, Mel was called upon to hurl himself on top of a fire in his prison cell. He refused to let a stuntman intervene. By this time, he was so patently fed up that no one dared argue when he insisted on doing the stunt himself. It was as if he wanted to vent his frustrations by letting studio executives watch him coat his body in gel before being set alight – just to make them that little bit more anxious. Luckily, he was not injured, but everyone on the set that evening could predict that Mel was heading for serious trouble.

At 8.30 pm on Wednesday, 25 April 1984, just a few days after Robyn and the children returned to Australia, Mel's rented Pontiac failed to stop at a red light on Yonge Street, Toronto, smashing into the back of unsuspecting 23-year-old Randy Caddell's car.

Seconds later, the young mechanic snatched the keys out of the Pontiac's dashboard and started screaming and yelling at the drunken figure behind the wheel.

Mel emerged smiling from the car and held up a hand to make peace with the guy whose car he had just hit, exclaiming, 'Hey, I'm for love, not war. How about we have a beer?'

Randy Caddell recalled, 'I was so mad, I was doing a little

dance in the street and using some terrible language. I mean, I was dangerous.'

It took a few minutes before he realised he had been hit by a car driven by Hollywood star Mel Gibson. When the police arrived, Mel was taken to the Five District traffic station where breath tests showed he was over the driver's legal alcohol limit. He had between 0.12 and 0.13 per cent alcohol in his bloodstream. The legal limit in Canada is 0.08.

Having got wind of the arrest, newspapers gleefully reported the next day that Mel 'could face six months in jail and fines of $2,000 if convicted'.

In Australia and Hollywood alike, there were fears that Mel might have blown his career. Any hopes of covering up the arrest were dashed. Mel's agents were trying to do everything possible to control the damage but, in the end, they all realised that it would either blow over and become yesterday's news or his career had just taken a huge backward step.

Back at MGM/UA, studio chiefs already split down the middle over backing *Mrs Soffel* were now petrified that their $15 million movie might have to be scrapped if the actor was jailed. They despatched a trouble-shooting lawyer and two minders to keep an eye on Mel.

One week later, while other members of the Gibson family were celebrating his parents' fortieth wedding anniversary in Australia, Mel kept a court date in Canada. Hair slicked back and dressed in a dark, double-breasted blazer complete with tie and grey slacks, Mel managed, typically, to turn up late for the commencement of court proceedings. His luck held out because his case was not the first one to be heard.

Hordes of female fans filled the public gallery of the court at the Old City Hall in Toronto. Many tried to pass him scraps of paper with their names and phone numbers. Resignedly, Mel told his lawyer William Trudel, 'It happens every week.'

Mel then pleaded guilty to the charge. His lawyer told Judge George Carter that his client wanted to record an apology 'to the court and the Toronto community and would like to thank the police officers who dealt with him … in a professional and courteous manner'.

Judge Carter banned Mel from driving in Canada for three months, fined him $300 and then, provoking a wave of laughter from his fans, warned that the star would get '30 days in jail if he doesn't pay'. Before banging his gavel and declaring the case closed, Judge Carter said warmly to Mel, 'I hope your stay in Canada is otherwise pleasant.'

Robyn was unsympathetic when Mel rang to tell her the news about his arrest, while Mel's mother, Anne, believed that her son's arrest for drunken driving in Toronto marked his moment of realisation that alcohol was taking over his life. 'That really woke Mel up. He realised he'd let the beer take hold. The boy changed after that. I was particularly happy no one got hurt. It could have been tragic,' she said later.

During that time alone in Canada, Mel's drinking capacity increased enormously. He sought solace in endless bottles of beer, where before he could have read the kids a bedtime story or enjoyed a quiet dinner with just Robyn for company. He was also painfully aware of behind-the-scenes problems, bad vibes, that were becoming an everyday part of life on *Mrs Soffel*. Director Gillian Armstrong felt persecuted by bullying studio executives angry at the way the shooting schedule had slowed to a snail's pace. She confessed that there were times 'when I wish I'd stayed home in Australia'.

Loyally, Mel and Diane Keaton supported Armstrong in her battle with the executives. But he was forced to question if it was all worth the stress – the freezing cold, the extraordinarily long hours, constant on-set tensions, the loneliness combined with the shame and embarrassment of that drink-driving incident (which provoked the studio into insisting he had those two minders with him the entire time). Mel was, he admitted eventually, at his lowest ebb. He could not see any light at the end of the tunnel, and he and the rest of the cast half-expected the studio to pull the plug.

Back at his rented house in Toronto, Mel shunned the concerned colleagues whom he had befriended during the earlier, happier stages of the shoot, succumbing to deep bitterness and resentment.

During *The River*, he had truly thought he had found happiness and contentment throughout the film-making process. *Mrs Soffel* had destroyed all those hopes and illusions. He was back at square one.

Both films opened in America just seven days apart, but the memories they held for Mel could not have been more different. *Mrs Soffel* had its première just in time to qualify for Academy Award nominations, not one of which it received.

Reviews off *Mrs Soffel* were astonishingly varied. Bill Collins of the Sydney *Daily Mirror* wrote, 'Like all great movies, *Mrs Soffel* lives on in the heart and in the mind for those movie-goers sensitive to the film's content as much as its sometimes casual, rarely obvious artistry.' And he registered Mel's performance as 'thoughtful and understanding. His characterisation is a personal triumph.'

The *Sydney Morning Herald*'s Paul Byrnes acclaimed Mel as 'demonstrating more ability as an actor in this part than I have seen before'.

But fellow Aussie critic Scott Murray said that *Mrs Soffel* 'is a very strange film and the love story does not work. Diane Keaton is miscast and the film never recovers. It was a failed project.'

New York Times reviewer Vincent Canby blamed much of

151

the failure of the film on Gillian Armstrong, saying that 'it more or less plods to its conclusion'.

Mel theorised that the film was misunderstood by its critics. '*Mrs Soffel* is a beautiful-feeling mood piece. I think it is a brilliant film,' he said shortly after the movie's release.

Besides being relieved that the *Mrs Soffel* shoot was over, Mel could not wait to get back to Australia for the birth of baby number four, named William, born in the middle of June, only days after Mel's return to the peace and relative sanity of Sydney.

But the three-month break changing nappies, recharging his batteries and catching up with his parents and his children just wasn't long enough. He had already committed to play Max Rockatansky one last time for *Mad Max Beyond Thunderdome*. It sent him over the edge and rapidly heading for what he termed 'burn out'.

In a remarkably candid outburst, Mel told one reporter, 'I'll probably be washed out in a couple of years. People get tired of seeing your face. They want to see another face. And there are faces better and there are talents better – or as good.'

TWELVE

WHEN I WAS 22 I WAS A RIGHT IDIOT.
I GUESS WHEN I'M 35 I'LL THINK I WAS AN IDIOT AT 28.

While *Mad Max Beyond Thunderdome* may well have done more than any other film to maintain Mel's reputation as an up-and-coming Hollywood star, it also sent him spiralling into an alcoholic haze threatening to destroy him.

His ordeal began the moment he turned up at the movie's isolated location, a dusty old mining town called Coober Pedy, some 800km north-west of Adelaide, but it could have been a million miles from civilisation as far as Mel was concerned. He had just done three movies back-to-back – *The Bounty*, *The River* and *Mrs Soffel* – and a 12-week break at the family home on the beach at Coogee could not offset that. Mel knew in his heart he should have taken six months, maybe even a year, off.

But, when Hollywood wants to make the third in a series of movies as phenomenally successful as *Mad Max*, they do not tend to take anyone's feelings or state of mind into consideration. Warner Brothers were willing to pay him $1 million, and Mel, ever the insecure freelance artist terrified that it might be his last job, took the money on the basis that it would provide his family with the security they deserved.

In Coober Pedy, temperatures regularly topped 40°C, and within days of setting up camp, seven crew members were taken to hospital suffering from heat exhaustion, and a dispute over the stunt work threatened the entire project.

Caught in the middle of all this was Mel. Already mentally and physically exhausted, worried about his career, anxious about his wife and children, no wonder he turned to the only immediate source of comfort – alcohol. Mel knew what happened when he drank too much but he could not stop himself. His drink-driving disgrace during the making of *Mrs Soffel* was only just behind him but he had no other way to turn.

Years later, he reflected on his excessive drinking in the course of *Mad Max Beyond Thunderdome*, admitting that life at that time had become nothing more than a blur.

'Not drinking certainly does make a difference to the tenor of my work. When you stop, your mind clears up a little, you're able to see things a little more clearly. Even one drink stays in your spine for months ... it's amazing how it can affect you. . . you don't realise it.'

Deep inside, Mel saw precisely what was going on. He had reached another crossroads and it was up to him which direction he took. 'I felt as if I was a juggernaut, hurtling down a steep hill, with the brakes not working and the controls all screwed up. Everyone expected me to live like a hard-livin', tough guy in real life, so I did.

'Sometimes I fought so hard and drank so much that I surprised even myself. But there were so many people hanging around me, assuring me I could do anything I wanted, that I believed them. I'd wake up in the morning with no idea where the hell I'd been the night before. And then I'd get dressed, stagger out and not know where the hell I was gonna finish up.

'I'd been a heavy boozer since I was 16. In Australia, you're not considered a proper mate unless you drink yourself stupid. I was a real hard case, a wild boy, knocking liquor back like there was no tomorrow. Then I'd get into fights because I was always shooting my mouth off.'

Adding fuel to the fires already banked within him, *People* magazine proceeded to dub him the Sexiest Man Alive. It infuriated Mel. His self-esteem was at its lowest-ever ebb and here was some magazine trying to turn him into the world's leading sex-symbol. He told friends the title was 'a joke' and steered journalists away from the subject if they were unwise enough to raise it.

By now, Mel was openly consuming five bottles of beer even *before* getting on to the *Beyond Thunderdome* set each morning. Uncannily – was it will-power or vitamins? – he still managed to give co-director George Miller 100 per cent effort when required. The problems were chiefly caused by huge lulls between set-ups when Mel would sit around playing cards, drinking more beer, smoking cigarettes, talking, cracking childish gags and swilling yet more beer. And this was only a few weeks into what was to be a gruelling four-month shoot.

The movie's producers – alerted by Mel's drink-driving offence – provided him with a driver and a minder so that their star would not end up in some small-town jail cell when he was supposed to be shooting a $10 million movie. But the actor's 'companions' could only keep an eye on him – they were powerless actually to take the endless bottles of booze away. In any case, he had no intention of stopping his drinking. It was, after all, his only means of escape.

155

Back home in Sydney, Robyn immediately sensed that Mel was in trouble. She told him to give up alcohol, but it wasn't as easy as that. He was stuck on a movie he did not want to be on.

'I was coming to the end of my rope. I needed help but I wouldn't admit it. My family went through hell,' admitted Mel, years later. Sapped of energy and enthusiasm, he felt as if his career was about to collapse and dreaded that his marriage also faced destruction. 'I was about to lose all the important things in my life.'

Sound technicians on *Beyond Thunderdome* began to notice that Mel's voice was getting raspier from such vast quantities of beer and cigarettes. However, throughout the entire shoot, he epitomised the perfect professional in other ways – always on time, acting with great competence and knowing every word of his dialogue.

His fuse became shorter and shorter as the film progressed. He clammed up completely during interviews with journalists and soon inevitable rumours about his wellbeing permeated the Australian film industry. It would only be a matter of time before word got back to Hollywood.

But Mel's attitude towards the press was not just a result of his own unhappiness at that time. While he had avoided any actual scandals, reports of his drinking were being openly published and he was especially sensitive towards his parents' feelings on the subject. After all, Hutton Gibson had never even allowed alcohol in the house throughout Mel's childhood. And then there was Anne Gibson – like any mother, she was increasingly concerned by stories of her son's hellraising.

'I never chastised him about it but he knew how I felt,' she said afterwards. 'Mel was tired and confused and missed the family. It was a matter of priorities.'

By the time *Beyond Thunderdome* ended, Mel had made up his mind – this time, he was going to take a complete rest from film-making for as long as it would take to recharge his batteries and get to know his family again. His newest child William was more than six months old, yet Mel had seen him for less than half his life.

Mel had no idea – possibly he hardly cared – whether *Mad Max Beyond Thunderdome* would be a hit movie or not. He certainly knew he was burned out and on the edge of a nervous breakdown. As it turned out, the film became a huge box-office success and his gamble paid off.

He promised himself then that he would never again make so many films in such a short space of time. But he managed to repeat that unforgiving marathon on at least two more occasions, with even more dramatic results. For the moment, Mel was happier. He had waved farewell to Hollywood, albeit temporarily.

'It was too much work. I just wanted to say goodbye and try something else. I felt I had to clear my head. It took nearly a year for me to get my strait-jacket off. I didn't know what to do with all the attention I had been getting. It was confusing and I needed time to see where I went wrong. I was starting to slip, I had to learn to relax and not take things in Hollywood too seriously. I realised you had to put on the brakes or go away and return to the fray with new armour.'

Mel rued the price of those three back-to-back movies. 'You can't do that much work and remain sane. You get off a plane somewhere and suddenly you're being steered towards this red carpet. Someone's handing you flowers, offering you a drink, telling you to relax ... it's really jarring, and you're sort of cringing, hiding.

'But then you realise that if you don't go along with it, then they resent you for it. And if you went the other way, became

157

a big asshole and made a big hoot and holler about how important you were, they'd still do it anyway. So what can you do? You're fucked no matter which way you jump.'

Most important of all was Mel's reunion with his family back in Sydney. He and Robyn wanted to bring the children up on a farm in the countryside, and they began looking at suitable properties. Besides swimming in the sea near their existing Coogee home, his only real exercise was 'lifting babies'.

As *The River* director Mark Rydell commented, 'He seems to revere his wife and children. He's a wonderful father, and the kids are hanging on him all the time ...'

Mel has always remained devotedly protective of his family. During his break from the limelight, he went out of his way to make sure they did not come under the public gaze. 'I've got a red light that goes on inside me ... I don't even like to say I go to the beach. If you don't say what you're doing, nobody knows where you're coming from!'

He even persuaded Robyn – a very traditional, self-sufficient kind of mother – to employ a nanny to help her with the four young children, and also give her and Mel a chance to get to know each other again.

Inside the Coogee house, Mel used tools that Robyn had bought him for Christmas and birthdays over the years to put finishing touches to the property. Visitors recall that the interior was like a huge football field with children running in all directions on the vast, open-plan ground floor.

Within months of starting his 'lay-off', Mel and Robyn paid $350,000 for a beautiful farm of 2,400 hectares in the picturesque Kiewa Valley district of northern Victoria.

Mel saw the purchase of the farm, called Carinya – which means 'happy home' – in Tangambalanga as a key move in his recovery from the strains of making those four films. Strolling between gum and willow trees lining the driveway, Mel trusted that he and his family could lead the ordinary sort of life they all longed for.

'I think everyone needs an interest apart from his work, another avenue of experience, something to be enthusiastic about. Working on my farm made me normal again. I looked after my cattle, ate snake pies and raw vegetables and got closer to my wife and kids again. I cut out the heavy boozing, although I wasn't teetotal, and I realised that I had used alcohol as a prop but it made me a bastard. I'd missed out on kids, family, all the joys of being a parent.'

Hutton and Anne Gibson joined Mel and his family for long weekends. For the first time in his adult life, Mel had an opportunity to re-bond with his father. Together, they tore down a cottage on the farm estate and rebuilt it brick by brick. Hollywood must have seemed a million miles away, even if the father–son scene cried out for cameras.

And Robyn insisted that Mel did his bit around the house like any other husband. Often she would stick a message above the telephone in the kitchen reminding Mel, 'Do the dishes.'

A thankful, mellowed Mel even tried to re-evaluate his relationship with the media, and with his own family. To one reporter he commented, 'This time last year I could never sit down and talk to complete strangers about myself the way I'm doing now. But I've emerged as a new, bold me. I've decided that life's too short … We all found so much happiness that I get tears in my eyes when I think how I nearly blew it.'

While Mel picked up the practical skills required for his second career – farming – he joined a consortium of actors, writers and artists resisting closure of Sydney's Nimrod Theatre, where he had so successfully portrayed Romeo just a few years earlier. Mel was regaining his appetite for life by doing the things he had missed out on for three or four years.

Naturally, it wasn't all play and no work. He was swamped

with screenplays sent over by agent Ed Limato from Hollywood. Among the movie projects that caught his eye was one about wayward soccer star George Best. The rags-to-riches-and-back-to-rags story of the talented Manchester United player seemed tailor-made for Mel. After all, Best's life of excessive drinking was not that different from some of the trials and tribulations that Mel had experienced. But the Best movie never got off the ground and Mel pledged that the next project he'd commit to would be in the traditional Hollywood action genre. Something very special indeed was called for to maintain his career in Tinseltown.

Pressures of life as one of the world's top box-office attractions would eventually push Mel back towards alcohol but, for the moment, he was content.

THIRTEEN

I USED TO MISBEHAVE A LOT. I DIDN'T HAVE ANY
DIRECTION. DOES ANYONE?

In April 1985, Mel met his Australian agent and mentor Bill
Shanahan in Sydney to discuss the actor's future. He was
slowly recovering from the burn-out suffered after those three
back-to-back movies and, once more, his career was at a vital
crossroads. Stardom had beckoned and proved disastrous.
Now Mel wanted guidance on what to do next. Hollywood
was the last place on earth he wanted to end up in, and he had
even at one stage seriously considered quitting the acting
profession altogether.

He also turned down the lead in *The Running Man* after
being pursued for three years for the part. So it went to
Arnold Schwarzenegger and is credited with having launched
the former Mr Universe on to an even more successful movie
career than Mel's. The project's producers let it be known that
Arnold came at about half the price of Mel – a situation
reversed within four short years.

Mel trusted Bill Shanahan more than anyone in the business

and this fatherly figure rewarded that loyalty by advising him to keep his roots in Australia. After all, the film industry Down Under had been enjoying a renaissance since the late 1970s. It seemed a perfect time for Mel to expand his interests and set up a company to make films in his homeland. It would also help keep him closer to Robyn and the children, whom he considered some of the few sane people in a very crazy world.

Shanahan suggested that Mel link up with Australia's leading female producer, Pat Lovell, and form a company to develop feature projects. The two had met and worked together five years earlier on *Gallipoli*, when Pat had been a second mother to Mel and his young co-star Mark Lee.

On a rainy day in May 1985, Pat visited Mel, Robyn and the children at their home in Coogee. The reunion was with a very different fellow from the fresh-faced actor of half a decade before.

Mel later told Pat Lovell that what saved him was reading Hollywood screenwriter William Goldman's book *Adventures in the Screen Trade*, considered by many to be the finest account of life inside the movie industry ever written. Evidently, he saw the theme of the book as a warning.

Pat Lovell was as well aware of the stories of Mel's excesses as anyone else, but she also recognised that the actor had made a conscious effort to turn himself around, and escape the trials and temptations of Tinseltown. Setting up a production company with Mel in Australia could only be good for all concerned. So, with Mel rocking youngest child Will in his arms in the garden of that rambling Coogee house, the two agreed to form a company called Lovell Gibson. As Pat explains, 'Mel told me that the eldest came first.'

Soon they were working on a project entitled *Clean Straw for Nothing*, about three Australians who go to Britain to seek fame and fortune and end up on a Greek island instead.

Gillian Armstrong – who had worked with Mel on *Mrs Soffel* – was slated to direct. The idea was to keep the company small and run it like a family.

But then Hollywood producer Jerry Weintraub came on the scene. He calculated that if he could get Lovell Gibson to commit to giving him a first-look deal on all their projects, then he must gain immense influence over Mel, one of the most exciting new stars in Hollywood. Pat and Mel were impressed by Weintraub's enthusiasm and soon struck a development deal that, on the face of it, seemed to be perfect springboard for Lovell Gibson.

Mel was as excited as a schoolboy over Lovell Gibson's partnership with Weintraub. He enthusiastically told Hollywood trade paper *Variety*, 'It's a tremendous opportunity to work hand-in-hand with them. I've been presented a lot of development deals before and Jerry has taken us on as a production company, not me as an actor.'

Headlines in Australian and US newspapers shouted about Mel's 'TEN MILLION DOLLAR DEAL'. However, like most Hollywood deals, it was not quite what it appeared; $200,000 a year for developing projects, a salary of just $50,000 a year, plus $150,000 a year to run an office. And most of that had to come from the budgets of any films that actually got made. The $10 million figure was simply a 'projection' of what he could earn if all the company's projects actually went into production. In reality, they would be lucky if just one left the pitfall-strewn runway.

As Pat Lovell agrees, ruefully, 'It was not the richest deal in Hollywood history.' She also discovered the sting – those notional millions of bucks were conditional on Mel starring in every single movie developed – exactly the opposite of what the actor had intended when launching himself as a serious producer.

The first instalment of money took four months coming through and Mel had to loan $6,000 of his own money to Pat to start up the office. Only a few months earlier, she had remortgaged her own house just to keep her business running.

Pat was also concerned by Mel's condition at that time. He admitted he had been drinking beer and blacking out. His virtual abstinence during the family sabbatical was over. 'He said he had been keeling over and had very low blood pressure. The whites of his eyes were yellow. I was quite worried about him,' Pat Lovell recalled.

After a visit to a homeopathic doctor in Sydney for treatment, Mel headed to Hollywood to star in *Lethal Weapon*. Lovell Gibson had not got off to an impressive start.

When Pat went to Los Angeles to discuss projects she had in development, she had to pay her own air fare and get it reimbursed by the company later. Pat was met at the airport by Robyn and whisked straight to their rented house in Beverly Hills. There, he found a completely different Mel Gibson from the exhausted man encountered in Sydney only a few months earlier.

'I did not recognise him when I saw him. He was tanned. His blue eyes were sparkling. The change in him was quite extraordinary. He looked absolutely glorious.'

It emerged that Mel had been to a nutritionist in Los Angeles who had discovered he was suffering from an illness derived from a build-up of the natural yeast present in our stomachs, called Candida.

'The yeast in beer was doing particular damage to him,' says Pat, who insists that the strongest thing Mel ever drank in front of her was either a natural fruit cocktail or mineral water. Mel had turned his back, it seemed, on late nights with a beer bottle for company. He announced his newest favourite drink was carrots, celery, raw beetroot, red capsicum, raw garlic and ginger, all combined and strained through a juice extractor.

'You drink a couple of pints a day and you have all this energy,' he told Pat Lovell enthusiastically.

During a later trip to Hollywood in September 1987, Jerry Weintraub laid on a stretch limo to take Mel and Pat to numerous development meetings. The meetings were intended to introduce Mel and Pat to writers with interesting projects that might be worth pursuing.

By this time, Robyn and the children had returned to Australia, leaving Mel staying alone at his apartment in Santa Monica. Unbeknown to Pat Lovell, he had resumed drinking heavily and enjoyed at least one encounter with a woman during the trip. He was also driving around in a gleaming, very noticeable turquoise Thunderbird classic automobile.

Some of the more important meetings with writers were held in the famous deal-making arena of the Polo Lounge of the Beverly Hills Hotel. Mel renamed it the 'Polio Lounge'. But, despite all their efforts, not one real project could be found during that trip to LA.

Pat Lovell has an interesting opinion of Mel's ability to judge the quality of scripts. 'Mel could be very intelligent about the structure and character and all those things. He is a highly intelligent boy. But he did have a weak spot and would say something was fabulous when all it had was a good part for him. Often, the rest of the script did not gel at all.'

One of the more interesting projects to surface at Lovell Gibson was a treatment about a petty villain with an absurdly hapless streak, called *Tetley*. The idea came from the pen of talented British writer Lynda La Plante, 'an old mate' of Pat Lovell's, well known in the UK for her television series *Widows*. Mel saw it as the perfect vehicle to expand his talents as a comedy star and catapult him above Paul Hogan – for whom *Crocodile Dundee* had become the Australia's most successful film ever – and, when he summed up the character, it sounded suspiciously like himself.

'He goes from bad to worse ... and worse and worse. The man is always getting himself into sticky situations but this one is way out of his league. At the end, he has to extricate himself from it.'

As part of their development of *Tetley*, Pat and Mel paid a very low-key visit to London just before the 1987 Cannes Film Festival. The couple stayed at writer La Plante's home in Kingston, on the outskirts of London, giving Pat a rare glimpse of Mel off-duty and among friends. She noted that the actor who claims to do no physical exercise went on long jogs around nearby Richmond Park every morning, as well as doing 50 lengths in the La Plantes' pool immediately after his run. Mel even taught the bubbly, attractive writer how to bake his favourite soda bread during the five-day stay.

Mel filmed the entire trip on a newly acquired video camera that he turned on whenever he felt like shooting some embarrassing scene or other. Pat said there were times when he behaved like an overgrown schoolboy. For Mel, it was a rare opportunity actually to sit with a writer and help develop characters and scenes – something that most actors crave without attaining.

Most nights Mel, Pat, Lynda and her husband Richard ate out at modest local restaurants. On one occasion, Mel and Lynda went out alone to the theatre to see the play *Les Liaisons Dangereuses*. Mel was delighted because his trip received absolutely no coverage in British newspapers.

Before going to England, Mel and Pat had both decided to go to the Cannes Film Festival, mainly to help promote their company. They also wanted to try and get some major financial backing for *Tetley*.

Pat Lovell remembers, 'We arrived at the Carlton Hotel in Cannes and all hell broke loose. There were hundreds of screaming fans. *Lethal Weapon* was about to come out and Mel was immediately cornered in the foyer, signing autographs. In the end, the manager had to escort him to his room.

Mel was also angry that he did not get a full-sized suite at the hotel. Pat went on, 'He was upset he did not have a larger room. He said it wasn't comfortable and then I had to smuggle him out of the tradesmen's entrance every time we left the hotel because of the fans.'

That first evening, Pat and Mel went to a party for Paul Newman at a restaurant in the hills behind Cannes. They were seated at a table which included such film notables as British producer and short-lived Columbia studio chief David Puttnam and highly respected actor John Malkovich. Intriguingly, Mel rejected an offer of an introduction to Paul Newman by Ed Limato. Ultimately, Malkovich, a renowned raconteur, entertained everyone by telling some very funny Hollywood stories, but Mel kept uncharacteristically quiet throughout the entire evening.

The next day, Mel was turned away from the British Film Industry's pavilion near the hotel, because he and Pat did not have tickets. It was the year of Prince Charles and Princess Diana's special dinner at the pavilion. Black market prices for tickets to that event were said to be upwards of $1,500. Demand for the 800 seats was so high that the organisers had deliberately avoided releasing the tickets until the day of the event, to foil forgeries.

A trip to the beach at Cap d'Antibes followed the next day, but Mel was getting increasingly restless and short-tempered. At a typical film industry ceremony for 50 movie stars to provide handprints, he pressed his palm into wet cement at the beachfront event and photographers caught him yawning. It was a broad hint of what Mel thought of being there in the first place.

Also at Cannes that year, besides his agent Ed Limato, was producer Weintraub, who chartered a yacht called the *Galu* at $30,000 a week to launch his own new company. Four days after arrival in the South of France, Mel took up Weintraub's offer to let him sleep aboard the yacht instead of that cramped, 'economy' $300-a-night room in the Canton Hotel.

Mel's contentment on the yacht manifested itself in a series of incidents sparking memories of those drunken, hazy Hollywood days a few years earlier.

The morning after one particularly alcohol-fuelled night, Pat Lovell appeared on the yacht for a meeting with Mel, to be greeted by a grim-faced Jerry Weintraub, who said, 'I think you better go down and see your boy.'

Pat gingerly opened the door to Mel's cabin, and remembers, 'I had never seen anyone look as ill as he did.'

Mel asked Pat to put him on a plane back to Sydney that night. He wanted to get home to Robyn as quickly as possible. Pat packed his bags and pushed him into a shower before taking him to the airport. There he discovered he had no cash on him so she gave him $100. It was never paid back. She even felt obliged to arrange for someone to meet him at London's Heathrow Airport, to make sure he caught the connecting flight to Sydney.

Once back home, Mel became increasingly obsessed with a role that he considered to be tailor-made for him – Captain Hook in *Peter Pan*. Weintraub had the rights to the classic JM Barrie work and Mel tried very hard to convince Weintraub that he was the right man for the job.

But Weintraub eventually passed the project to Steven Spielberg and Mel's incredibly successful role in *Lethal Weapon* pushed *Pan* into the shadows. He was, by all accounts, positively heartbroken when the coveted Hook role went to Dustin Hoffman in the movie *Hook*, which eventually hit the screens in 1991.

At around that time, Ed Limato had moved to the giant ICM organisation and was, naturally, anxious to keep Mel in Hollywood on a virtually permanent basis. One day, Pat picked up a film industry magazine and read, to her surprise, that Mel had formed an LA-based production company without her knowledge. 'I could sense that Mel was not happy. We were getting loads of "No"s on projects,' recalled Pat. Even so, she was stunned to read that Mel had even appointed a development person at his new company in Los Angeles. 'I was so relieved that it had come to an end. I was basically being buffeted by all these people who wanted a piece of him,' said Pat.

At a meeting after the announcement, Mel took all phone calls in a next-door office, carefully shutting the door behind him as he went. Pat, close to tears, left the building. She never saw Mel again and was left to deal with Bruce Davey as lawyers tried to unravel their complicated business partnership.

She is not bitter about what happened with Mel because it gave her 'an incredible insight into Hollywood'. But she says her biggest sadness has been caused by the end of their friendship. 'It was more than just a working relationship. I miss Robyn and the children very much. She was such a sensible influence on him.'

After months of negotiation with Davey to close Lovell Gibson, she received a cheque for one dollar as her share in the company. It was merely a legal formality as the company had been effectively worthless – no projects had actually been made. And, to Pat, it seemed a hilarious way to end a partnership.

Pat says that Bill Shanahan's death in 1990 marked the final cutting of Mel's umbilical cord with Australia and the people she believes truly cared for him.

'He was very truthful to Mel. Mel was very upset when Bill died. It was a turning-point for him.'

Lovell Gibson officially folded with a low-key announcement in the film industry trade papers on 14 January 1989. In a carefully worded statement, Pat Lovell told reporters, 'Mel is a very fine actor with boundless potential so his acting career should take priority.'

Behind the scenes, Pat's lawyer Michael Frankel dealt with Bruce Davey – who just three years earlier had been a run-of-the-mill accountant – on winding up Lovell Gibson.

A few months later, Mel was nothing if not philosophical about his experiences at Lovell Gibson. 'It's disappointing. I tried to get projects up in Australia, and it's impossible. So I decided I'd rather be rich, and plan to have fun for a change.'

'Being rich' meant that, in Hollywood, Mel's LA-based company Icon Productions was already gearing itself up to start seriously developing big-budget vehicles for him. He had gradually come around to agreeing that, if you can't beat 'em, join 'em.

FOURTEEN

HOLLYWOOD IS A FACTORY. YOU HAVE TO REALISE
THAT YOU'RE WORKING IN A FACTORY AND YOU'RE
PART OF THE MECHANISM. IF YOU BREAK DOWN,
YOU'LL BE REPLACED.

Mel had just walked in from castrating a bull at his farm
in the Kiewa Valley when the screenplay that would
change his life arrived by courier from Los Angeles. He had
spent 18 months seriously reconsidering his entire future. He
wondered if movies were worth all the emotional upheavals
he had been through during the previous five years. He had
already decided that, unless the right sort of projects were
offered, he might as well stay on the farm with Robyn and the
children. He had the resources to do it. Why return to brutal
pressure and risk going off the rails again?

But within minutes of picking up that script – entitled
Lethal Weapon – Mel recovered his appetite for work. He
was hooked by the project after the first five pages. It had
action, humour and a leading character strikingly similar to
Mel. In many ways, it was Mel. The more he read, the surer
he was that this was the movie to revive his career.

LA cop Martin Riggs – Vietnam vet, suicidal following the death of his wife, on a fuse so short it would take a split-second to ignite – this was Mel's world, all right. Riggs was merciless in his pursuit of the bad guys but able to weep at the memory of his dead wife. He was a hero given extra dimensions of pathos and tragedy.

Within days, Mel was bound for Los Angeles, a city he continually cursed and swore he would never live in, the city that was the key to his success whether he liked it or not. On arrival at LAX airport, Mel went straight to the impressive Hollywood Hills home of director Richard Donner, already attached to *Lethal Weapon*. A film-maker whose best-known project to date had been *Superman*, starring Christopher Reeve, Donner had had Gibson and Danny Glover recommended to him as the unlikely pair of hero cops by casting director Marion Dougherty.

At Donner's house, Mel was introduced to Glover. Contrary to popular opinion, the two stars had a few creative problems to begin with. They came from completely different schools of acting.

Glover – the quietly spoken, San Francisco-born, one-time economics student – had not even decided to become an actor until he was 30. He also had a partial affliction from the learning disability dyslexia. But, once the decision had been made, he threw himself into studying every aspect of the art and a steady stream of very respectable movie roles followed. Now – fresh from his success as Mister in *The Color Purple* – he was being offered a buddy-buddy role in a cop film.

But Glover saw a great deal more in the role. 'I jumped at the chance to play the intricate relationships and subtle humour that exist in every close family group. It was an intriguing challenge,' he said.

Glover was a Method actor and, for Mel, that took some

getting used to. Glover's movement classes at acting school ran parallel to his reading and study. Among his books was one on the life and work of Konstantin Stanislavsky, the guru of Method actors such as Marlon Brando, James Dean and Rod Steiger. Glover was a product of exact, meticulous training – the opposite of Mel, who had his own opinions of his Method colleagues: 'I find that each one has their own, totally different way of getting into what they do. It's sort of a hard sell – sort of get yourself up to a higher pitch and be really positive. Australians, I think, do tend to come underneath that a bit.'

Mel believed firmly that 'the only way to get there is to be relaxed and happy. There can't be a conflicting attitude that's in there already for me. Otherwise, you have to rip that down and just be open and accessible and be an instrument.'

He also confided to one associate that he believed he could 'fake it' if necessary – something that purists like Danny Glover wince at hearing. 'I think it is possible to fake it – to go into something you don't know about and get away with it provided you do your groundwork.'

Mel has acknowledged, privately, that he and Glover did not hit it off immediately. It was to be a gradually improving relationship that reached the height of familiarity only in the *Lethal Weapon* sequels. And it wasn't helped by Mel's honesty about his attitudes towards Method acting. 'Some actors – Method actors – remain as the person they are playing during the whole working day. For me, the Method is to get away from it. If you're enjoying yourself, even showing grief, then it comes across better in acting.'

Although Donner knew after a couple of hours of rehearsal at his house that Mel and Glover were perfect for the key roles, he also knew that their professional conflicts might send either of them over the edge at any time – Mel particularly. 'I was expecting to have problems with him. I thought he was going to be a Method actor, somebody who wanted to know where everything came from and why. But give him one word and he runs with it. Half the time he doesn't even need that.'

But this was a different Mel. He was refreshed and invigorated by his lay-off. He had a new appetite for work and he believed that *Lethal Weapon* was going to be 'something very special'. He had also just celebrated his thirtieth birthday. It was time to consolidate his considerable gains, take a grip of his responsibilities.

Robyn and the children settled into a rented home in Beverly Hills within days of Mel signing contracts with Warner Brothers – his fee was a very healthy $1.2 million. His human sheet-anchor mattered more, though.

During the preparations for *Lethal Weapon*, Mel and Danny Glover wanted to get the feel of what it was really like to be LA cops by going out on patrol with the real thing. The naked truth about being a police officer in a crime-riddled city is that it is a tough, dangerous and exhausting profession in which you go to work every day wondering if this could be the last day of your life.

'It's hard to imagine what it's like to be a policeman until you find yourself in that situation,' said Mel. 'You feel very vulnerable. I was never involved in anything big. They obviously weren't going to throw me into the middle of a hot-spot in LA. But it's just your whole perception – and your imagination starts to get to you. You even start to look at little old ladies walking along the street in a different way.

'You can see why these guys are wired up and ready for action all the time. You can also see why they have a lot of problems in the police force. There are many marriage break-ups, a high suicide rate. I gained a lot of respect for them ...

I'd hate to do it. It must be terribly hard and you don't get many rewards for it.'

Despite initial problems over Method acting, Mel and Danny Glover forged a partnership that had all the ingredients for a buddy-buddy cop movie, which is exactly what they turned it into. Early difficulties were perfectly reflected in the way that Glover's structured, uptight character in the film starts by completely mistrusting Mel's wilder figure, Riggs. Once again, real life had spilled over on to celluloid and provided Donner with the love-hate chemistry he sought.

Mel granted that the character he was playing was 'fairly unbalanced. Now, I'm not as unbalanced as him. I would not try to shoot myself. I would not jump off buildings.'   H i s intensive martial arts training before shooting began, and the very physical aspects of the character he was playing, threatened his life at one stage during filming. For it is little known that by shooting ten, sometimes twenty takes on difficult chase sequences, the actor – still smoking two packs of Marlboro a day – was running up to 16km daily. Once he was so exhausted that he collapsed on the set and had to be given oxygen. Paranoid studio executives ordered a cover-up of the incident, fearful that any shadow over Mel's health might seriously affect the image of the movie – which was about a super-fit ex-soldier, after all. From that moment on, Mel sustained his high-energy antics by being administered oxygen between most takes.

Just a few months earlier, he had visited an iridologist in Sydney who had told him to stop ingesting certain meats and beer and too much coffee. He lost ten kilos and began yet another new lease of life.

Mel was convinced the appeal of *Lethal Weapon* lay in the relationship between the cops played by him and Glover.

'This thing is going to work simply because it has a strong

basis, a strong foundation. You are going to care about all the action because you care about the characters ... that's what I like about the script – those two guys are great,' he explained enthusiastically.

According to cast and crew on the first *Lethal Weapon*, it was an exhilarating, happy shoot – something which Mel had rarely experienced in his previous movie outings. It was also reflected in Mel's willingness to expand his character of Marty Riggs. He wanted to put a personal stamp on the tale and director Downer was more than happy to permit that.

In fact, Dormer recognises that Mel rapidly became more than just another actor doing a job of work. He found the star prepared to add nuances to his character that were not even touched upon in the script. It was something that can mean the difference between a satisfactory performance and one that lights up the screen. Mel added little touches of humour here and there, but it was the movie's most emotional scene that probably did more for his career than any other sequence.

A despondent Riggs decides to end it all, puts his police revolver in his mouth and starts to squeeze the trigger. It was a familiar set-up, repeated many times over on the big screen. But Mel decided to take it one stage further, with literally dramatic results, as Dormer confirms. 'Because the scene was so intense, and shot under extremely difficult, cramped conditions inside a trailer van, only the camera operator was in there with Mel as he went through his paces. I checked the revolver myself before it was handed to him by the unit's official armourer.'

Even a blank would inflict terrible damage if it went off when the barrel was near the mouth – wadding from a blank killed actors Jon Erik Hexum and Brandon Lee in separate incidents on movie sets in subsequent years.

Mel gripped the pistol tightly and rammed the muzzle into

his mouth. Dormer and his crew gasped. This was definitely not in the script.

'I watched the scene on a video monitor outside the van. I watched ... I couldn't believe what Mel was doing. It was so real. I thought, Hell, he might have put a shell in the gun ... things rushed through my head. Did Mel ask the armourer or special effects guy to put one in there to give him motivation? I tell you, I was terrified as Mel started to choke on the barrel, his finger tightening on the trigger. I was torn between rushing in and stopping the scene in case there was a shell in the gun and getting this amazing performance. I was glued to watching the video screen. The crew was spellbound. A couple of girls were choking, beginning to cry behind me.

'I figured we had what we wanted and was about to call "Cut" into the radio mike that went to the cameraman's earphones. But Mel kept it going, adding a final few tears of frustration and mental anguish as he wept, apologising to a photo of his dead wife. I can tell you I breathed out loud when he stopped the performance and I called a meek "Cut" to the operator.

'I rushed into the van and hugged Mel. Told him it was great, fantastic. He looked around, shook his head. "Want to try another one, for safety?" he said to me quite innocently, wiping a real tear from his eye. I gave him another hug and said, "You were perfect, the film gate is clear. We've got it."

'I could never have gone through that again. But Mel would have done it again, gladly. When I saw the scene intact as part of the finished film, it still took my breath away. My hair stood on end. This sort of thing rarely happens. With Mel, I guess anything is possible. He's one of the greats and he seems to be cruising most of the time.'

What Dormer failed to mention is that, after that sequence,

Mel sat down, blew his nose, took a breath, reached into his pocket – and pulled out a red clown's nose and put it on.

When the actual gun-in-the-mouth scene appeared during screenings of the movie in cinemas, voices would erupt from the audience, 'No, don't ... don't do it.'

One person who saw that scene and was deeply moved by it was eminent Italian director Franco Zeffirelli. He made a mental note to approach the actor about a special project he had been trying to get off the ground for years.

'It was a scene in which he has a kind of "To be or not to be ..." speech with a gun. But he's not able to pull the trigger. When I saw that I said, "This is Hamlet. This boy is Hamlet!"'

The essence of *Lethal Weapon* is that it is a violent film and there can be little doubt that Marty Riggs is a violent character, to the point that his partner Roger Murtagh (Danny Glover) asks, 'Have you ever met anyone you haven't killed?'

Mel later explained that this underlying current of violence was one of the main reasons for injecting his own throwaway lines into the dialogue. 'I wanted to give the character a bit of life. I thought that to give a man who was in so much pain a bit of light relief would be interesting. I got that idea from a Shakespearean play,' he explained.

At the time, this injection of humour was revolutionary because the characters Mel had portrayed up until that point tended to be stern, distinctly unfunny people like Mad Max or Fletcher Christian.

But, as Mel's confidence grew during the making of *Lethal Weapon*, so did his comedic talents. Eventually, those awful one-liners and constant bad jokes became his stock in trade. 'He could have been a Marx brother, there's something undeniably zany about the man,' says Robert Towne, who later directed Mel in *Tequila Sunrise*. 'Beneath the romantic exterior, there is this preposterous farceur longing to get out.'

Richard Dormer had a slightly different take on Mel's humour level. 'He is God's gift to a director. But he tells the worst jokes in the world.'

A higher opinion is held by *The Year of Living Dangerously* co-star Sigourney Weaver. 'He can sing and dance and he's all over the place, and he's very funny. Mel is all the Three Stooges rolled into one.'

Mel himself has admitted that 'horsing around' is just part of his work ethic. 'I figure, if you have to work for a living, you might as well make fun of it. What I do certainly isn't a cure for cancer. And one of the best things about this job is that you can enjoy yourself at it almost all the time.'

The 'new' Mel had secretly got himself into shape before *Lethal Weapon* began by lifting weights in preparation for those martial arts. It was a fascinating about-turn in his attitude towards keeping fit. Previously, his most strenuous exercise had been lifting babies. He kept his painstaking fitness routine out of the public eye because it worried him that his fans might think he had completely abandoned all those Hollywood-won't-get-me statements from earlier in his career.

But Mel needed no telling that *Lethal Weapon* was his biggest and best movie opportunity to date and he did not intend to blow it. He was only too well aware that, if the project had landed on his lap two years earlier, he might well never have coped with it because of the disarray of his life then.

Yet probably the most significant evidence of the change in him came when two young fans approached him for an autograph on the set of *Lethal Weapon*. The old Mel would have gruffly refused to oblige. The new version smiled warmly and wrote, '*To Michelle and Karen – Mel.*' Then, pondering for a minute, he inserted the word 'love' as if afraid to seem cold, but reluctant to appear too demonstrative.

Lethal Weapon represented another important first for Mel. It was the first time he had actually based himself in Los Angeles, instead of flying in for two- or three-week bursts of meetings. It had a profound effect on the actor; his attitude towards Hollywood as a place, if not its society, began to soften.

'You see, when I first went there you'd go over and you'd talk to guys in studios about deals and you'd feel uncomfortable because you didn't know how the place worked, you were somewhere else and you'd get a very slanted idea of it. You'd be staying at a hotel somewhere in Beverly Hills and you'd have these kind of "dying to meet you" lunches. It's not a natural sort of environment at all, so that you can get very sort of uptight and you can find it repulsive, you know you want to get away from. it. But when I was there to work and do a job it was a total joy. I really enjoyed it.'

His fitness became a vital factor in the original *Lethal Weapon*' especially the climactic scene in which he ends up in a life-or-death struggle with the villain, played by Gary Busey, on the front lawn of partner Roger Murtagh's house.

'Yeah. That was a hell of a scene,' said Mel afterwards. 'Water pouring from a burst main, hovering helicopter with its blinding light, cop cars and uniformed cops everywhere, chanting for Riggs to "kill the bastard". When we finished the scene, after four days of being so wet, I could feel every sore bone in my body. It was like I'd been run over by a bus. But when I watched the rushes the next night I knew it would all come together as a great final piece. I felt it was all worth it, even though the bones still creak.'

The most extraordinary thing about the first *Lethal Weapon* movie was that it had no romantic interest. In fact, as Australian film critic Scott Murray pointed out, 'It was all about the relationship between Mel and Danny's characters.

There is such a fusion between them, despite the fact they came from two completely different schools of acting. It is almost a love story between them.'

Before shooting was completed, Warner Brothers executives had decided that a sequel had to be made. There was a constant buzz on the set that 'this is going to be a big one'. The first *Lethal Weapon* eventually grossed around $120 million worldwide, making Mel Gibson what everyone had been expecting – a box-office star who could write his own ticket. He even started taking Robyn out in Tinseltown, to movie premières like the new Bette Miller/Danny DeVito comedy *Ruthless People*. The town he said he would never become a part of was starting to suck him in.

Critics in the US did not really know what to make of *Lethal Weapon*, but, in Mel's adopted homeland of Australia, there was no such confusion about it. 'Gibson clearly relishes a role that gives him a chance to show that he's more than just a pretty face,' wrote Bev Tivey in the Sydney *Telegraph* in June 1987. And in the Sydney *Sun* critic Peter Holder wrote, 'Mel proves once and for all he is an accomplished actor first, with the "sex-symbol" tag running second.'

However, controversy erupted in August 1987, when the movie was released in Britain just after the tragic massacre of 16 people by a gun-toting maniac in the quiet Berkshire town of Hungerford. The movie – with its virtually non-stop depiction of trigger-happy cops and robbers – was withdrawn from a cinema near the scene of the killings. A local vicar attacked a London newspaper for carrying a full-page colour photograph of Mel pointing a gun in the same issue that reported church services mourning the victims of the massacre the previous week.

Just after the release of *Lethal Weapon*, Robyn weighed in with her own production, giving birth to the couple's fifth child, a boy called Louis. Hollywood noted with glee that Mel was proving very different from their traditional, multi-divorced megastars.

Mel had so enjoyed the happy-family atmosphere of the first *Lethal Weapon* that he was delighted to make a sequel less than 18 months later. Hollywood was much more surprised by director Donner's decision to take charge of it. He had never before agreed to direct a sequel, despite the fact that five of his previous films had been turned into series.

The sequel proved an even bigger money-spinner than the original – which is virtually unheard of in Hollywood – by grossing $147 million in the US alone. Marty Riggs was on his way to becoming one of the biggest-earning creations in movie history.

'It was Donner and the boys again. There's a great sense of freedom on these sets with this crew and it's pretty familiar territory, so it's easy to just step into it and feel free to experiment and push it to the edge,' Mel observed. He'd been pleased to settle Robyn and the children in another rented house (its $23,000-a-month rent was picked up by Warner Brothers), this time in Malibu, for the duration of the shoot.

Lethal Weapon's original creator – a shy ex-film school student, Shane Black – refused to help write a sequel because he felt he had taken the characters as far as he could. So Donner turned to writer Jeffrey Boam for some new ideas. He came up with a ludicrous plot concerning evil South African diplomats running a drug cartel, which predictably sparked mild outrage from non-fiction South African officials, who claimed the film was yet another example of 'the villainisation of South Africa in films'.

But, this time, the film had a definite love interest in the shape of young British star Patsy Kensit. It looked like a match made in heaven to the British tabloids, determined to create a romance between Mel and his blonde, 21-year-old co-star. But her presence was much more significant for Detective Marty Riggs. Jeffrey Boam had – by introducing the love interest – changed the perceptions of *Lethal Weapon* and in the process set up the formula for the series. Sexuality had been virtually non-existent as far as Riggs was concerned in the first *Weapon*.

Mel reacted to this new situation with a measure of reluctant pleasure. His character had to have romantic touches if the *Weapon* series was to remain fresh and appealing. It also enabled Mel to add another dimension to the role.

And Patsy Kensit – herself only recently married (and only a year away from divorce) – proved the perfect female lead, though she confirmed coyly that her passionate love scenes with Mel were not the real thing. 'We are both married, both Catholics, so it was a little weird. He was as uncomfortable as I was, but he was a real gentleman about it. He was very delicate.'

During the kissing scene, impish Kensit said she mouthed the word 'vomit' to her handsome co-star. He, in turn, told her dirty jokes. Their most physical moment was, according to the blonde actress, 'when I had cold feet and warmed them up on him. But apart from that, I just lay there with my legs open ...'

The rest of the time on set, Mel kept up a constant stream of antics and gags, entertaining anyone who happened to be within earshot.

He would appear wearing a coffee filter on his head like a Jewish yarmulke. He bellowed never-ending renditions of 'Edelweiss' from *The Sound of Music*. And he had the set in stitches as he would criticise himself out loud, 'What! Oh, no, you're terrible. Gibson! Lighten up. Stop twitching.'

Director Richard Donner explained, 'He's crazy. He lives on

the edge, full of energy and excitement. If Hollywood was still doing drugs, I'd say Mel was taking lots of drugs, but the truth is that he is crazy naturally.'

That led to the oddest scene in the entire movie, when Danny Glover's character is sitting on the toilet and discovers it is rigged to explode, so he cannot leave the throne. The whole sequence was created the day before, much of it by a very amused Mel who thought 'it would be a gas' to have his partner 'stuck on the john with his trousers round his ankles'.

Some of the critics were just as bemused as before: afraid to condemn the film completely but remaining unconvinced. 'It's a potentially interesting film, but it leaves a bad taste in the mouth because it pretends to treat us as a mature audience capable of judging difficult moral dilemmas while leaving little doubt that Gibson's line is the one we are supposed to agree with,' wrote Lynden Barber in the *Sydney Morning Herald*.

But the authoritative *New York Times* positively glowed in its praise. 'Gibson, Donner and Glover have concocted the best action-buddy-comedy formula since *Butch Cassidy and the Sundance Kid*.'

After it was released, Mel announced he would never make another *Lethal Weapon* film. His commitment to the sequel had meant having to turn down the lead role in *The Untouchables*, a part which springboarded the lesser-known Kevin Costner to even greater fame and fortune than Mel.

In any case, he was excited by the prospect of playing opposite a young actress dominating Hollywood's female marketplace – Julia Roberts. The two were slated to star together in *Renegades*, a western told from the woman's point of view.

Mel's first meeting with the still shy (and very young) Roberts occurred at Hollywood agents ICM in Beverly Hills. He and the actress exchanged few words but Hollywood remained convinced that they would make a lethal box-office combination. Mel, on the other hand, thought otherwise. Without any explanation, he pulled out of *Renegades* within days of that meeting.

It took just one phone call to his farm, to which he had immediately retreated, from larger-than-life Hollywood producer Joel Silver to get Mel to change his mind about making *Lethal Weapon 3*.

In this film, Murtagh is seven days away from retirement when the pair investigate the disappearance of firearms from a police lock-up, finding a trail leading to a crooked cop.

Trying to do their job – despite interference from a beautiful, martial-arts-trained Internal Affairs detective played by Rene Russo, and the egregious informer, Leo Getz (Joe Pesci again, after Mel had lobbied hard for Pesci to return), still keen as ever to play amateur cop – Mel and Danny take their audience on yet another action-packed adventure, considered by many critics to be vastly superior to its predecessor's plodding, unbelievably formulaic progress.

There were rumours that Robyn was concerned that Mel was taking too many risks by doing many of his own stunts. One source even claimed that Mel had been told to 'go away' by his wife and think about his actions and not come back to his family until he had agreed to stop taking such risks.

She had never forgotten how Mel's hyperactivity on the set of *Lethal Weapon 2* nearly cost him his life, when a stunt went horribly wrong. The actor had insisted he could handle a sequence where he was tied up in a sack and dumped in a water tank. In theory he was supposed to unravel the rope with ease and come to the surface. But Mel stayed under the water for a dangerously long period. Professional stunt divers were poised to plunge into the tank and rescue him when he finally emerged.

'His cheeks had ballooned up and his eyes were popping out of his skull. We thought he was a goner,' said one shaken member of the crew.

Obviously well aware of the concern, Mel looked at all the anguished faces, smiled and moved on to the next scene as if nothing had happened.

All the *Lethal Weapon* films did get a lot of criticism for their high violence quota. However, Mel – who sees the series as being comic-strip-comes-to-life – defended them stoutly at a press conference just before release of *Lethal Weapon 3*. 'It drives me nuts when people say it's violent and offensive and going to scar people's minds. It's entertainment. There are a lot of problems in society and they like to lay blame on things like this. But I don't think that's fair. If there is anything harmful in a movie, it's wrong. But who's going to be a judge of that? In my case, it's me.'

When the film was released just after the LA riots erupted – the worst civil unrest in US history – he refuted suggestions that his movie might incite more violence by saying, 'What happened in Los Angeles is lamentable. But I don't think a film like this threatens to incite anything. When John Wayne got hit on the head with a shovel in *Legend of the Lost* in 1959, I can't recall a rash of shovel-hittings.'

But Mel is nothing if not inconsistent. In an interview with *Cleo* magazine in Australia, he admitted, 'I loved violence in films as a kid, especially when you realise it's not really happening. It depends on how it's put out. Every cartoon I saw as a kid had cats and dogs blowing each other up and shooting each other – hilarious fun. Knowing that violence exists is a necessary part of your education.' Mel did, though, insist later that he would never let his own children watch the *Lethal Weapon* films.

The media continued to heavily criticise violent aspects of

all three films. The Sydney *Telegraph Mirror* even went so far as to publish a tally of comparative totals for everything from car wrecks to killings in the *Lethal Weapon* series:

Numbers of cars wrecked: 7, 14, 5
Number of people killed: 24, 29, 16
Number of explosions: 3, 7, 4

Interestingly, there had been a definite effort to cut down on mayhem in the third instalment, but by then perhaps it was too late.

In an effort to defuse the criticism, Warner Brothers gave proceeds from the first few Hollywood screenings to help the victims of those same LA riots that tore the city apart in the final days of April 1992.

Prophetically, in one interview to publicise *Lethal Weapon 3*, Mel compared the phenomenally successful series with that supposedly dying breed of movie – the Western. Just a few months later, he was persuaded by director Donner to play the lead in a Western that, if successful, could once again alter the course of his career.

True to form, reviews for *Lethal Weapon 3* were just as mixed as for the previous two films. Hollywood's *Entertainment Weekly* magazine claimed, '*Lethal Weapon 3* is like a pile of odds and ends that never made it into the first two movies. It zips around without any true forward momentum.'

And the *New York Times* could have spotted a recurring theme in Mel's life when their critic wrote, 'Gibson looks tired – and has every right to. The movie isn't going anywhere but it goes in circles at top speed.' But the *Hollywood Reporter* said that Mel's performance was 'a bullseye'.

Lethal Weapon 3 – which cost $40 million to make – grossed more than $300 million worldwide during the summer and autumn of 1992. Yet again, it outdid its predecessor, just as that movie did better than the original. Warner Brothers were so happy they presented Mel, Danny Glover, Richard Donner and Joel Silver with brand-new, four-wheel-drive Range Rovers as a token of appreciation. Silver immediately commissioned *two* separate writing teams to prepare *Lethal Weapon 4* screenplays at a cost of more than a million dollars, despite the fact that neither star was prepared to commit to another sequel.

Having completed *Lethal Weapon 3*, both Mel and Danny Glover agreed that it was getting hard to keep up enthusiasm for the series. Ironically, the third film marked the first time Danny Glover had truly sat down and talked on a proper personal level with Mel.

On *The Arsenio Hall Show* on US television in May 1993, co-star Glover made it absolutely clear that he had no wish to make a fourth film. 'It's time for us all to go on to other things,' he told Hall. But would money eventually speak louder than words?

FIFTEEN

IF I'VE STILL GOT MY PANTS ON IN THE SECOND SCENE,
I THINK THEY'VE SENT ME THE WRONG SCRIPT.

After the incredible $30 million-plus opening weekend at
the US box office for *Lethal Weapon 3*, rumours swept
Hollywood that Mel was paid an extra $5 million to bare that
famous bottom in the movie. Industry experts estimated that
the sight of the actor's rear would automatically add $20
million to overall takings of any film.

He made light of the tales with, 'I haven't got anything that
no one else has.'

But the truth was that, every time he showed his naked
backside, women wanted him to turn around and then went
home from the movie and told all their friends what
wonderful shape Mel was in.

Although he doesn't like to admit it, he bared all (very
briefly) during a mooning scene in his first film *Summer City*.
That should have provided him with a taste of what was to
come. Then there was a brief glimpse of that famous rear in

189

Gallipoli. A four-year hiatus followed. Mel's bottom came back with a vengeance, as it were, in the original *Lethal Weapon* – and it has rarely looked back since!

Initially, Mel's family were 'very concerned' about the embarrassment caused by his nude scenes, but, when he continued to do them if they were part of the story, they reluctantly approved. He is also well aware of the financial value of his best-known asset, not counting those eyes.

As one Hollywood producer said, 'You've heard of the $6 million man? Well, this is the $20 million bottom!'

There is a nudity clause in every movie contract Mel signs and, though $20 million may be nonsense, his fee does increase if there is a scene in which he shows a lot of skin.

'People want you to take your clothes off,' says Mel with feigned bewilderment. He even sneaked into a movie theatre one night to see *Lethal Weapon* only to flee by the back exit in embarrassment when that famous nude scene flashed on the screen.

Hollywood gossip had it that an indignant Mel refused to strip for any of his naked scenes – and that a lookalike bottom was used on each occasion. That is patently untrue. He confessed to one producer that he was surprised by the sight of his bottom on the screen because 'my bum's got a fair carpet. I didn't realise I was so furry on my back end.'

And, in August 1992, American magazine *Women on Top* even went so far as to claim that Mel had bared his bottom more times than any other Hollywood star.

In *Bird on a Wire*, a comedy in which he starred with Goldie Hawn, he even had a bullet sliced out of his rear by a beautiful vet. And by the time his slushy romantic comedy *Forever Young* hit the screen in late 1992, Mel's naked rear caused nothing more than a ripple of excitement, after his earlier stripteases.

But there is absolutely no question of upping the ante by trying full-frontal nudity in the future. 'He draws the line at that for the sake of his family and his pride!' said one Hollywood associate.

However, Mel's continual exposure in movies did foster another line of thought among more cynical members of the Hollywood establishment – that this very heterosexual star was unintentionally attracting a large number of gay men to his films.

The irony cannot be lost on members of US gay groups such as Queer Nation, which selected Mel as its *bête noire* of the season after he made a number of controversial comments to the Spanish magazine *El Pais* in December 1991. In the article, Mel said that, when he first took up acting, he assumed many people would think he was gay.

'When you are an actor, they stick a label on you. I went from playing rugby one day to taking dance classes in black leotards the next. Many of the girls I met in school took it for granted that I was gay,' he told journalist Koro Castellano. 'But I did it. I became an actor despite that. But with this look, who's going to think I am gay? It would be hard to take me for someone like that.

'Do I look homosexual? Do I talk like them? Do I move like them?' he was reported as saying, before going into a graphic description of sexual activity which included getting up from his chair, bending over, pointing to his posterior and saying it was for use only in the smallest room in the house. Those gestures were described as being 'crude and disgusting'.

The comments caused an outcry across the US, and *The Advocate*, a gay and lesbian weekly newspaper, took waspish revenge by naming him Sissy of the Year, in its annual Sissy Awards for allegedly homophobic, anti-gay actions. They had been looking for ammunition to fire at Mel ever since his 'mincing portrayal' of a supposedly effeminate hairdresser in *Bird on a Wire* had enraged many members.

A spokesman for the powerful Gay and Lesbian Alliance Against Defamation (GLAAD), the media organisation that 'watchdogs' the press for derogatory remarks about gays, said, 'If Mel Gibson has such deep religious views, he should be using his status to educate and not to spread hate. There are many people of deeply religious views who certainly are very tolerant of gay people and who don't find it necessary to insult or degrade. Mr Gibson seems to be hung up on some stereotype of how gay men are supposed to look or behave. If, as he says, he knew gay people in drama school, then he would know that there is no particular way in which gay men look or behave.'

Even top US syndicated columnist Liz Smith joined in the row shortly after the Spanish interview occurred by snapping that 'Mel Gibson lives in the dark ages ... Mel Gibson is so divine on the screen, it is awful to discover he thinks this way. I find his remarks astounding.'

In Hollywood – where a high percentage of people inside the industry are homosexual – a vicious verbal hate campaign was launched against the star. Two muscle-bound bodyguards were hired to keep an eye on Mel, prompted by serious fears of physical attacks being launched by members of Queer Nation.

Ed Limato ordered an immediate 'damage-control' operation. But, by trying to dampen the flames of a crisis, he unleashed even more publicity through calling Liz Smith (presumably after consultation with Mel) and insisting that the actor had never even had an interview with *El Pais*. It was a disastrous move because Mel then did a movie promotional interview on TV's *Good Morning America* and immediately confessed that he did make the comments, before accusing Liz Smith of 'violating my right to have an opinion'.

Smith – whose column is read avidly in Hollywood – then ran an interview with GLAAD spokesman Robert Bray, hitting back, 'He can't defame gays and then try to wriggle out of it by blaming the translation. Gay fans of Mel Gibson need to throw out their *Mad Max* tapes and stop going to his movies until he stops defaming gay people.'

In 1988, Mel received what was for him probably the most offensive role offer anyone could make. As his career bloomed, his commitment to God and the Catholic Church had deepened, even though – under Papa Hutton's strict instructions – none of the Gibson offspring attended church any more, due to modernisation of Catholic observances.

However, when Ed Limato contacted Mel in Australia to say that pre-eminent director Martin Scorsese wanted him to play Jesus in the *The Last Temptation of Christ*, Mel was outraged and told Limato, 'I would not touch that one!' He simply did not think any actor was capable of portraying the Lord.

At home in Australia, Mel's new-found confidence manifested itself in many different ways. Gone was the shy, reluctant star who dreaded every press interview. Visitors now found a determined character who had finally found his place in the world – and, like his father before him, had some fairly rigid views to lay on the community.

Mel the farmer was as determined as any family man to make sure the wholesome values that come with living in such a rural area were kept up. Working in Hollywood had made him all the more determined to avoid becoming another multimillionaire star with a string of broken marriages and a worthless private life. He had long since seen past the tinsel and come to the conclusion that La La Land had a lot of problems he hoped would never emigrate to his beef farm near Tangambalanga.

In 1987, with his box-office presence confirmed by the success of the first *Lethal Weapon*, Mel took a step that disturbed many of his advisers and fans. He hooked up with Australian right-wing politician Robert Taylor and actively campaigned for the return of what Mel called 'old-fashioned values and traditional family values'. It was a dangerous move.

In the week that a poll carried out in singles bars in the US found that Mel was the man with whom most American women would like to be marooned on a desert island, he was out voicing his support for a return to a puritan lifestyle, in the town of Albury-Wodonga.

Taylor never had a bigger audience. As an independent candidate in the 1987 Australian federal election, he was more used to addressing tiny groups in roomy halls or from the back of a truck in a dusty township. Most voters tended to ignore people like Taylor because they were not aligned with the three major parties. He was also against many of the products of democracy like unions and support for the needy. His dislike for government bureaucracy, heavy taxation, Fabian socialism and humanism had been heard 1,000 times before. But, to Mel, Robert Taylor represented all the values he believed in – and he was determined to help him get elected.

The Australian media were sardonically amused. One local paper seemed to sum up feelings in the area with the headline 'MAD MAX WEIGHS IN FOR A TRUCKIE'. It must have made Mel cringe.

But none of that deterred him. At every gathering, he voiced his support for Taylor, often standing next to him on the platform as he ranted about 'the evil vices plaguing today's society'.

'Our nation today is suffering a massive increase in child abuse, drug abuse, suicide, pornography and the AIDS thing,' thundered Taylor as Mel led the applause. 'Our nation is in the grip of hopelessness. That's why you're here today, because you're dissatisfied.' The truth was that much of the audience of teenage girls were only there for a glimpse of Mel. 'Abortion is legalised mass murder,' continued Taylor, and Mel backed his candidate to the hilt, recognising that he was Taylor's only chance of being successful in those elections. Newspapers and television were all giving him the sort of coverage he could never have dreamed of before a star came on board.

'I couldn't even get my press releases in the paper before Mel came along,' enthused the young politician. Mel turned to Taylor because, in the couple of years since buying his farm, he had seen at first hand all the problems and frustrations attached to trying to earn an honest living from the land. 'People think these guys sit in their properties in front of their fire and it all just happens. That's crazy. I've never met such hard-working people in my life as I have in the country areas of Australia.'

He considered himself one of them. In the area near the farm, Mel went to great pains to be just another farmer. Instead of displaying his wealth with pride, as has always been the American way, he drove around in a scruffy Volvo Estate, chewing bits of straw and talking about the cost of cattle.

But there was one aspect of his involvement in local politics that was bizarre, to say the least — he could not vote in Australia because he still carried his American passport. In fact, that explained in many ways why he exposed his views so publicly. It was the only method he had to give his beliefs any influence.

'I haven't got a vote, but I certainly give a hoot about what's happening to this country, because I'm responsible for bringing six Australians into the world. I can't think of anything more challenging or important than making sure we guarantee the future of our young ones,' stated Mel.

His somewhat surprising foray into politics began after chatting to a neighbouring farmer, Ed Jacobs, who happened to be an adviser and long-time family friend of Taylor. But then Mel did not take much persuading that the young politician was 'on the right track'.

'Mel was committed to helping me,' Taylor said. The Hollywood star also reckoned he could help the small-town politician's 'stage performance'. He began secretly coaching him on speech delivery, using all the tricks of the stage and screen, learned so carefully over the previous ten years.

'There were little hints about my wording in speeches, my delivery. Mel was great at helping without interfering or treading on toes. I was so lucky having a famous person supporting my own long-held beliefs,' continued Taylor.

Mel threw himself into the thick of the battle. Opposition politicians were ridiculing Taylor for needing a film star to get sufficient attention. But the actor ignored the criticism and stuck by his man throughout the campaign. He not only attended meetings, he also drove Taylor's truck around the constituency. In the middle of all this, he also found time to visit the Children's Hospital in Camperdown, Sydney. Many of the young patients were victims of brain tumours and Mel showered them with attention, oblivious to long, adoring stares from nurses and parents alike. Mel, unusually, endured all that and willingly signed autographs on anything thrust under his nose.

'It's five minutes of magic. If they saw me for an hour they would find it boring,' he said to a reporter at the hospital.

But the newly politically charged Mel managed to turn his goodwill visit to the hospital into electioneering, when he publicly accused the Australian Government of failing to give sufficient funds for the running of the hospital. According to newspaper reports, he was 'sickened' by the state of the unit and made a 'sizeable' donation towards the hospital funds.

Mel even persuaded Warner Brothers and the Australian distributors of *Lethal Weapon* each to give $5,000 to the hospital's fund-raising body. Mel and co-star Gary Busey also signed a poster to be raffled to raise further cash for the ill-equipped hospital.

Some Australian politicians were outraged by what they saw as an actor sticking his nose into something that was none of his business. MP Peter Anderson, during Question Time in the State Parliament, dismissed actor as 'mistaken Mel' and went on to say, 'He may well be beyond the Thunderdome, but in this case he is off the planet in regard to the things he had to say.' Refuting Mel's claims about government underfunding, a government spokesman added, 'He had not checked his facts out beforehand like any good politician.'

Later, he let slip another of his strong-willed opinions – no doubt passed on by his father Hutton. This time the subject was capital punishment. 'I think capital punishment is a valid issue. In today's world, I support it. I back it 100 per cent.'

In a typical Mel comment, he informed one reporter that executions were 'no different from when they hooted and cheered John Wayne when he shot the bad guy'.

He was even more blunt a few months later. 'It's a sick violent world out there and a humane form of capital punishment is a valid way of dealing with that sickness.'

Gradually, his fans were being shown an entirely different picture of their hero.

On election night, Mel and Robert Taylor sat together to watch the resultsbut, as it turned out, not even Mel could help Taylor to victory. His final share of the vote turned out to be just 9 per cent.

Taylor claimed after his defeat that 'big bucks and the system beat us in the end'. Cynical observers insisted that Mel's involvement had cheapened Taylor's campaign and exposure of his fiercely right-wing beliefs had come as quite a shock to his previously unquestioning public. For someone who, only a few years earlier, had complained bitterly about having to talk to the press, Mel had gone to the other extreme and his fans did not necessarily approve.

Reflective after that defeat, Taylor was unswerving in his loyalty to Mel. 'I learned a lot from that plunge into politics. And quite a lot of it came from watching Mel in action. It wasn't like watching him on screen playing a character. He was speaking from the heart. Mel Gibson the Aussie ... Mel the father, the family man. He wasn't acting, and the people who came to our campaign meetings knew it, too.'

Back in Hollywood, Mel's extreme right-wing views did not go unnoticed. In one camp, there was delight that he was proving such a traditionalist – it would obviously do nothing but enhance his reputation as a strait-laced action hero. But there were others who were muttering jibes like 'redneck' and 'right-wing extremist'. He was treading a very thin line.

Three years later, Mel proved that, once you get a taste for politics, it is hard to resist the temptation to get involved. It was federal election time once more in Australia and this time he was throwing his weight, influence, charisma and wallet behind another independent candidate, Barry Tattersall.

Mel was even more sure of himself than on his previous political outing. He appeared in television advertisements for Tattersall, championing the value of independents in politics. Some of his friends and advisers believed that his first outing with Taylor could hardly be described as a public-relations triumph, but Mel was his own man and no one could stop him standing up for what he believed in.

If anything, in the three years between campaigns he had become farther right-wing in his beliefs. Just like Hutton Gibson, he saw things in purely black-or-white terms. There was no centre ground. Mel seemed to be preparing himself to take on his father's mantle in every sense. Already, he was financially assisting many of his family. That was fine with Mel; keeping the Gibson clan intact was his number-one priority.

Independent candidate Tattersall insisted that his famous backer was 'talking straight from the heart. The value of the individual is important to us and I want to serve the electorate, not dictate to it.'

But once again, Mel's ability at getting his candidates publicity was not enough to persuade a very cautious electorate to vote for such a radical change in power.

However, none of this altered his political standpoint. He still believed that Australia, along with most of the Western world, was going downhill fast. It was an attitude that had made his father up-sticks and abandon the United States 20 years earlier. But this time, there was nowhere to escape. Mel just had to keep preaching what he believed when the opportunity arose. For the first time in his professional career, he had discovered that his stardom provided a very useful platform from which he could seek to influence others. He was determined to spread the word about right-wing conservatism; but his experiences during those two elections persuaded him that politicians were the lowest of the low ... along with journalists, naturally.

During an extraordinary outburst while being interviewed on Australian television's *The Midday Show* by Ray Martin in 1990, he showed frustration when asked what he thought about high interest rates and taxation.

'1 suppose they're going to have a nose-picking tax next. I just don't think the people in power in the government have in their hearts anything good for the country. I think it's nothing short of traitorous what they're doing.'

But he invited criticism about where his loyalties really lay when he also admitted, 'I haven't been home in a long time but I keep getting reports that there's a recession.'

Privately, he was voicing his disillusion and reactionary aspirations even more bluntly. He believed that he really had something to offer the world of politics. With that in mind – plus the runaway success of the *Lethal Weapon* series – he surprised (and delighted) Ed Limato in 1989 by deciding to splash out $2.4 million on buying pop star Rick Springfield's luxurious Malibu mansion.

The town he had once said he would never ever live in had become a much more attractive proposition. The financial incentives of living 'nearer to the office' were growing into the tens of millions of dollars zone and there was also a germ of an idea about one day putting all those political ideals to the test.

On his less frequent trips back to the farm in Australia, he continued the political rhetoric. In February 1993, Mel told the *A Current Affair* programme that he was deeply saddened by a federal government he described as being 'like a liability'.

'Australia was the greatest country, the most affluent, with the highest credit rating in the world, with the most natural resources, with the least amount of people in it ...'

Then he lashed out at former Labor Prime Minister Bob Hawke, who had told the star to 'stick to acting' and keep his nose out of politics. 'I was very offended. To actually say that I have no say in what is happening is a very scary thing to say ... a very fascist thing to say.'

Mel's opinions on a whole variety of topics have startled many people. While many like him in person, they do not agree with any of his outlandish opinions.

'Mel is a great guy in many ways. He has a superb sense of

humour, a deep commitment to his family, but there is another side to him. It is almost as if part of his personality is still back there knocking back beers in a neighbourhood bar in his teens. His bluntness is sometimes quite astonishing and he does tend to say the first thing that comes into his mouth,' one actor acquaintance said.

Not surprisingly, Mel's more extreme opinions have not been revealed outside a small circle of his personal friends and acquaintances. But the actor friend says that in the past few years – as evidenced by his continuing interest in right-wing politics – Mel has 'grown steadily more and more extreme' in his beliefs. 'It is almost as if fewer and fewer of his friends have the courage to stand up to him and tell him to cool down and take stock of some of the things he is saying,' said the friend.

Many of Mel's opinions were moulded by his father Hutton, of course. Belief in the old-style Catholic Church goes hand in hand with attitudes towards race, other religions and even feminism. Even the loving son has admitted that his father is an extremist.

'People see him as an extremist. He certainly doesn't ... what's the word? ... compromise in any way.'

But, he was asked, does he share his father's views?

'I share them because I believe them to be true,' replied Mel loyally.

Back in Tinseltown, Mel and Ed Limato were flooded with screenplays. In fact, just about every major US film during that period was offered to Mel. It was a remarkable achievement considering that, at the start of the decade, he had been earning $300 a week in theatre in Sydney.

There were also some rather eccentric proposals like the time *Dallas* star Victoria Principal begged the show's producers to sign Mel up for the Texan soap saga.

In an extraordinary move, Mel was offered a staggering $2 million a week to join the cast of the programme, once reputed to be the most-watched weekly television series in the world. But then the *Dallas* producers and Ms Principal were not aware that Mel had sworn he would never touch television again after his experiences as a young actor on a handful of dreadful Aussie shows. The offer was rejected instantly.

SIXTEEN

I'M GOING TO CHANNEL THE MANIAC INSIDE ME.
I'M GOING TO GET HOLD OF IT.

The Hollywood buzz on *Lethal Weapon* had been so good that Mel was inundated with screenplays – often poor imitations of the movie he had just made. But he and Ed Limato had already decided that – with a sequel already in the works – they would look for something completely different. They found it in *Tequila Sunrise*.

Mel adored the script from the moment he read it. 'I was intrigued as soon as I started reading it, although I didn't understand it – "Just be patient ... eventually, it'll pay off." It's one of those things that sucks you in slowly, but surely,' he said at the time. It was also scheduled to be shot in Los Angeles and Mel had grown accustomed to going home every evening to Robyn and the kids, during *Lethal Weapon*. He did, after all, have a seven-month-old baby in the household, not to mention four other very active children.

The actor was still being dogged by that 'Sexiest Man in

the World' title bestowed on him by *People* magazine five years earlier. No matter where he turned, another publication would find an excuse either to repeat it or, worse still, give him a new label. In Britain, the tabloid newspaper the *Star* announced that Mel had been voted Mr Wonderful after nearly two-thirds of readers polled said he was their favourite actor. On this occasion, Mel beat *Magnum* star Tom Selleck to the title. Then a Los Angeles-based women's group called Man Watchers Inc selected Mel as one of the ten most watchable men in America.

Mel laughed it off, as usual, when asked how he dealt with such tags. 'You deal with it by a trick of the mind. You figure: Is it worrying me that much? Does anybody else give a damn as much as I do? So you decide not to. It's easy.'

But all this renewed press attention caught the eye of singing superstar Madonna, according to the *Daily Mirror* newspaper in Sydney.

An article by Rosalind Reines reported that this unlikely pair arranged to meet in a Los Angeles restaurant – with Mel almost having a punch-up with Madonna's loud-mouthed then-husband Sean Penn. The accuracy of this article is impossible to verify.

But, away from fantasy romances, there was another reason why Mel was so attracted to *Tequila Sunrise* – the presence of outstanding writer/director Robert Towne, who won an Oscar for his screenplay of the private-eye classic *Chinatown*. Ed Limato, though, had an ulterior motive for persuading Mel to attach himself to the $25 million budgeted project; he believed that matchmaking one of his other up-and-coming clients, Michelle Pfeiffer, with Mel would virtually guarantee the film's success. Former Miss Orange County 1976 and LA check-out girl, Michelle was definitely 'bubbling' in Hollywood terms after starring roles in *Scarface* and then *The Witches of Eastwick*.

But there was one snag with Dale (Mac) McKussic, the character Mel was to portray for a fee of $1.5 million. He was a former drug-dealer, no longer in business, but living comfortably on the proceeds of distributing cocaine. This in itself presented Mel with a moral dilemma. How could he play a guy whose entire lifestyle was based on his earnings from drug-dealing?

Seven years earlier, as his former business associate and *Gallipoli* producer Pat Lovell disclosed, he had rejected an offer to play a drug addict in *Monkey Grip*, an Australian movie. At the time, Mel felt that he could never play anyone involved in drugs. But here he was accepting just that role.

In fact, Mel thought long and hard about his role in *Tequila* and, as usual, came up with his own unique piece of logic as to why the role was acceptable. 'Look, no one's perfect, and most of us have done something in life we regret or may even be ashamed of. I felt the character of McKussic was legitimate. He wasn't pushing any more; he saw the future of his son as more important than his own or his past. I mean, sure, he dealt in drugs ... but when the story opens, he's clean.

'Personally, and it's well known publicly, I detest drugs, hate the damn things ... I won't go near them, and I would hate to think my kids or anyone's kids could get hooked on them. We are the ones that make sure they don't get hit.'

But then what Mel did not mention was that he had an addiction of his own. He was hooked on nicotine. He had tried everything to kick his daily intake of two packs of Marlboros but the anxiety he so successfully hid on the big screen had to be soothed by something and, in his case, it was cigarettes. The booze he could cut down on, sometimes even give up for a few weeks at a time. But the dreaded weed was another matter. He could not – or maybe would not – give it up.

'I have to have some vice in my life,' Mel would always say. During one moving interview, he even confessed that his smoking was causing endless anxiety at home.

'One of my kids came up, saw me smoking and said, "Please don't. I don't want you to die." They really believe that, if I have another one, I could drop dead on the spot. And I could. That's a pretty strong motivation to quit.'

But, even after that candid admission, it was noted that Mel immediately picked up a packet of Marlboros, took out a cigarette and lit it.

Before shooting of *Tequila* began, Mel attempted to get inside the mind of the character he was to play by talking to a real drug-dealer, recently released from jail.

'I'm sure he regretted what he had done, although he never apologised for it, and never used the stuff himself,' explained Mel. 'He didn't consider the end result; he was just the middle-man, exactly like Mac, enjoying the thrill, not to mention the money ... He wasn't thinking about the drugs making some kid jump off a roof or shoot his sister. In the film, it's Mac's own little boy who prompts him to rethink his profession.'

In *Tequila Sunrise*, Mel is at odds with a high-school friend, played by Kurt Russell, who is a narcotics cop. Michelle Pfeiffer is the beauty caught between the two men.

Many of Mel's female fans who saw the film were convinced that Mel used a body double during the movie's highly charged love scene. Certainly shots of Mel's body from some angles do not look like the original, but both stars have kept a discreet silence about the subject.

The sequence involved Mel and Michelle in a hot tub for what director Towne called a 'pretty explicit' sex scene. But Mel and his beautiful co-star prevented the temperature in the bath from reaching boiling point by playing Scrabble between takes.

While Mel enjoyed the same sort of at-a-distance working relationship with Michelle Pfeiffer that he had with Diane Keaton during *Mrs Soffel*, the actor became close pals with co-star Kurt Russell. It was a friendship that blossomed into something even more significant when Mel and Kurt's lover, Goldie Hawn, agreed to team up in *Bird on a Wire*.

When *Tequila Sunrise* came out in late 1988, Mel's performance received reasonable praise, but many of the critics questioned the drug background of the character he portrayed.

'Can you accept a cocaine dealer as a romantic, lovable, even admirable character, even if he is as handsome as Mel Gibson and is presented as a loyal friend, an ardent lover, a caring father and a connoisseur of food?' wrote highly respected Sydney *Daily Telegraph* critic Bev Tivey.

Matt White in the *Daily Mirror* was more positive about the film. '*Tequila Sunrise* is certain to sustain Mel Gibson's regained popularity while it waits for the second *Lethal Weapon* movie.' In actual fact, the movie took a very modest sum at the box office and became known as one of those projects that never really lived up to its real potential.

But, for a different reason, Mel has never forgotten the launch of *Tequila Sunrise*. Shortly before a celebrity screening in Los Angeles, he had an encounter with veteran actress Jane Wyman, former wife of President Ronald Reagan.

The two were alone in a lift together when Mel became aware that the 70-something actress was casting seductive glances in his direction. 'Hey. You're a good-looking boy. Ever considered a career in the movies?'

Mel, highly amused, replied, 'Yes, ma'am. I have given it some thought.'

Ms Wyman realised her mistake within minutes, when she attended the screening of *Tequila Sunrise* and saw Mel up on the screen.

During the round of meet-the-press gatherings that had become a part of Mel's staple diet in the run-up to the release of every film he was involved with, the star showed an uncharacteristic side after agreeing to be interviewed by Australian journalist Nancy Griffin. Ten minutes after meeting Mel, she found herself being driven off in his rented red Mercedes to look for a car among the dozens of dealerships that line a two-mile stretch of Santa Monica Boulevard, near the apartment Mel had bought in 1988.

Eventually, reported an astonished Ms Griffin, Mel spotted a used navy-blue Mercedes 560SL for a bargain $52,900.

'Do you want to drive it home?' asked the star-struck dealer. Mel replied that he had forgotten his chequebook.

'We trust you,' replied the dealer, handing Mel the keys and telling him to come back with a cheque when he was ready.

After *Lethal Weapon 2*, Mel headed back to Canada – for the first time since his embarrassing drink-driving run-in with the police in Toronto – to star in a 'frothy piece of fun and action' called *Bird on a Wire* with Kurt Russell's live-in love Goldie Hawn. Once again, Mel had chosen something different from the *Lethal Weapon* series in the hope that it would help him break free of typecasting.

Before signing for the movie, he turned down a host of action-oriented projects including a film about motor racing, *Champions*, which became *Days of Thunder* starring Tom Cruise. Stories circulated in Tinseltown that Mel was offered the lead role in *Batman*, later taken by Michael Keaton. Mel denied, joking, 'I think I would have felt silly in rubber.' There was also much speculation about how Mel's millions of women fans would have reacted to him being dressed up in a skin-tight Batsuit.

Another much steamier project he rejected out of hand was the lead role in *Final Analysis*, about a psychiatrist who falls in love with his patient. Mel found the *Fatal Attraction*-style project deeply offensive. His judgement was vindicated when the movie was released in 1991, starring Richard Gere and Kim Basinger. It was universally slammed and did not perform well at the box office.

More surprisingly, Mel rejected the role of Robin Hood that his chief rival Kevin Costner made his own – and a $100 million-plus box-office success. There was a suggestion that Mel 'did not fancy prancing around screen in a pair of green tights'. For the second time, he had passed on a project that would strengthen Costner's grip on that slot as number-one male star in Hollywood.

There was also talk of a comedy in Australia, the reality being that Mel was now such a big star that the Hollywood gossip machine attached him to just about every project in town. Mel was as choosy as ever. He was increasingly keen on doing comedy. Every time he made a movie, everyone from the director down would heap praise on his comedic skills and he convinced himself that he had a long-term future doing something considerably lighter than the cops-and-robbers format of *Lethal Weapon*.

During the making of *Tequila Sunrise*, Mel, his wife Robyn, Kurt Russell and Goldie Hawn had become firm friends and, inevitably, conversation kept coming round to the possibility of Mel and Goldie making a movie together. But both stars agreed that it would have to be just the right project. Before meeting Goldie, Mel expected her to be 'dippy and goofy'. That most emphatically was not the case.

'She certainly has a vivacious quality that never lets her down. I mean, it's like she's always smiling and cheery. But there's certainly more to her than the dumb blonde.'

Goldie had had her own reservations about Mel before they met. 'I had trepidations because I thought he'd have no sense of humour or be stuck on himself. But Mel is bursting with humour and very self-deprecating.'

Goldie Hawn was, if anything, even more careful about selecting projects than Mel. She was painfully aware that it had been ten years since her last major hit, *Private Benjamin*. Other movies like *Wildcats* and *Overboard* had sunk without trace. Hence, *Bird on a Wire* became a very important project for the blonde star. Mel had no doubt it would do them both good.

'This is funny and warm,' he said of *Bird on a Wire*. 'I've always been afraid to try things like that, but I thought I'd just dive in and see what happened.'

But Mel did expose his own lack of intensity towards the role – for which he got $3.5 million – during one interview when he said, 'The title, it's an old Beatles song, isn't it?' An assistant immediately corrected him. 'Oh, Leonard Cohen, right.'

Bird on a Wire turned out to be a very basic, $20 million chase movie with Mel playing a former sixties radical living a secret life as a government-protected witness after blowing the whistle on two corrupt drug-enforcement agents. Goldie is his former girlfriend who accidentally rediscovers him. So do the bad guys. They chase Mel and Goldie through a zoo in cars, on motorcycles, in a plane and aboard a roller-coaster.

The movie's director was experienced Hollywood hired hand John Badham. But he had huge problems with Goldie over those roller-coaster scenes. She was so jittery that her participation was limited to a small section of the track.

'They fork-lifted me up to the roller-coaster like a jackass,' she said later. 'I think I risked more doing that than if I had gone on the whole roller-coaster ride. Every fear I've ever had I faced in this movie. I think I'm a new woman now. I can do anything.'

Goldie's main fear was of heights. During one stunt, she had to climb around the ledge of a 20-storey building, not an easy task for anyone but especially frightening for Goldie. Vertigo took over and she completely froze as Mel and the rest of the cast and crew looked on.

Noticing her distress and just like a Saturday matinée idol, he came to his beautiful co-star's rescue. 'Mel grabbed me in his arms and hauled me back. I was shaking and crying. He saved my life.'

A close and lasting friendship grew between Mel and Goldie and their respective families. Crew members say that the noise of children (Goldie has three) coming from the two stars' trailers was deafening and her caravan wall was plastered with Polaroids of her youngsters. There were champagne toasts when Robyn announced she was pregnant for the sixth time.

But the two stars infuriated director Badham by secretly agreeing to tone down the film's most important love scene during secretive late-night phone calls during shooting.

'It just wasn't right to see these two people go at it together. It would be a turn-off,' Goldie admitted after the movie's release. As the scene was rewritten, Mel and Goldie landed up in bed together in a motel room, but their lovemaking was funny rather than sensuous.

Critics around the world dismissed *Bird on a Wire* for having a paper-thin plot and scorned Goldie Hawn's performance, but Mel's acting abilities were generally well received. 'It was an indescribably bad film but Mel came out of it OK,' said Scott Murray of *Cinema Papers* in Australia. And Evan Williams in *The Australian* commented, 'The less said about *Bird on a Wire* the better. It is an ugly, witless, hyperactive film which tries pathetically hard to outdo Spielberg or George Lucas at their own game.'

Despite all the criticism, *Bird on a Wire* became one of the bigger-grossing films of that year, proving that Mel had well and truly arrived as a box-office star who could attract customers even when the product was sub-standard.

After two films in quick succession, Mel was feeling almost as exhausted as during that perilous period a few years earlier which threatened a nervous breakdown. He had been giving round-the-clock press interviews to promote *Lethal Weapon 2* while still shooting *Bird*. He reckoned that it was time to take off for Australia and a long rest on the farm. 'It's just a matter of getting back into a more sedate rhythm of life which is well needed at this time,' he said, just before the end of the *Bird on a Wire* shoot in Canada.

Mel was on a genuine work high at the time. Word of mouth from Warner Brothers about *Lethal Weapon* was that the movie was a sure-fire hit that would rocket Mel to superstar status. But his drinking had reached almost epidemic proportions. Sometimes he would down five beers before breakfast and as the shoot had progressed his capacity had increased. Now, back in the security of his hometown of Sydney, he was finding it just as difficult to say no to a round or three of drinks in one of the city's most notorious drinking clubs. And once there, he was prey to every pretty girl with come-hither eyes as the booze and the testosterone coursed through his body. British-born Miranda Brewin was just 19 when she met Mel in a bar, where they allegedly shared lethal cocktails called Kamikazes and chatted away like lifelong friends. They then went off to a club together, and Miranda claims to have stayed with Mel at a house in Coogee where they continued drinking until dawn. Miranda stated in an interview after her night with Mel, 'There is no doubt at all that he loves his wife. He is completely crazy about her. But he is also basically a fun person.'

One year later, Mel was linked by a British tabloid newspaper with another young English blonde, whom he was alleged to have met in a trendy Los Angeles boutique called Maxfields.

The 24-year-old Hertfordshire-born shop assistant was reported to have moved in to Mel's Santa Monica apartment, in an article headlined, 'MAD MAX STAR DITCHES WIFE FOR SHOP GIRL'.

The article was met with furious denials from Mel and his representatives, who dismissed it as nonsense. The actor rounded on dozens of reporters who had gathered near his home in the Kiewa Valley, and angrily announced the story was 'absolute rubbish'.

Mel's fury was followed up with threats of legal action against any paper that repeated the story. Ed Limato and his team launched a damage-control operation and contrived to prevent further coverage of the alleged affair. The promised legal action never materialised. But it had the required effect of scaring off scandal-hungry tabloids.

The girl – who still lives in California – insists that there was a relationship although she never moved in to Mel's apartment. She described their brief friendship in very similar terms to Miranda Brewin. She even looks similar – blonde, English and pretty.

Talking for the very first time about her friendship with Mel, she insisted, 'I was nervous about it because I had never been out with a married man before.'

The couple met when he walked into Maxfields to buy a shirt for his flamboyant Hollywood agent Liorato. Then he decided he wanted to buy a pair of trousers and she measured him – so that they could be taken up in a spacious rear changing room. The girl says that Mel 'kept making flirty comments and I sensed there was an attraction between us'.

Mel spent thousands of dollars on suits, shirts and ties that day. He also ended up insisting that the girl walk him to his rented car in the parking lot nearby, much to the amusement of the store's other assistants.

Next day, Mel called Maxfields and asked the girl when his trousers would be ready to be picked up.

'He was really nagging me to deliver them in person and he made a point of saying where he was staying,' recalled the girl in an interview in November 1992. But she refused to go to his house as the shop rules forbade that.

Mel was not deterred. He rang her back a few days later.

'This time he did not even ask me about the trousers. He just asked me out instead,' says the girl.

The blonde shop assistant agonised, she says, about accepting his invitation to dinner, before agreeing. That night she turned up at the apartment in Santa Monica that he had bought some years earlier. (She has since pointed out the apartment and it is indeed the place where he was staying at that time.)

'Mel was already a little drunk when I got there,' said the girl. But within minutes he started kissing her. After 'a lot of kissing and cuddling' on a sofa, the couple went out for dinner at the nearby Chez Jay's restaurant. The girl was struck by the fact that the Hollywood star was unconcerned that he might be spotted out with another woman. At one stage in the restaurant, a customer at the table next to them began taking photos of him but it did not stop Mel from smooching with his new friend.

'He just couldn't stop touching me. He did not seem to care that people were watching. He just laughed when I said I thought they had just taken our picture.'

That night the girl drove Mel home in her car.

The girl believes that Mel 'just let himself go and acted really naturally' during their brief relationship.

'He was so relaxed. Laughing and joking,' she says.

But, despite wildly exaggerated claims that the girl moved in with Mel, the young store assistant never saw Mel alone again after that night, although the actor did ring her from the airport to thank her for a great time. It was a touching gesture that the girl says she will never forget because 'he did not have to bother, but he did'.

However – six months later – after the dust had completely settled over his alleged affair with the girl, a piquant incident took place when Mel walked into Maxfields boutique – with his wife Robyn and all their kids.

'I was flabbergasted. Then she insisted I measure her up for a dress. All the time I could see how tense and uncomfortable Mel was,' says the girl.

She managed to avoid embarrassing eye contact with Mel because the children were running around the shop causing chaos, but she has absolutely no doubt why they came into the shop. 'She made him come in just to see how he would react.'

Despite that scene the girl does not show bitterness towards the actor. 'Essentially he's a good person. A very genuine person,' she stresses to this day.

The girl believes that Mel suspects she leaked the original account of their relationship back in 1987. But the truth is that she had nothing whatsoever to do with the one and only article that saw print. Her decision to talk about it now, almost six years later, was inspired by a wish to put the record straight.

Mel's aides set up another damage-control operation in January 1993, but this ended in the biggest embarrassment of all for the actor and his family. On this occasion, Mel had gone on a bar crawl with three pretty young students in the northern Californian town of Modesto. The night of drinking, smoking and smooching ended with Mel apparently cavorting with a blonde named Shawn.

But it wasn't until more than two years after the incident that Mel's antics reached the eyes and ears of his adoring public. Stories of his fling had fuelled gossip in Modesto ever since Mel left town following a cattle-buying trip in October 1990. But no one passed these rumours on to the notorious American tabloids and Mel must have thought that his drunken encounter would never be revealed.

However, muck-raking experts on the *National Enquirer* were determined to find evidence of the much-talked-about fling in Modesto and they pulled out all the stops to unearth concrete evidence of Mel's two-timing. Eventually, they tracked down the three girls concerned and unintentionally initiated a frenzied attempt by Hollywood to cover up a scandal about one of its most happily married stars.

One of the girls involved was Wendy Kain. She explained that, as soon as the tabloid's enquiries reached their ears, the father of one girl called up the actor's agent 'looking for a deal'. Within hours, one of Mel's lawyers went to Modesto. His mission – to investigate the claim that three girls were about to sell their story to the US tabloids. There was even talk about a blackmail plot by someone involved in the story who had threatened to take photos to the papers unless a six-figure sum was paid over by Mel.

The lawyer's swoop on Modesto was provoked by a genuine concern over what appeared to be a very damaging situation. Wendy Kain explained, 'I refused to talk to Mel's lawyer. The approach made me real mad.'

'Confidentiality' and 'non-disclosure' agreements were then drawn up for the girls to sign. 'But I did not like how aggressive they were being,' added Wendy.

Furious at being pressured, Wendy eventually co-operated

with the *Enquirer*'s biggest rival, the *Globe*, and supplied them with details and photographs showing Mel kissing one of the girl's high-heeled shoes, burying his head in another girl's lap, downing a vodka cocktail, and sucking one girl's fingers, with his arms round two others. Wendy claims that, if Mel's lawyers had kept away from Modesto, she would never have considered giving her account to the tabloids.

Lawyers also threatened to sue the *Globe* if they published an account of what happened, warning on Mel's behalf, 'If you run that story, whoever writes it, the *Globe* will be the recipient of a lawsuit. I intend suing the *Globe*.'

Six months after the story appeared, no legal action had been taken. Mel's lawyers said this was because the most flagrant inaccuracies had been deleted.

The articles that were eventually published gave the distinct impression that Mel's fling with Wendy's friend Shawn and his bar crawl with her and the other two girls was something that happened in a drunken moment.

However, Wendy has disclosed for the first time that Mel actually met with Shawn the previous night and arranged a date with her. Then he carefully checked out of the Holiday Inn in Modesto and booked himself into the Red Lion to cover his tracks by staying an extra night in town to have some fun with the girls. The customary bar crawl that followed involved Mel admitting that he had a foot fetish and that he was also in love with women's high-heeled shoes. Just as on those earlier misadventures, vast quantities of cocktails were consumed between never-ending impersonations of the Three Stooges.

Wendy recalled a boorish incident which she says completely changed her attitude towards him.

'We were in one bar when I saw Mel go over to this girl we knew at the bar and just rip her top. That girl got really mad at him but he was too drunk to work out what he had done. He seemed so male chauvinistic.'

Wendy also recalled characteristics which previous friends have commented on.

'He had such bad manners. He never opened a door for us. He never even bought us a drink all night.'

At one stage during their crawl through this quiet cattle town, Mel was challenged by a local cop to prove he was the famous movie star, because no one believed him or the girls. The actor pulled out an American Express Gold Card and showed it to the cop. His name was clearly printed on it but the girls were more surprised by the fact that he never once volunteered to spend any money on them.

All three girls plus Mel returned to Angela's father's house, later than evening. Mel continued downing hefty quantities of alcohol and, at one stage, ate catfood out of two tins – something he did with dogfood in *Mad Max 2* and later *Lethal Weapon 3*.

Mel and Shawn enjoyed a cuddle together and the married star was not the slightest bit embarrassed when Wendy walked into the room.

She had already noted that the actor had an 'almost exhibitionist-type habit of walking around the house stark naked'. She also said that Mel was 'very sheepish' the next morning. 'He would not talk to us at all and in the end Shawn drove him back to his hotel,' added Wendy.

Shawn did tell her friends that the star called his wife in Australia when they got back to the hotel and he admitted sheepishly to the student, 'She's not too happy with me.'

A strange twist was that Mel was extra co-operative when the girls took photos of his antics – because he had had a punch-up the previous evening with a local newspaper photographer who started snapping him in a Modesto parking lot. Mel smashed the journalist's camera, only to apologise later and offer to pay for the wrecked equipment. It had the effect of calming him down and making him less neurotic about having his photo taken. He lived to regret that day ...

Mel and his advisers are doggedly determined not to allow his image of a family-loving man to be shattered. The star frequently makes a point of talking about the importance of being faithful while married. He has also publicly insisted that he hates women who throw themselves at him. 'I'm a romantic but I don't expect women to tear their clothes off when they meet me. That sort of thing only happens if you're nosing around asking for it – I've got everything I need at home. Some women do come on strong though.'

Mel is especially prone to retell a story of how one Hollywood actress tried to chat him up at a Tinseltown gathering in front of Robyn. Mel was holding baby Will in his arms at the time. Deeply embarrassed by this flirtatious blonde, he plonked the child on the woman's lap and told her to hold him while he went to the lavatory. What he did not bother to add was that Will had just 'done a present' in his nappy.

'When I came back, she stood up and screamed. There was a big brown stain in the middle of her expensive white dress. She couldn't get away from me fast enough,' chuckled Mel.

In fairness, within months of that last serious incident in Modesto, Mel recognised that he risked losing his family and agreed to consult Alcoholics Anonymous. And, according to sources inside his production company, he really has calmed down, avoiding nights on the town with dangerously pretty blondes ever since.

In the past, he has always tried to get his family to accompany him on location shoots at least some of the time.

And cast and crew on those films vividly recall how Mel pleads with Robyn and the children to stay with him as long as possible because he knows there is a very real danger he will transgress if they are not around.

Sadly, with his children getting older, Robyn has made it clear that their education must take precedence over Mel's loneliness on a movie shoot. That is believed to be one of the main reasons why he is especially keen to shoot films either in Los Angeles (like all the *Lethal Weapon*s) or at least somewhere not too isolated in the United States.

Long-term damage control, after the Modesto revelations were published in January 1993, came in the shape of a carefully orchestrated campaign to project Mel's image as a clean-living family man. In the notoriously inoffensive magazine *Hello!*, Mel was photographed in France during the editing of his directorial début movie, *Man Without a Face*, just a few weeks after the Modesto incident was exposed. The article referred repeatedly to the actor's commitment to his family and old-fashioned morality. 'Mel Gibson may be famous for his on-screen sexuality, but he's longing to show to the world that he's an old-fashioned romantic, who truly believes in gentlemanly behaviour,' trilled the magazine.

There was also the very real and scary problem of lovesick fans. Some of them would follow Mel out of supermarkets near his Malibu home. One woman rang his doorbell and dropped her coat to the floor, revealing nothing underneath, when he answered. Another started leaving pornographic notes on his car and erotic messages on his answering machine.

Naturally, Mel and his family were irked by these weird incidents but they also helped Mel to smokescreen his own activities by claiming that women like the LA shop girl and Shawn were just nutty fans who had become obsessed with him. Unlike many of his film roles, it seemed to suit Mel in this instance to play the victim, rather than the main protagonist who should be held accountable for his actions.

SEVENTEEN

AS AN ACTOR, YOU'RE AN EMOTIONAL PROSTITUTE –
YOU GET CAUGHT WITH YOUR PANTS DOWN. IT'S LIKE
PUTTING YOUR DICK ON A CHOPPING BLOCK WITH
THE KNOWLEDGE THAT NO ONE IS GOING TO CHOP
IT OFF.

Mel Gibson hates flying. He looks at aircraft with the
same suspicion a desert dweller might have for a
canoe. But he overcame his fear in exchange for a $4.2
million fee for *Air America*, a film in which the actor spent
almost as much time in the air as on terra firma.

The star confronted his fears very simply – by taking flying
lessons. Mel never got an official flying licence but he did
learn to fly a helicopter.

'When I started, my instructor told me putting a helicopter
down was like landing on a greased golf ball. Well, it wasn't
just like landing on a greased golf ball. It was like trying to
hump in a hammock. Very, very tricky.'

As it turned out, flying was the least of Mel's problems on
Air America. The film was shot entirely on location deep in
the Golden Triangle of Thailand, an area of jungle-clad
mountains and almost constant steamy rain showers. Opium

poppies bloom in the small clearings between the highlands and drug-traders are the main employers in the region.

Mel had already discovered during a stopover in Bangkok *en route* to the jungle that any ideas he might have had about not being harassed in such a distant land were far-fetched. Everywhere he went, a chorus of 'Mad Mack!' rang out.

'They didn't know what my name was but they knew I was Mad Max,' recalled Mel. 'That was the thing that really surprised me.'

Air America had been pitched to Mel during earlier discussions in Hollywood, as a serious action-adventure movie about the covert airline which the CIA ran out of Laos during the Vietnam War. The real Air America had been a remarkable operation, the fruit of United States paranoia and run by a group of CIA operatives with fewer scruples than a ticket tout. Basically, Air America would fly literally anything across the area if they thought it would combat the spread of Communism.

'Air America flew everything from elephants to opium to monkey embryos. It was amazing. It was the world's biggest airline at one time and you could get anything, anywhere, any time on these planes,' lectured an enthusiastic Mel before he got to Thailand.

And the CIA devised some ludicrous schemes in an attempt to demoralise the enemy; they dropped vast boxes of oversized condoms behind Vietcong lines, convinced that the enemy would be so overawed by the size and virility of American troops they would surrender instantly. But the Vietcong were far from impressed. They put the condoms over their rifle barrels to keep them dry, making them all the more effective for shooting American soldiers.

The pilots who worked for Air America were a law unto themselves. Although undeniably brave, tough and skilful, they were avionic cowboys – and quite a number were crazy from having lived too long in the jungle and sampled too many narcotics.

Initially, the project – which was backed by the Carolco company that had created *Rambo* – was to feature Sean Connery and Kevin Costner, following their phenomenally successful pairing in *The Untouchables* (in which Mel had regretfully rejected a role two years earlier). But when their joint fee was rumoured to have risen to $15 million, the producers decided to look elsewhere for their stars.

Mel was then signed to play the younger of two Air America pilots, but he felt that, at 34, he was 'too wrinkly to get away with that new-kid stuff any more'. So, the movie's producers cast Robert Downey Jr as the rookie and Mel played Gene Ryack, a world-weary pilot and gun-runner who finds the Laotian way of life to his liking and wants to get out of the dirty tricks business. The female interest was provided by American actress Nancy Travis.

Yet again, Mel was tempted into playing a character he felt was not that far removed from his own personality. In Hollywood, scripts were now being virtually tailor-made for the star with writers casting their main role in the Mel mould before even starting a project. And, as Mel explained before setting off for deepest Thailand, those sort of parts did attract his attention.

'Ryack was born in the USA, he is Captain America but he's been so long away and has became so cynical and jaded that he's Asian on the inside. In a way, I'm a bit like that. I was born in the US, moved away and became something else, a creature not of my own creation.'

Mel landed in the Golden Triangle in early 1990, together with British director Roger Spottiswoode, a large cast, 15 cameras, three units, 500 crew, 30 aeroplanes and helicopters rented from the Thai military, plus a physician to treat all afflictions, of which there were many.

And there was Mel's companion – a tall, well-built lady, Terri DePaolo. She had become a development executive at Mel's production company two years earlier but, to everyone else on the shoot of *Air America*, she was 'Mel's minder'. The idea was that, everywhere Mel went, Terri would follow. Unfortunately, she was not very effective in her nanny role. Having signed a confidentiality agreement, Terri confined herself to saying, 'It's a very difficult situation ... we had a kind of bitter-sweet relationship but I still care about him a great deal.'

Before shooting of the $35 million movie could begin, there were major obstacles to overcome. Tragedy struck the project when an Israeli first assistant director died before work got under way. Talk among the cast and crew was that the technician had picked up a deadly virus while scouting for locations near a huge waste dump on the outskirts of Chiang Mai. Then there was the script. Mel decided he wanted to 'lighten it up', and it became a trivial treatment of a serious subject.

Finally, there was Khun Sa, reputed to be the world's most powerful heroin dealer. *Air America* was to be filmed right in the middle of his territory. And Khun Sa happened to be protected by a well-equipped private army which was in the habit of taking pot shots at any aircraft daring to fly over the region. Considering that more than 50 per cent of *Air America* was scheduled to take place in or around aircraft, the drug lord did pose something of a hazard.

According to production staff on the movie, fears over Khun Sa were quelled when it emerged that the drug baron was a keen 'Mad Mack' fan and an autographed message of greetings from Mel would probably go a long way to promoting peace and harmony for the duration of the *Air America* shoot. Reluctantly, Mel agreed and a peace deal was struck.

Filming took place in mountainside communities that had experienced little or no contact with the outside world. Hollywood meant nothing to the indigenous population and Mel found it all very refreshing at first. It appealed to his sense of humour.

'It was fun, a great deal of fun, although it looked tough. The Thais are very hospitable. The guy who managed the place where we stayed – I won't call it a hotel because it was something else – would go down to the river, catch an eight-foot snake, come back, throw it in the pot and eat it.'

At Chiang Mai, the main town in the hill country, 'Mad Mack' attracted a lot of attention from the locals during a long series of night-time shoots. Crowds would gather every evening outside the Arun Rai Chinese restaurant, which had been transformed for the film into the White Rose, an establishment fondly remembered by those who frequented it during the Vietnam War. In those days, everything was available at the White Rose, from bar girls to guns to marijuana carefully rolled into cigarettes, and sold in Marlboro packets. *Plus ça change* … all the same vices were available to everyone who descended on Chiang Mai.

Mel – suffering from chronic back problems that had plagued him since he played rugby at St Leo's College 20 years earlier – surrendered his tired flesh to the ministrations of local masseuses. With a broad smile, he enthusiastically told one visitor to the movie set, 'It's the best massage I've ever come across. It's miraculous. This is a stress-free country. Everyone's cool.'

In Chiang Mai, Mel was being harassed by prostitutes the whole time. Virtually every time he walked through the lobby of his hotel, lithe teenagers would approach him. Many of the hotel staff were used to Westerners ordering girls every night and they presumed Mel was no different from just about everyone else. Even when the movie switched locations to the more isolated Mai Hong Son, many Chiang Mai prostitutes simply took a bus to where the 500-plus cast and crew were based and began bargaining for sex all over again. With only two bars in the entire town, it was hard to avoid them.

One of the Thai crew – an attractive mother – took Mel under her wing and kept him on the straight and narrow. 'I wanted to protect him from the obvious temptations. Many girls would have viewed it as a feather in their cap if they slept with a movie star like Mel!'

After Mel's wife Robyn and two of his children arrived in Chiang Mai, the actor – even when he was shooting elsewhere – would join them on his days off. And he kept a generally low profile, developing his new-found love of sketching by carrying a pad of artist's paper wherever he went and drawing some very lifelike pictures of members of the cast. But Robyn did not show up until the last couple of weeks of the four-month shoot. And there were many incidents before she appeared.

Among the extras used in some of the night-time scenes at the White Rose bar was United States Ambassador Charles Ray and his 13-year-old daughter. 'I did it to keep the peace in my family,' he sighed when asked why on earth he was at the location in the first place. 'My daughter said, that if I had a chance to be in a movie with Mel Gibson and I didn't do it, she would never live under the same roof with me again. I figured it better to spend five nights out here in the streets than the next five years with an irate daughter,' explained the Ambassador.

But as the boredom set in, Mel began enjoying the

occasional drink with crew members after a long day's shooting. Sometimes, he would wander around the town with his video camera pretending to be a television reporter. In one restaurant, he approached a bemused-looking couple and asked them, 'What brings you to Chiang Mai on a night like this?' They looked completely aghast when they realised the man doing the talking was a Hollywood superstar.

Mel kept the gag going for about five minutes before admitting who he was and cheerfully posing with the couple for photographs, and signing autographs. But his antics were really nothing more than evidence that he had got very bored with *Air America*. He yearned to go home to Robyn, who was about to have the couple's sixth child and did not want to give birth in the middle of the jungle.

At another location, the *Air America* production benefited the local economy by paying for the construction of an entire hotel, built especially for the crew. They also brought hot water and Western toilets to all their other hotels. Even the airport runway was improved and a whole new hangar built for one important scene in the film.

The relationship between Mel and Robert Downey Jr was, by all accounts, 'businesslike' but not close. Mel, of all people, complained that his co-star's sense of humour was 'weird'. 'Downey was a typical Hollywood actor, out jogging at dawn every morning and in bed early most evenings, whilst Mel just wanted to be out with the boys,' said one crew member.

Probably the busiest man on the entire film was the unit doctor, a British medic from Fulham, in south-west London. He was constantly warning the cast and crew about the presence of AIDS in Thailand. An estimated 80 per cent of prostitutes in the province where *Air America* was being filmed were said to be carrying the virus and it was well known that a number of people from the production had succumbed to temptation and paid for sexual services.

And in addition to the many non-sexual diseases in the region, let's not forget the mosquitoes. Vast armies of the insects were making mincemeat of most members of the cast and crew at night, as Mel recounted in his inimitable way, 'They had mosquitoes there armed with machine-guns, it was so bad. We were pumped with so many holes for inoculations I thought I would leak.'

Then he decided to give up smoking. It could not have been at a worse time. He began frantically chewing gum and crew members on *Air America* swear that he became visibly more nervous. Occasionally, he would sneak a sly draw on someone else's cigarette and eventually took up the habit again. Mel's attempt to quit had been a painful experiment for all those in close proximity. With no Robyn about, he would disappear some weekends by flying to the beach resort of Phuket where he would swim and sleep on the beach away from the rest of the all-too-familiar team.

As filming progressed, events became increasingly bizarre. The crew was homesick and fed up with having to deal with the locals. And there was the rain. It didn't just shower occasionally. It came down in torrents for sometimes as long as 36 hours at a time. At one point, Roger Spottiswoode even consulted a village soothsayer to find out when the rain would stop.

Then an earthquake struck in the middle of the night. Although many of the film team were used to the occasional tremor back in Los Angeles, this was a big quake. It turned out to be 6.1 on the Richter scale.

One night, he got involved in an incident with definite echoes of those distant days when he got in so much trouble during shooting of *The Bounty*.

'Mel turned up in the bar with a beer bottle already in his hand and came over and greeted us. He was already very drunk and he kept on about how much he was missing his wife and kids. It was really sad to see,' recalled a British member of the crew.

As the night progressed and Mel and his two companions began swallowing quantities of the local beer, the star became more and more incoherent. Mel spoke in slurred terms about the 'marvellous massages' he had received from some of the local girls.

'At first he was a bit reluctant to talk about them but he soon came out with it,' said the British crew member.

Suddenly, one of the other two men made a blasphemous remark. It was enough to send Mel into a fury. 'Mel looked daggers at this guy and got up and walked out, slamming the bar door so hard that the glass broke,' the British crew member told me.

Then Mel – who has always been proud of the way he used to feign head-butts on other pupils when at school – walked back in and readied himself for action.

'He went head to head with this guy. They were eyeball to eyeball. It was serious stuff and it was really scary. He was quite prepared to have a fight just over some throwaway remark about God.

'To make matters worse, the manager of the bar was screaming at Mel, demanding that he pay someone to clear up the glass window he had smashed. Eventually, the other man paid him off to keep him quiet.

'Finally, I calmed him down and he just staggered off outside with another beer in his hand,' added the informant.

But the incident did not finish there. As so often with Mel, he awoke next day riddled with guilt about his actions and stumbled on to the set trying to find the man he had appeared ready to kill with his bare hands.

'But he'd gone back to England that morning. That's the thing about Mel. He gets really drunk and then the next day regrets his actions. It seems to be the story of his life.'

About halfway through the shooting of *Air America*, Mel got uncharacteristically involved in a row with the film's producers. He wanted to get home to Australia for the birth of his sixth child. He had never forgiven himself for missing the birth of Hannah all those years earlier during the filming of *Gallipoli* and, in any case, he was fed up to the back teeth with being in Thailand. Excessive drinking sessions were leaving him with a sore head and a short temper most mornings.

But Carolco were worried that, if they let Mel go, he might never come back and, besides, he was needed on set for virtually every set-up. There was no question of him pulling out. But the producer's response sent him into a deep depression. He withdrew from most of the friendships he had made during the shoot.

When Robyn did give birth to their sixth child, it should have been a time to celebrate, but Mel was in such a bad mood that most colleagues avoided anything but essential contact with him. In fact, he had ended up listening on the phone to the details of new baby Milo's birth, from nine-year-old daughter Hannah, who had 'stood in' for her father at Robyn's side and gave him a 'blow-by-blow' account.

Mel got back to being his sunnier self when Robyn flew in to Thailand following a series of appeals from the actor, who was seriously worried that his drinking would escalate unless she came to his rescue.

As a result of his disagreements with the movie's producers, when it came to pose for a traditional photograph of cast and crew in front of one of the vast Hercules transport planes used during the filming, Mel refused to play. It was his way of protesting against the decision not to allow him home for the birth of his son. The outcome was a vast photograph showing everyone involved in *Air America* – and an empty canvas chair with Mel's name emblazoned across the back, but no sign of the star.

'He was very angry about it,' one British crew member told me later. 'Mel felt betrayed and, quite frankly, just like the rest of us, he was desperately homesick by that stage!'

Air America's problems were compounded six months later when the producers decided that the movie's ending was not 'upbeat enough' after it had been previewed for audiences in the United States. With just three weeks to go before the film's scheduled release, they tracked Mel down in London where he was shooting the final scenes in *Hamlet*. Awkwardly, he had grown a beard and had his hair dyed for his new role. Carolco were in a state of complete panic and mounted the sort of salvaging operation only Hollywood is capable of.

An *Air America* unit booked into London's costly Savoy Hotel and waited patiently for Mel to complete *Hamlet*. Then they rushed him to Shepperton Studios, on the outskirts of London, and filmed an entirely new scene with co-star Robert Downey Jr. Mel got $100,000 for the one-day shoot after Ed Limato demanded that his client be 'compensated' for the extra work.

But when *Air America* finally hit the screens, they need not have bothered. A happy ending was the least of its problems. Just as Mel had privately predicted, it was a disappointing movie. In fact, the most entertaining moments came when veteran Chinese actor Burt Kwouk – star of such classics as *Thunderbirds* and the *Pink Panther* films – appeared on screen as a crooked general.

Some claimed *Air America* lacked true direction; others,

like British journalist Christopher Robbins, on whose book the film had been based, said that Hollywood had ruined the story by sanitising it. 'The film is a very trivial comedy about a tragedy – 100,000 people were killed. The one thing, had you asked me, not to do with the book would be to make it into a comedy ... I just couldn't believe it. I thought that at least it would have been interesting. But it went the way of many things in Hollywood. They put $35 million in one end and a turkey came out the other!'

Australian film critic Matt White, writing in the *Daily Mirror*, said, 'It's time Mel took things a little more seriously and showed us some more of the Gibson acting talent that doesn't have to rely on charm and scripted heroics.'

More criticism came from the very pilots upon whom the film was supposed to be based. And one former pilot accused the movie's producers of making a 'political obscenity' and asked, 'Did Hanoi make this film?'

But the most damning remarks came from Mel himself when he insisted that Australian showbusiness writer Dan McDonnell switch off his tape recorder during an interview to promote *Air America*. 'He said he hated the movie but he had to promote it. He was very tired and very pissed off. He felt he had just spent four days promoting a film he did not like.'

Mel was exhausted after *Air America*. He rejected the lead role in *Ghost* that earned Patrick Swayze worldwide acclaim and at least $10 million. Those earlier problems in the mid-1980s were drifting back to haunt him. He knew he could not afford to burn out again because Hollywood might not give him a third chance. He even admitted that his state of mind was such that he 'never wanted to work again'. But he would not take such drastic action – yet.

Instead, he planned to take time off, continue breeding his

cattle and get to know his sixth child Milo. *Hamlet* was beckoning and he considered that to be the most important challenge and prize of his career.

EIGHTEEN

YOU QUIT DRINKING, YOU WORK MUCH BETTER.
YOUR HEAD IS SO CLEAR.

Mel's battle with alcohol has been a persistent cloud over much of his career. The star has often given up the bottle for months at a time only to lapse when the pressures are mounting.

But in late 1990, Ed Limato and Robyn decided that the time had come for Mel to take positive action to beat booze for ever. They persuaded the star to enrol in Alcoholics Anonymous near the family's main Californian home in Malibu, near Los Angeles.

At first, Mel was reluctant to get involved with AA. He felt that the only person who could get him to give up drinking was himself. His attitude towards AA matched his opinion of psychiatric therapists – if you can't sort yourself out then don't bother.

But both Limato and Robyn feared that if Mel did not go completely on the wagon then there was a danger that his career could self-destruct. Stories about his early days boozing were well known because Mel had publicly admitted them, but few people realised that the announcement that he had given up drinking in 1987 had marked nothing more than a temporary abstinence. He had returned to the bottle with a vengeance.

In the depths of the Thai jungle, his fondness for beer with a whisky thrown in for good measure had stunned colleagues. And while in London making *Hamlet*, there had been similar incidents, including one occasion when he turned up at a nightclub whose owner was later exposed as a drug-pusher. With a neat vodka in one hand, Mel leaped on a table and led revellers in a version of 'Waltzing Matilda'.

According to eyewitnesses, Mel started urging three friends, cast members from *Hamlet*, to 'have a party'. The star eventually rolled out of the club in London's West End at 3.30am.

The main problem was that booze and Hollywood no longer mixed. The days of drunken stars causing chaos in bars across Tinseltown had long since gone. Many celebrities turned teetotal in the early 1980s and studio executives were making it plain that they would not tolerate actors with drink issues. In some cases, stars were being required to take medical tests to uncover what level of dependency they had on alcohol or drugs. There was a genuine fear that, if Mel did not give up the demon drink, then he could be quietly but systematically stripped of his top-billing status.

Yet Mel – despite all the boozing – was never unprofessional when he was working. He always knew his lines. He was always on time and he never burdened anyone with his 'problem'.

Lethal Weapon director Richard Donner was astonished when he found that Mel was secretly knocking back five bottles of beer before reaching the set. Coolly, the veteran film-maker made no effort to make Mel feel guilty about his drink problem. Donner went so far as to tell friends that the star drank beer like water and so long as it did not affect his performance then he was prepared to tolerate it.

Photographs in the Hollywood press at the time frequently portrayed Mel as the friendly drunk: eyelids drooping, glass of booze in one hand, cigarette in the other. He started showing up at tacky film premières 'just for the free drinks'.

While at the Venice Film Festival in the mid-1980s, Met bumped into a little-known actor called Kevin Costner in the bar of the Excelsior Hotel. They struck up a conversation and it emerged that Costner was attending the festival to help promote his films *Fandango* and *Silverado*, movies that marked the start of what was to become a phenomenal career. Mel, already deemed a box-office attraction, was considerably the more famous of the two at the time. Both men took to each other instantly and started drinking at a most convivial rate.

Costner recollected that the two of them – both married with families back at home – stumbled outside the hotel and decided to 'borrow'a couple of locked bikes and go for a spin.

'We went outside, and they were all locked. So Mel went off and found one, but not two. I said, "I'll ride"; I'd just done this bike picture. And it was great. There we were, on Lido Island, and Mel's on the goddamned handlebars looking like ET! I even think there was a full moon.'

Rather sadly, Mel and Costner did not keep up their initial friendship as the Californian actor headed for the same goal of all-out Hollywood stardom and even, to a certain extent, overtook his one-time drinking partner. The two did not keep in touch even though their careers collided frequently in the late eighties and early nineties.

In Australia, Mel's drinking continued at a ferocious pace when he consumed vast numbers of tequila stammers in a hotel bar with local pop star James Reyne and his three pretty backing singers.

And on the set of *Tequila Sunrise*, his drink quota steadily rose, although once again, neither his co-stars Michelle Pfeiffer and Kurt Russell, nor director Robert Towne, were concerned, since he was still delivering superb performances when required.

Mel's other big fear about AA was that his attendance would become public knowledge and he hated the very idea of anyone finding out that he was associated with such a place. But Robyn and Ed Limato would not take 'no' for an answer. They agreed that there was a risk that Mel's membership of AA would become public knowledge, but they insisted that there was no room for excuses and they would face that problem if and when it occurred.

It took a few weeks for a British tabloid newspaper to get an exclusive tip-off about Mel's membership of the Malibu branch of AA. When Limato got wind of the rag's intention to run a story, he mounted yet another damage-control operation to keep the story out of the press. Tens of thousands of dollars were spent on trying to convince a high court judge in London that, if the story were published, it would be a serious breach of privacy. After days of legal deliberation, the judge threw out Mel's lawyers' claims and the *Sunday Mirror* carried the following headline in its issue on 15 September 1991: 'MEL'S SECRET VISITS TO AA TO BEAT BOOZE HELL'. The paper quoted unnamed fellow AA members about their astonishment at seeing Mel alongside them. 'There he was one day, just sitting with us – then he introduced himself as Mel Gibson and said he had a drink problem,' said one AA regular.

Another told the paper, 'Mel said a couple of weeks ago that if he didn't get his drinking under control it could start to affect his family. That's why he was there, he told us – because he needs help in fighting this problem. Drinking is the one thing in his life that really frightens him.'

The paper recorded that Mel had been attending the Malibu branch of AA – which meets in such venues as community halls and church buildings – for the previous six weeks.

'When he first came in he looked sad and unsmiling. We could see he had his demons too,' said another member. 'But soon he was opening up to us. That's part of the therapy. Mel said that he couldn't be with us too frequently because he was dividing his time between his home in Los Angeles and his ranch in Australia.' This member added, 'All the girls at the meeting were bowled over. He looked so cute in his blue jeans and denim shirt.'

According to the paper, Mel confronted his problem head on by standing up and talking to the rest of the group.

'Mel told us that nothing worried his wife as much as his boozing, and she encouraged him to join AA. There were about twenty people in the group that night. You could see it was hard for Mel, admitting he had a problem over his boozing.'

The *Sunday Mirror* had been startled by the legal battle with Mel's representatives, because it was hardly as if Mel's problems with alcohol were novel. But Limato and his LA lawyers believed that it was essential to promote a new image of Mel being whiter than white. They also wanted Hollywood to believe that Mel was the victim of a vicious smear campaign. The story came and went, despite them, prompting sympathy for Mel from within the film community. Truth had proved stronger than hype and whitewash.

Mel has been off alcohol for several years now. There are no longer bloodshot or black eyes to be worked on by anxious make-up artists. In their place, Mel's most famous trademark – those exquisite orbs, the colour of bright, fresh cornflowers – gaze out more clearly than before.

'Whenever I'm tempted to go back to my drinking days, I know I can turn to Robyn. One look at her and I know it's not worth it,' Mel assured one friend.

Through those difficult days of Mel's induction into Alcoholics Anonymous in the summer of 1991, the actor tried to keep himself occupied, and away from the bottle. He even agreed to record a guest appearance with fellow Aussie Dame Edna Everage – alias actor Barry Humphries.

The television special was being filmed in Hollywood and featured other stars like Julio Iglesias and Charlton Heston. Dame Edna's treatment of 'her idol' Mel was hilarious and did more than anything else at that time to prove that the old Mel sparkle had not died.

The offbeat chat show host insisted that Mel share a sauna with 'her' and grabbed his hand and greeted the actor with, 'You're huge, aren't you? Professionally huge. And your *Lethal Weapon* – well, two, as a matter of fact – were tremendous. You really are very big, Possum!'

Mel was in stitches even though he had to cling to his skimpy towel on getting out of the sauna – in case Dame Edna tried to pull it off. But 'she' insisted she had seen it all before. 'I'm safe – I'm a happily bereaved woman, so you don't have to cover up. Women all over the world would kill to be here.'

Mel lapped up every moment of it. Usually, he tended to be shy and reserved and 'hated' one-on-one TV encounters like the disastrous Barbara Walters show he did during the making of *Hamlet*. But, as one of the Dame Edna show's producers said, 'Mel was so happy to be amongst other Australians. He seemed so relaxed.'

Around the same time, Mel's younger brother Donal took

his biggest step towards a major acting prize when he starred in a film produced by Phil Avalon – the same character who had given Mel his first break 15 years earlier in *Summer City*.

Fatal Bond, co-starring ex-boxer Joe Bugner, was a thriller and Phil Avalon says that Donal, two years younger than Mel, was paid considerably more for his starring role than the $400 Mel made (or didn't make, depending on whom you believe) from his feature début. Donal was reluctant to be drawn into comparisons with his famous older brother.

'Mel and I are not the same character and we have different attitudes,' said Donal, who also starred in a low-budget movie with Linda Blair, star of the original *Exorcist* film. 'It would be foolish to match myself against Mel. Most actors are never going to be as successful as him.'

But he did hope that both of them had an ability to turn any part – however small – into something memorable. 'Mel and I can take a part which looks like nothing on paper and do something with it.'

While Donal might have been confident that he could make something of a role which 'looked nothing on paper', Mel was about to bring his talents to bear on perhaps the greatest role ever written. The Four Seasons Hotel in Beverly Hills was the fairly remarkable setting in which Mel agreed to star in a project that would profoundly influence his career – more than any other film he had made up to that point, and probably will ever make. Sitting opposite him in the quiet hotel restaurant was Italian director Franco Zeffirelli, a notoriously eccentric, bombastic and influential man. There was a loaded silence because Zeffirelli had just asked one of the most commercial movie stars in the world if he would like to play the lead in *Hamlet*.

Mel was aghast. His first reaction was that it would be madness to film a play that's been around for 400 years, that some of the finest actors in the world have failed to master – he would be making himself a target for every critic in the world.

However, as the two men enjoyed a light lunch of spaghetti, Mel started to wonder. Maybe it wasn't such a mad idea after all. He was always bemoaning the fact that Hollywood rarely stretched him. Now, here was an opportunity to prove that he was capable of anything. In any case, there was something intriguing about Zeffirelli's proposal. He was offering Mel a chance to get back to his acting roots.

By the end of that lunch, Mel was halfway to being convinced. After a reading for Zeffirelli the next day, he was desperate for the job and. refused to listen to Ed Limato, who tried desperately to persuade his star not to play the role, even though he had been instrumental in getting the two men together. There were fears in Tinseltown that Mel might damage his lucrative career as an action-adventure hero. But the actor did not see it that way.

'I don't care what they say ... I don't give a shit,' he growled. And Mel had a very distinct handle on *Hamlet* as a serious subject. 'All the images ... people listening to one another and spying on one another and all the intrigue and blackness and darkness in people's souls. It was almost pre-Christian – Christianity had just arrived – it's dark and decayed and rotten with death everywhere.

'I'm very excited about Franco's vision. He'll do it in a very rotten, pre-Christian state of Denmark, where pagan Vikings kill each other and scheme all the time.'

Signing Mel for the part was a terrific coup for the Italian director. Now there would be no shortage of financial backers for the project. Some Hollywood sceptics suggested that Zeffirelli's main motive in casting Mel was to guarantee he got the film made. And it was well known that Warner Brothers – makers of the incredibly successful *Lethal Weapon* movies –

were hoping to sign Mel (they eventually did in February 1991) to a long-term contract. An investment in *Hamlet* would be their way of showing good faith to Mel, but both men maintain that was not the case and, to prove the point, Mel's own production company was widely reported to have helped finance *Hamlet* – although it is unlikely that the cash they provided came from anywhere other than Warner Brothers' coffers.

Zeffirelli observed, 'Mel put his life and career there. Imagine if he did not succeed. He would have been the joke of the industry.'

Mel did not see it in quite such dramatic terms but he was alert to the professional risk of the $15 million project. Yet, taking his father's advice to him as a boy, he was not that bothered. He knew he was going to get some flak but he quite enjoyed the thrill of defiance. He agreed to take a greatly reduced fee of less than $1 million (plus a percentage of the profits if it made any money) as a gesture of absolute commitment to the project.

In a phone call to actress Glenn Close, chosen to play Hamlet's mother Queen Gertrude, before any of the actors met for rehearsals, he admitted, 'Everyone's laughing at me over here. But screw 'em.'

Many people in the industry *were* laughing at him. They saw it in terms that were perfectly reflected by a tabloid newspaper headline shortly after the official announcement of his involvement – 'MAD MAX TO PLAY CRAZY DANE'.

Mel relished every bit of snobbery that came his way. After all, he was following in the footsteps of some of the greatest actors of modern times – Laurence Olivier, John Gielgud, Alec Guinness, Derek Jacobi and Nicol Williamson to name but a few. Not only did he have something to prove to the critics who said he was only capable of playing one-dimensional action-packed heroes, he also liked taking on the British establishment, with an outsider's chance of beating them at their own game.

Many of those laughing and sneering at him had conveniently forgotten his background in classical theatre. Shakespeare had been part of his staple diet at the National Institute of Dramatic Art in Sydney. After all, he had played Romeo and had been considered for Hamlet, only to be rejected for being too young at the time.

Masterful director Zeffirelli had already successfully translated Shakespeare on to the screen with. adaptations of *Romeo and Juliet* (which grossed $90 million) in the late Sixties and *The Taming of the Shrew* starring Richard Burton and Elizabeth Taylor. Zeffirelli had been trying for years to film *Hamlet* and had directed it on stage in 1964, then failed to mount a stage production in Los Angeles in 1979 with Richard Gere in the title role.

Before the cameras rolled on this latest version, the director declared, 'I must break with tradition. I never loved this self-masturbating, blond, impotent, supposedly romantic prince who is presented as the definitive Hamlet. Hell, the role has been so emasculated, it has been played by women. He is fit enough to duel and I think he is the opposite of vulnerable. He knows about the dealings of the world but he has a divided heart. He sees his duty but can't bring himself to do it.'

Zeffirelli claimed he was, in fact, a long-time admirer of Mel's work, including the *Mad Max* films. 'I responded to the energy, the violence, the danger of this character and it made me think of him a bit as an Elizabethan character.'

The same went for Marty Riggs in *Lethal Weapon* and, as we've seen, that especially tense suicide attempt. 'He has stature. I was impressed by him. I began to think here is my Hamlet ... It was the voice. I was madly in love with the voice,' enthused the director as word of his 'surprise' choice spread through the film industry.

Zeffirelli began signing up Mel's supporting players and they all sounded equally intrigued by the choice of leading man. Glenn Close said her initial reaction was, 'Why not? I've always loved his work. I think he has the imagination of an actor who has resources which are yet to be challenged.'

British actress Helena Bonham-Carter, who was to play Ophelia, admitted she was 'sort of surprised. But then I thought it could have been a genius move. First of all, I realised Mel was not going to be a fool and, if he couldn't give a good shot at the part, he wouldn't do it.'

The star of such diverse projects as *A Room with a View* and *Miami Vice* later reversed her stance on Mel by making fun of him just before *Hamlet* opened in London.

'He's got a very basic sense of humour. It's a bit lavatorial and not very sophisticated. His face is wonderful and his eyes are extraordinary but, physically, he is not in proportion. He's got this odd sort of body. He's got short legs, a slightly over-long body and a concave chest,' she told one reporter.

Meanwhile, Mel had to go into training. Once again, he tried to give up smoking and, by all accounts, managed to stay off cigarettes for parts of the five-month shoot. His voice coach Julia Wilson Dickson warned him that the long passages of Elizabethan dialogue were going to be easier if he could regulate his breathing. Having cut out his usual two packs of Marlboros, he replaced them with jaw-wrenching mouthfuls of nicotine chewing gum that he would only remove when actually speaking his lines.

Another hurdle was the sword-fighting. Mel – more used to handling a gun than any other lethal weapon – had to master the ballet-like intricacies of fencing, as Hamlet was an expert swordsman. Finally, he had to learn to ride a horse –

something that the purchase of trail motorbikes on his farm back in Australia had helped him avoid until then.

Before shooting began, Mel was being made painfully aware that he had taken on the Everest of his career. He could not have the occasional cigarette to soothe his nerves and he was starting to be haunted by the character of Hamlet. Mel could not decide precisely how to play the role – and that was bothering him the most.

'I couldn't sleep at night with this character. It was like something that kind of ruled your whole life ...'

Mel disclosed even more frustration a few months later when he admitted, 'There are moments playing Hamlet that make you want to rip your hair out because he is the most confounding character ever written. The only consistent thing about Hamlet is his inconsistency, and you're chasing your tail. You feel like you're going mad – and you do, a little bit ...'

Just a couple of weeks before filming was scheduled to begin, he booked himself and Robyn into the $175-a-night Henlow Grange health farm, in Bedfordshire, to limber up with a few days of seaweed baths, saunas and aromatherapy.

The film was shot at Shepperton Studios near London and at locations in castles along the Kent and Scottish coasts. Mel moved his family into a $14,000-a-month, eight-bedroom house with an acre of land at Ascot, Berkshire, on the outskirts of London. The garden of the $2 million estate was soon strewn with skateboards and bikes and the whole neighbourhood was abuzz with news of the movie star tenant.

Teenager Debbie King got to meet her idol when he strolled into the local newsagent where she worked. 'I couldn't believe my eyes. It was just like a dream. He asked me for twenty Marlboro and a packet of mints.' So much for abandoning his smokes ...

Any hopes Mel had – despite his beard and dyed hair – that his stay at the estate might go unnoticed were soon dashed. But then the same house had been rented to singing star Diana Ross the previous year and, according to neighbours, 'she was much noisier, with helicopters flying in and out the whole time'.

Mel had got into the habit of enrolling his children in schools wherever he happened to be filming. On this occasion, he put them into what he later told friends was a particularly 'snotty' establishment. Within weeks, Mel and Robyn took the three eldest children out of the school because of what they considered the poor quality of teaching and the fact that there were too many children to each class. Privately, Mel was angered by the school's attitude towards him and his wife.

He also claimed that all three children asked to leave because they hated the drudgery. Mel claimed to be appalled by the British school system, saying that it had stifled his children. There was also talk of an incident involving one of the Gibson children and a bullying classmate. Mel was disappointed and somewhat diverted by his children's temporary educational problems. He felt that it was a typical example of British snobbery at its worst.

Very occasionally, Robyn would visit the set with some of the children, but this was not like *The River*, a few years earlier. Tensions on the set of *Hamlet* were intense. Not only were Mel and his classically trained co-stars trying to concentrate on every move, but emotions in the heat of the moment were running high and Mel felt under enormous pressure.

As usual, Robyn was providing Mel with a little bit of sanity at home. It was his way of escaping the pressure. He even flew his parents Hutton and Anne over for a month. Mel overcame his misgivings about England by strolling around the streets of London, sometimes with just Robyn for company – eating in one particular Chinese restaurant on a number of occasions.

He also enjoyed long walks in the Berkshire countryside with the children, and narrowly avoided danger when a bull charged the family. There was also hide-and-seek with the children in the grounds of the country mansion, which prompted one neighbour to comment, 'You'd never have thought this was the man you see in films blasting people with a shotgun.'

However, some of the family Sundays were ruined by Mel because he was so hyped up over his role, and insisted that Robyn read all the other parts to him as he ran through his lines over and over in a bid for perfection in his performance the next day.

Mel had got his favourite make-up lady Lois Burwell – with him on *Air America* – to join him on *Hamlet*, and together they pressured the producers to allow him to grow the beard he deemed essential for the role. There was anxiety that none of his fans would appreciate a hairy growth but Mel got his way in the end.

For *Hamlet*, Dunnottar Castle in Scotland became Elsinore. But the gloomy weather so carefully emphasised by Shakespeare was nowhere to be seen when cast and crew turned up. Blazing sunshine, cheery blue skies and a holiday camp atmosphere prevailed. Long delays were endured while technicians spent hours attempting to block out the sun. But it was still cold, bitterly cold, and Mel and his co-stars had to trek half-a-mile to a portable loo every time they needed to go to the toilet. And photographers popped out of the bushes at regular intervals.

Later, back in London, Mel got so fed up with being hounded by one 'little bastard' that he had a bet with a friend that, if he failed to stay off cigarettes for the duration of *Hamlet*, then he would allow the photographer to take his picture. He lost the bet. The role was proving physically demanding for Mel in many ways; he had to be sewn into his costume which caused him to sweat profusely beneath the hot lights. At one stage, he was losing four kilos of body weight every day. Then his back started playing up again. Filming was delayed for 24 hours after he pulled a muscle while lifting another actor.

Mel's on-set relationship with Glenn Close was said by onlookers to be that of soulmates. The actress admitted that she found the most effective way to stop Mel telling incessant bad jokes was to ... kiss him. 'They weren't sexual kisses. I really kissed him in order to stop him talking!'

Those awful jokes included altering the whole meaning of the movie's library scene which featured Ian Holm (Polonius) with Mel sitting on a ledge above a ladder with Holm climbing the first few rungs as he speaks. With Hamlet's line, 'For yourself, sir, shall grow old as I am ... if like a crab you could go backward', Mel suddenly gave the ladder a push with his foot, knocking Holm to the ground. A brief, tense silence followed, then a smile invaded Zeffirelli's face. 'Yes, yes, leave that in and do it again.'

One of the most dreadful jokes of all came when Mel impaled Holm's character with a single sword stroke as he cowered behind 'the arms'. Mel immediately piped up, 'There's an arms-hole for you.'

He defended his wisecracking by telling bystanders that he would 'go really nuts' if he had to stay in character the whole time. Despite all that, Mel felt wary respect for the actors surrounding him.

'It was rather like that nightmare where you have been thrown in the ring with Mike Tyson. Well, I felt I was in there with him – only I was awake.

'When I looked around me on the set I was so intimidated.

At times, I almost felt like running home because of the illustrious acting company I was in.'

And through all this, his co-stars kept up a constant theme of praise to anyone who would listen. Alan Bates, who played Claudius, said emphatically, 'Mel Gibson is brilliant. He is going to surprise a lot of people.'

Ian Holm said he had nothing but admiration for Mel. 'It's a hell of a thing for a megastar of his magnitude to put himself on the line playing Hamlet with a lot of Brits. He does just fine!' Mel, for his part, described Holm as 'a great guy – for a Pom!'

Helena Bonham-Carter – despite her reservations – conceded, 'He's a real clown, a buffoon. He is so relaxed when you're actually with him.'

Not for the first time, Mel was using humour as a way to camouflage his deep-set fears. He felt intimidated by the cast that had been assembled in his honour and non-stop praise from his co-stars was starting to sound just a little hollow, patronising. It was almost as if they were saying, 'Considering it's Mel Gibson, he's not that bad.'

Mel did not want it to be like that. He saw Hamlet as being a logical extension of his stage roles back in Australia – yet everyone was treating him like some crass Hollywood star trying to prove a point.

He took his role in *Hamlet* so seriously that Universal had to spend an estimated $200,000 flying dozens of journalists into London to interview him about his previous film *Bird on a Wire*, which was about to open.

Explained Hollywood-based reporter Dan McDonnell, 'Mel refused to go back to the States to promote the film so we had to go to him. It cost Universal a fortune.'

The reason behind Mel's stubborn refusal to travel was that he feared he was close to a nervous breakdown. The stresses and strains of working on three consecutive films had combined with his own insecurity about the *Hamlet* project. He confessed to a film industry figure that he 'had run out of gas'. It was Mel's own way of saying that if he did not take a long break after Hamlet, be might not be in a fit state to make another movie – ever. All that pent-up tension had finally got to him and what was even more frustrating was that he knew he had yet again pushed himself too far. He had recognised the symptoms but he had tried to beat them by slogging on.

When American television's Barbara Walters interviewed Mel on the set of *Hamlet* for a special, aired in the United States on 14 November 1990, he seemed tense and very tired. He told friends he was annoyed when Walters tried to suggest he was a hypocrite for acting in films that did not coincide with his deeply religious beliefs. Mel did vaguely open up about his 'dark period' of alcohol abuse five years earlier, but said that was all in the past.

In truth, Mel, who had suffered a dreadful day of take after take performing the difficult soliloquy which starts, 'O that this too too solid flesh would melt ...' was in no mood to be interviewed. He struggled and stumbled and dried up when Walters asked him, 'Can you say a bit of Shakespeare for us?' Mel looked positively relieved when the interview came to an end.

Oh yes, and there was the ghost of all those previous Hamlets. Mel really did believe that the role was 'haunted', as was shown by a bizarre incident during the last few weeks of production. Exhausted after another hard day's filming at Shepperton Studios, he headed for his trailer to find a gift-wrapped box awaiting him. Gingerly, he untied the unmarked package to find an elegant, hand-stitched shirt with a bloodstain on one sleeve. Mel gasped as he read a note lying on the shirt. It said that here was the very shirt worn by

Laurence Olivier in his film version of *Hamlet*. He snapped the box shut instantly.

But later at his hotel, he found himself irresistibly drawn to the package. Once again, he looked down at the shirt and then, unable to stop himself, slipped it on. For a few moments, he stared at himself in the mirror. Shivers ran down his back. He felt a strange presence in the room. Hastily, he pulled the shirt off and packed it back in the box and has never opened it since.

Mel has never discussed this incident, but according to one person who met him during the shooting of *Hamlet*, it 'completely freaked him out … He felt as if the spirit of Hamlet was close by him the entire time,' said the source.

When *Hamlet* finally wrapped, Mel experienced an overwhelming sense of relief. He knew from viewing the rushes with Zeffirelli each evening that he had done reasonably well. In fact, he was quietly confident. But Mel expected that the biggest obstacle of all would be the critics. This was no *Lethal Weapon*, where any amount of criticism would be ignored by the public, desperate to see action. *Hamlet* had to be well reviewed, as the people who read film criticism in newspapers and magazines would make up the majority of the movie's potential audience.

Within days of finishing filming, Mel also kept another promise to Robyn – to take her for a romantic weekend in Paris without the children. In the French capital, the couple spent two days wandering around shops and restaurants as Mel pondered on what direction his career should take next.

Determined to make *Hamlet* a success, he embarked on an exhausting worldwide publicity tour to promote the film, still ignoring all the danger signs looming in front of him. The buzz surrounding the project was phenomenal. Everywhere he travelled, journalists wanted Mel to talk about *Hamlet*. For

Mel with Goldie Hawn, his co-star in *Bird on a Wire*.

Above: Mel as Hamlet, the role that haunted a host of actors before him.

Below: Julia Roberts and Mel taking direction from Richard Donner in *Conspiracy Theory*.

Above: With Helen Hunt in box-office smash *What Women Want* – most men including Mel still don't really know!

Below: Mel scoops his *Braveheart* Oscars for Best Picture and Best Director.

Above: With Madeleine Stowe in Vietnam War epic *We Were Soldiers*.

Below: Mel plays psychiatrist Dr Gibbon to Robert Downey Jr's tortured novelist in *The Singing Detective*.

Providing the voice for Rocky in *The Chicken Run*.

The truth is out there … *Above:* With the director of *Signs*, M. Night Shyamalan.
Below: With co-star Joaquin Phoenix.

The controversial *The Passion of The Christ*, which attracted no end of publicity. *Above:* Setting up a shot.

Below: Directing James Cazaviel.

Mel attends a première with his wife Robyn.

once in his life, the actor was happy to oblige. He was anxious to spread the word and his new-found fondness for talking to the press did not go unnoticed. Reporters had not forgotten how awkward he usually was; some were speculating as to whether Mel's new charming front could be attributed to the film's obvious lack of commercial appeal.

Another part of his pre-release preparations was an hour-long educational video on *Hamlet*, which he did in co-operation with the students of the tenth grade at University High in Los Angeles. It was titled *Mel Gibson Goes Back to School* and Mel talked to the students about *Hamlet* in their own language: 'great story ... eight violent deaths, murder, incest, adultery, a mad woman, poison, revenge ... and sword-fights'.

The students took to Mel's interpretation with great enthusiasm, much to the actor's delight.

'I asked them a lot of questions. They couldn't answer them but it got them thinking about the play. Some of these questions I couldn't answer myself because Shakespeare doesn't come to any answers. He was just raising the questions; that is what is so intriguing.'

The video has been a solid seller through Mel's Icon Productions ever since, although teachers don't know if it is because it provides a fresh insight into Shakespeare or simply a showcase for a Hollywood heart-throb.

Then, in December 1990, just a few weeks before *Hamlet* was scheduled to open in the US, tragedy struck when Anne Gibson – who had been ill for some time with diabetes and a heart condition as well as rapidly failing sight – died at the age of 69. The cause of death was a heart-attack, in Wodonga Hospital, northern Victoria. Mel was shattered and caught the first available flight from LA to Australia to be with the rest of his family.

In the Kiewa Valley area where his farm is located, friends and neighbours threw a protective screen around the Gibson family. Reporters dispatched from Melbourne for an update on the situation were told to keep away from the Gibson compound.

By all accounts, Mel found it very difficult to grieve openly over his mother's death. He admitted to respected writer Linda Lee-Potter, 'I don't cope very well with grief. I don't think it's unmanly to cry. But,' he added bluntly, 'I'm not going to tell you if I ever do.'

He was particularly saddened because his mother would never get an opportunity to see him in *Hamlet*. The whole family had been proud of the actor when he landed the role. Just a few days after the funeral, Mel surprised Hollywood by putting his grief behind him and flying back to Los Angeles to continue his publicity tour.

'We're surprised that he came back to do this but, of course, we're delighted,' said a Warner Brothers executive. 'It's an indication of how important he feels this film is, that he would lay himself on the line for the press and all the public appearances, at a time when this must be the last place he would want to be.' Journalists at press conferences that followed his mother's death were warned not to mention Anne Gibson or even offer condolences. They all noticed that Mel was back to virtually chain-smoking.

At one gathering, dressed in a sombre black suit with a black-and-beige polo shirt, he was asked what it had been like to have Glenn Close, who, at 43, was not that much older than himself, playing his mother.

'It was fantastic,' came the reply. 'She was so good I think I'll adopt her.' Then Mel's voice dropped to a whisper. 'She's great to work with ... but young to be my mother ...'A silence filled the room as he trailed off, close to tears.

A few minutes later, Mel dived outside the room for a puff

of a cigarette in a corridor. He looked tense and nervous and told one journalist wearily that he was 'gonna stand here and let some steam off'.

Later, he talked about what he perceived as the similarities between himself and Hamlet. 'He also has this volcanic range of expression bubbling up inside of him. And he doesn't know if it's justified. He's a very honest and just person ... that's the way he was raised. He holds it in ... but sometimes it bursts out.'

And, it seems, that just about summed up Mel's attitude towards director Zeffirelli by the time the shoot wrapped. There were few public rows between them on set but Mel found the Italian's hysterical method of film-making very wearing. He told friends that the director used to stomp around the set 'like a madman who thinks he is Napoleon'.

'I don't want to bag the guy ... we got along all right,' was about all he would say when asked about his relationship with Zeffirelli.

With the film days from opening in the United States, Mel anxiously awaited the reviews. He later admitted to having suffered from his biggest crisis in confidence during that period. In the United States, reviews turned out to be very impressive. 'Gibson's Hamlet is strong and intelligent. The film is controlled by his dignified yet explosive presence ... a compelling Hamlet,' said the *New York Times*. And *Time* magazine described Hamlet as 'being almost perfect for Gibson with his neurotic physicality and urgent baritone'.

The *New York Post* raved, 'Mel Gibson makes a very good Hamlet. It's a doubly pleasant surprise since we've had to judge him by the likes of *Mad Max* and *Lethal Weapon*.'

The Los Angeles première of the film helped raise $1 million towards the revival of Shakespeare's Globe Theatre in London, after three centuries.

Relieved by the first wave of reviews in the States, Mel returned to Australia something of a hero, especially when he visited his old home ground of the National Institute of Dramatic Art. The main reason for returning to NIDA was to announce the Mel Gibson–Village Roadshow–NIDA scholarship for a student on either technical or creative courses. But he also wanted to talk to and encourage the students. The school theatre was packed for his appearance and a barrage of questions were thrown at him. Asked if he would be forever haunted by the role of the tormented Hamlet, Mel stated bluntly, 'I'm not going to let the bugger bother me.'

One student wondered how he had reacted to the fanfare of jeers that greeted his decision to play the part. 'Who cares? I don't. I'm rich.'

But Mel's biggest fear on returning to NIDA was that one of his old teachers would see *Hamlet* and give him a no-holds-barred criticism of his performance. He told a college lecturer he was 'quaking in his boots' in case she cornered him.

Mel then got himself embroiled in a row about the recruitment of foreign actors for Australian productions and became a victim of angry responses from Aussie actors. He enraged the local actors by accusing the Equity union of Australia of stifling the local film industry by not allowing foreign stars to work.

Actress Penne Hackforth-Jones accused Mel of 'forgetting his roots – the days when he was a struggling actor', and actor John Hargreaves accused Mel of being 'naive'.

The star himself pointed out the irony that he was not even an Australian citizen, but insisted that local stars could make it abroad just like he had if they tried hard enough. It took a phone call from his old *Mad Max* and *Summer City* flatmate Steve Bisley to advise Mel to keep a lower profile on the subject. In the eyes of his friends, he was treading on very thin ice.

Before the Australian première of *Hamlet* in Sydney, Mel attended a party in his honour. For the first time in years, he looked relaxed at such a gathering, mingling with guests with a Perrier in one hand and a cigarette in the other. Seven of his brothers and sisters turned up along with Hutton Gibson. For Mel, having his family there was very significant, as he believed that *Hamlet* was the first movie he could truly be completely proud of. Pursuing their own interests as Mel ascended through Hollywood, the Gibson siblings had become, among other things, a professional singer, an X-ray technician, a business executive, a store manager and a moderately successful actor, not to mention two 'home-makers'.

He told one fellow guest why *Hamlet* was so important to him. 'I want this production to be successful because I love Shakespeare and the world needs more Shakespeare ... because it's full of wisdom, wit and beauty. We need more of that ...'

Following that party, guests moved on up the street to the cinema for the screening of *Hamlet*. Mel did not bother acting the star and riding the few hundred yards in a limousine. He strolled into the auditorium with a handful of relatives, took an unreserved seat well away from the VIP area and disappeared before the end of the final credits as the audience applauded.

Reviews in Australia were glowing. 'This film literally pulsates with dramatic energy. Despite minor wear and tear, Gibson automatically notches up Brownie points as a believably youthful Hamlet,' wrote Rob Lowing in the *Sun-Herald*.

But not everyone in Australia was completely won over by Mel's portrayal. Scott Murray of *Cinema Papers* magazine said, 'Hamlet is a puzzle. A lot of the favourable reviews were just because he did not muck it up. But it is so thin. It is a big nothing. Every scene is meaningless. Mel did not give it a proper spin. It's neither good nor bad. But I suppose he did help make Shakespeare more accessible to a younger audience.'

But Murray insists that making Hamlet was 'not a good career move for Mel. It was partly ego. He wanted to see if he could do it.'

The toughest territory of all for Mel to conquer would be Britain, where the classical traditions and Shakespearean heritage originated. Many critics had felt intimidated and appalled by the Hollywood star's decision to play Hamlet.

There was a royal première for Hamlet at the Odeon Haymarket in the West End of London. However, Mel – not the biggest fan of the British Royal Family at the best of times – managed to upset the Duchess of York by being late after getting held up in traffic.

'ALAS, POOR FERGIE AWAITS PRINCE MEL' read the headline in one newspaper, which reported that the Duchess had greeted Mel with the words, 'It is very good of you to come …'

British reviews for Hamlet were predictably lukewarm. 'He makes a plain-spoken, rather uncomplicated Hamlet who sometimes seems scarcely to know what's hitting him but bravely tries to mould fate to his own ends all the same,' said the Guardian.

The Times critic accused Mel of 'enunciating with the unreal clarity of a speaking clock. He is grave, anguished, tender, playful, all the things Hamlet should be. Yet, though Mel Gibson is never for one moment bad, almost everybody in the cast is better. And for all his effort, we never get under Hamlet's skin.'

Mel told friends that playing Hamlet had had a very deep effect on him, something that will stay with him for the rest of his life. In a diary he kept during the long and arduous shoot, he wrote, 'As I began to fight for Hamlet, I started to understand him. In the thick of the fight, with no time to think, only to react, and completely absorbed in Hamlet's actions, I am him. His spirit enters me and somehow we're fighting each other and we're fighting together at the same time. He makes you grow up a little bit.'

Hopes were high at Warner Brothers in early 1991 that Mel would be nominated for an Oscar for *Hamlet*. The film was even specially released before the deadline for entries that year. But members of the Academy overlooked him and he has privately admitted his disappointment, although friends say he is philosophical about winning such awards. The one gong he did get was a prestigious Will Award from the Shakespeare Theater in Washington. He was the fifth recipient, joining Joseph Papp, Kevin Kline, Christopher Plummer and Kenneth Branagh.

With *Hamlet* up and running throughout the world, Mel retired gracefully to his farm. He badly needed a break after three virtually back-to-back projects. He had to avoid the pitfalls of overwork and he was seriously thinking about what the future held for him.

'You work because you want to work and you're hungry. Then you wait 'til you're full and you take a break. You have to take a break, to do things that you work for, or you couldn't survive. I've got to go away and learn some new tricks. I've got to replenish my creative energy because I'm out of it.'

NINETEEN

MY FAMILY MEANS MORE TO ME THAN THE ARTIFICIAL
TRAPPINGS OF MY CAREER. IF EVER I HAD TO CHOOSE
BETWEEN MY CAREER AND MY FAMILY, THE WIFE AND
KIDS WOULD DEFINITELY COME OUT ON TOP.

Overworked, stressed to the point of burn-out, Mel had
to get home to Australia before something very serious
happened to his health, following his whirlwind global
publicity tour to promote *Hamlet*. Those gruelling back-to-
back movies had made him desperate for the peace and quiet
of his Victorian cattle farm. Privately, he was admitting to
associates that, if he tried to make another film, he might have
a breakdown. He felt as if he never wanted to go near a movie
set again.

Mel even managed a complete reversal in his long-held
disdain of therapists and consulted one in Los Angeles before
returning Down Under. It was a remarkable about-turn for
someone who had ridiculed psychiatrists so fervently, but he
had to take some action to sort himself out. Mel described
his visits as having his body 'switched off', and he told one
associate that the sessions with the psychiatrist left him

feeling totally drained for three days but 'after that you feel great, like a dancing bear'. Soon, he was even able to laugh off his own hypocrisy and has continued receiving regular treatment ever since.

Top of his list of priorities was to see Robyn and their six children. The whole family was aware that Mel was heading dangerously close to burn-out. Showbusiness friends and associates had noticed how much more serious and less inclined to crack jokes and pranks he became in the closing months of 1990. There was none of Mel's inarticulate sidestepping. His eagerness to return to his true home was clear for anyone to see.

Mel was only too painfully aware that the last time he had to take a year off to recharge his batteries was after *Mad Max Beyond Thunderdome* in 1985. This time around, he was even more tired but he seemed a little more in control of his own destiny than in those days which he now described as his 'bad period'. But the actor was alarmingly open with anyone who asked him if he was feeling the strain. 'I have a hunger to work. To work is to create. But for the moment, I have sated my hunger. I need a holiday, a year off,' he confessed to one showbusiness writer.

The Carinya farm, in the small township of Tangambalanga near the banks of the Kiewa River in Victoria, represented Mel's little piece of sanity and he fumed every time journalists dared to mention it during his publicity tours. And when US television host Robin Leech tried to persuade the star to let his property be featured on *Lifestyles of the Rich and Famous* Mel exploded at the indignity. As far as he was concerned, the farm and his family were off-limits to the media.

He was still angry over the way one Australian magazine had invaded his privacy by sending photographers to take pictures of his house, plus a team of reporters to question locals and farm workers nearby about their famous movie star neighbour.

The only photographer allowed into the farm throughout this period was freelancer Mark Griffin, after a deal was struck between a local paper and Mel for coverage restricted to his agricultural business alone. The first thing that struck Griffin was the lax security. 'No electronic gates, no barbed-wire fences … it was completely open. Mel turned out to be a very affable bloke. I shot him on the tractor and riding his four-wheel motorbike. He was very relaxed.'

But Mel changed when the photographer innocently asked about taking some pictures of his children, who were playing nearby. The actor completely ignored the question and changed the subject instantly. However, Griffin said he was impressed by Mel's knowledge of the farming business. 'He seemed to really know what he was talking about.' After being given a cup of coffee and some of Robyn's homemade cake, Griffin departed and never heard from Mel again.

Gradually, Mel had expanded the red-brick farmhouse with an additional double-storey extension, to cater for his huge family rather than a desire for a grandiose home. Locals note that the farm does not have any of the whitewashed post-and-rail fences or huge signs common to many cattle properties where big money has been invested.

In fact, the farm has a fine range of sheds, yards, bales of hay and wrapped silage, and excellent lush pastures nurtured without the use of chemical fertilisers, the kind of things that are essential on a working farm of 2,500 hectares. Then he bought an 800-hectare property next door, Limerick Springs, followed by about 1,600 hectares of rough hill country at Bullioh, in the upper Murray region close by. Finally, Robyn bought a rundown hotel in nearby Yackandandah for a bargain $75,000 at an auction. Local gossips are predicting that Mel will refurbish the place in due course and reopen it for business. All four properties are said to be worth in the region of $2 million – and he has still held on to that house at Coogee, in Sydney, worth at least another $500,000.

Just before Anne's death, in late 1989, Mel moved his mother and father into a property on the estate. At least she got to be with Mel and his family. Hutton stayed on after his wife's death and became the property's unofficial caretaker when the family was away.

When he first bought the place, Mel had little or no intention of going into cattle farming in a big way. His only aim had been to find a place to escape that now familiar burn-out scenario. But, he told friends later, the land 'needed something on it' so he bought a herd of commercial Hereford cattle. Then, after a year of making endless mistakes, Mel hired 28-year-old Peter Ford, a sixth-generation farmer from nearby Dederang. Originally, he asked Ford to be farm caretaker, but then Mel decided to give the farmer a full-time job.

Mel also had to face the fact that, since making the first *Lethal Weapon* film, Los Angeles had become his main home. In 1989, he paid $2.4 million for a vast eight-hectare spread a mile into the Serra Canyon, just behind Malibu, that belonged to singer Rick Springfield. It was the perfect retreat for the star and his family with a 24-hour armed guard at the gate to the private road leading to the property – visitors are by invitation only. Mel and Robyn fell in love with the property the moment they saw it because it is surrounded by horse stables and its dusty terrain reminded them of Australia.

There are a couple of tight turns on Serra Canyon that lead to a narrow street that passes the electrified gates to Mel's palatial home. You cannot see the modern building from the road. You identify yourself over the intercom and face a solitary video camera that automatically tightens focus on the subject. Then there's a buzz and the gates swing open.

Mel was advised to put even more of his many millions into property straight after purchasing the house in Serra Canyon, so he started looking for another place in early 1990. During one bizarre, only-in-Hollywood scene, he spotted a house he liked the look of in Beverly Hills, and got the real-estate agent to persuade the owners to vacate for one night so that he could sleep over in the house and 'get the feel of it'. The flattered owners allowed the actor to put them up in a luxurious hotel suite but then Mel changed his mind because he 'did not sleep well'. He shelled out $3,000 to the owners for their trouble.

Then, in February 1992, Mel purchased what real-estate agents describe as a 'beach house filled with rustic charm' in Malibu for $2.5 million. Initially, it was bought just so that Robyn and the kids could swim in the sea in privacy. The sky-blue-painted house – with 20 metres of private beach that comes complete with a golf buggy to get down to the ocean – was built in the 1940s and had three bedrooms and three bathrooms, so it was not even big enough for the entire family to stay in at one time. Neighbours include such Hollywood luminaries as Sylvester Stallone, Robert Redford, Dustin Hoffman and an immediate neighbour, Emilio Estevez. Just like his house a few miles away in the canyons behind Malibu, this one could only be reached by passing an armed guard at the entrance to a private road.

It transpired that Mel had been looking for the perfect, private beachfront property for his family for years and he intended to move the entire family in after conversion work was completed. Building got under way in early 1993 and was completed 18 months later for a Southwestern-style house with a swimming pool and waterfall constructed alongside the existing home.

Despite being a property-owner in California now, Mel continued to criticise Hollywood. 'You get spoiled in Hollywood, they throw it at you. But it's like joining the police force and trying to stay straight. Sure, I like the things they throw at me. I like nice hotels and I like nice food. And I like cars.' But he added quickly, 'I like the farm more ...'

In 1989, he bought the 5,000-hectare Beartooth Ranch in Montana in partnership with Queensland breeder Don Anderson. Gradually, Mel developed an interest in the highly controversial genetic engineering of certain breeds of cattle, which had been going on at Beartooth for years. The property had been home to one of the world's finest Hereford studs. Within weeks of buying the farm, Mel invested $120,000 in a prize Saler bull and got himself hooked on genetic breeding.

Former Beartooth owner George Ellis was left in no doubt that the star is serious about running a successful cattle business. 'I believe he plans on doing it for a major means of income. He's not just doing it for home entertainment. Mel is very athletic and handy with the equipment and anything else he puts his mind to. He's learned to know the difference between these critters very quickly.'

Over the next two years, Mel poured hundreds of thousands of dollars into cross-breeding Salers, Gelbviehs and Angus cattle; he and his farming advisers believe that they will eventually make a fortune out of his investment. However, a worldwide recession had hit Australia particularly badly and Mel has privately admitted that he has lost upwards of a million dollars over the first few years of owning the ranch.

'Luckily, I don't have to eke out a living as a farmer or I'd go broke trying to feed my family,' he says.

But Mel had another, more human motive for raising the cattle – he loved eating the organically raised beef and vegetables from the garden knowing that none of them had been sprayed with 'horrible toxins'. Mel fervently believed that avoiding such chemicals would enable him and his family to live healthily and happily to a 'ripe old age'. He often jokes that his next plan is to brand the rear end of every piece of cattle with 'Mel's Organic Meat'.

To Mel, being on the farm was a soothing antidote to the movie business. Riding around his vast estate on a 200cc trail bike, chopping wood and 'lugging things around' were the perfect ways to escape the pressures. The other reason why he was stuck in Hollywood for long periods of time, whether he liked it or not, was that his company, Icon, was attached to Warner Brothers in Los Angeles and Mel was expected to get involved in many aspects of the day-to-day running of the business. Hundreds of scripts flood in each month for his consideration either as producer, director or star – or all three.

But trouble was brewing at the Beartooth Ranch. Mel, who'd originally bought the property because, as he told one reporter, 'Ranching's good for you, good for your mind, your spirit,' was discovering that his onscreen adventures were nothing compared to what happened when he encountered cattlemen Dan Ellis and his father George, who'd owned Beartooth for 23 years before selling it to Mel.

The actor had originally hired both men to stay on as his ranch managers then, in 1992, he suddenly fired both men and George collapsed and died. The Ellis family linked his death to the incident. One family member said, 'The death was hastened by events at Beartooth. George suddenly fell ill and no one expected that. He went into a coma and just died. I know that the whole cattle industry he worked with is upset about this. He was respected, popular.'

Just a few days before Mel retreated to Australia after *Hamlet*, he had no idea what he was going to do next. In fact, he wanted to keep his plans deliberately vague to give himself a chance to recover from all that previous work. He wanted to disappear.

'Hollywood impedes my ability to be an observer. This visibility you have taints everything. It's hard to explain but, if Joe Blow goes into a department store to check out how sales assistants behave and how they do their job, the assistants are going to behave differently in front of him than in front of me. And this visibility I have changes things for my kids and it is starting to get difficult to take them out. I do ... I make the effort but sometimes it's just not worthwhile and that chokes you. If you have a farm, like I do, it's great; nobody's going to come up. Life comes to me rather than me going to it. That helps put everything back into perspective.'

There was another thrust behind Mel's decision to retreat into the bush. He worried that there was a danger of over-exposing himself to the public. With his Hollywood agent and other advisers urging him to accept more and more roles for increasingly large fees – of which they took a healthy cut – Mel fretted that people would soon get 'sick of the sight of me'. And he infuriated Ed Limato by refusing to give him the main phone number of the house ... allowing him to get on with his other career as a farmer.

On Sundays, Mel and Robyn hold barbecues for local friends. People who have attended say they are fairly quiet affairs where Mel makes a point of personally handing out dishes of meat and salads and behaving like anyone else there. It all boils down to the type of outback living that Mel hankers after more than anything else in the world. And he showed just what a local sport he was when he witnessed a hit-and-run accident involving a German Shepherd dog. Mel immediately rushed to the animal's aid and drove 30km to the nearest vet where he left a cheque for $1,300 and asked that they call him if the money did not cover all the expenses.

British-born Amanda Palmer worked as the Gibsons' daily helper/nanny for three years and she provided an insight into the real home life of Mel and Robyn down on the farm.

'Mel only ever wore jeans and a T-shirt and would be barefoot and unshaven with his hair in a mess most of the time. He would love getting stuck in at home, cooking sausages, making toast and frying eggs and bacon. Then he would feed the younger ones and change the nappies.'

Amanda Palmer revealed that Mel's household had a strict routine. 'I would arrive at 7.30 in the morning and get the children moving, dressed and downstairs for breakfast. If Mel wasn't filming, he'd be down helping with everything. The first thing he said when I started was, "Do you want a cup of tea?" then went off to make me one!'

She travelled with the family to Los Angeles on a number of occasions, but Amanda Palmer insists that Mel and his family led a 'hermit-like' existence for much of the time at the farm. 'Their whole way of life is no big deal. The house is in a state of semi-chaos.'

He is also very strict about what films the children arc allowed to watch. All the *Lethal Weapon* films are banned, as is *Tequila Sunrise*, although he did allow them to watch *Mad Max 2* because he considers it harmless fun. The only other films of his they were permitted to view were *Tim* and *Air America*.

There in the background, making sure Mel's feet remain on the ground, is Robyn. Mel loves the fact that, to her and the kids, he's just a husband and father and he absorbs the criticism Robyn regularly heaps upon him. 'She says I've got short, skinny legs, a big bum and a hollow chest. And when she tells me to get out in the kitchen and wash the dishes, I jump to it,' Mel grins.

Amanda Palmer recalled, 'Robyn spends her whole time

with the children. She's very much the traditional mother and wife. She just likes to run the home. If people saw her, they'd probably be very surprised. Glamour and expensive clothes don't interest her at all. With six children, and given that she doesn't want any staff, it means she's on the go the whole time.'

Farmer Mel is not shy about handing out corporal punishment to his children if he deems it necessary. It has been reported that he has often smacked or spanked his offspring for bad behaviour. Another case of 'like father, like son'.

Mel believes that his children should respect him and corporal punishment is part of that scenario. He has described to friends the type of punishment he hands out to his children as 'the type of crack that will sting and bite'. But, usually, he warns each child three times before handing out a punishment. 'He firmly believes that you cannot raise a decent human being without using a little force at times,' says one friend.

Yet like most disciplinarian fathers, he believes that after hitting a child 'you're all back to square one'. And his friends and associates have noted that he never talks down to his children. Mel regularly picks them up from their schools when they are all together in Australia, and he believes that constantly moving them around the world with him will do them nothing but good. And both he and Robyn have promised they will never send their children to boarding school. 'I'd rather take them to wonderful places and get a whole new culture spat in their faces,' he says. 'Make them learn conversion rates and pick up on different cultures.'

In a lighter vein, he succumbed to pressure from the children and agreed to appear on a *Muppets* television special aired in Australia, Britain and America in late 1992. He happily hammed it up as Hamlet in a short comedy sequence with the grotesque puppet megastars.

Mel never uses bodyguards or even barbed wire to repel prying fans in Australia. The only time he has ever considered some sort of protective action was when a number of 'sick and twisted' letters turned up at the main farmhouse. He took the intrusion in his stride and felt strangely reassured that at least the threats were put in writing. He believes that the ones who don't write are the types who might end up paying a dangerous visit.

A similar problem at the family's main home in Malibu surfaced with a stream of fan mail that frequently included telephone numbers, raunchy letters and even ladies' underwear. Mel sabotaged such approaches by having the mailbox removed from the bottom of his driveway. All his post is now diverted to his agent's home. He also took security measures that he would never consider in Australia.

Accordingly, Mel loathes annual lists such as the *Forbes* world's richest entertainers, which in 1990 proclaimed him the thirty-seventh wealthiest person in US showbusiness with a fortune estimated in the region of $24 million. He worries that there are people who read these lists and then target a personality.

When, in August 1992, an Australian TV channel decided to run a current affairs programme on how easy it was to computer-hack into personal backgrounds and featured Mel plus one of his Malibu homes as an example, he was enraged.

The programme had a Hollywood private eye use Mel's tax file number to track down personal details on the star, including what he paid for that house in Malibu ($2.4 million), when the house was built (1980), and that he was paying $9,000 a year in land taxes alone.

Towards the end of his year off, Mel allowed himself to see that it was time to start thinking about work again. His attitude towards Hollywood had mellowed. It seems to be best summed up by his insistence on wearing a fake Rolex watch, much to the consternation of many so-called movietown players. In Tinseltown, almost everyone wears expensive watches. But not Mel. 'It is as if he is saying, "Take me as you find me or don't bother,"' said one friend.

TWENTY

PEOPLE MUST BE SICK OF ME, OR THEY WILL BE SOON.

It was one of the biggest-grossing movies of all time, spawning soaraway careers for all the actors and technicians involved. Mel – resting on his farm – eyed the phenomenal success of Kevin Costner's *Dances with Wolves* with envy. As an artist, he respected Costner's work. In the hands of a different director, he reluctantly recognised that *Dances* would never have been the epic sensation it turned out to be.

When Costner went up and collected his Oscar for Best Director, it fulfilled the American Dream. Mel had enjoyed his share of that dream but he wanted the same as Costner and embarked on the daunting task of finding a similar project to direct and star in. It had to be something that would close the gap between him and Californian Costner. Mel believed he had it in him to equal Costner's directorial début. He had the charisma and allure of a major movie star and Warner

Brothers would give him a chance if he found the right project.

Mel had his eye on several film properties by the end of 1990. He was particularly interested in finding the sort of romantic adventure that would salute and evoke the days of stars like Cary Grant and Gary Cooper. The frenetic violence and non-stop action of the *Lethal Weapon* series had pushed him in the opposite direction. His partner, friend and accountant Bruce Davey instructed their development executive at Icon Productions to keep a special lookout for such a screenplay.

Eventually, Mel settled on a script entitled *The Rest of Daniel* (later changed to *Forever Young*), a fantasy adventure about a man frozen for 50 years in a cryogenics experiment. He committed himself to the project and, as a measure of how important Mel was to Warner Brothers, the studio shelled out an extraordinary $2 million to buy the script from writer Jeffrey Abrams. It became the most expensive script of its kind in Hollywood history when Warners announced they had purchased it specifically for Mel, in November 1990. Interestingly, he passed on the opportunity to direct it, preferring to wait for something on a smaller scale.

But even multimillion-dollar screenplays have to be polished a little and while Mel awaited a new draft of *Daniel*, he became intrigued by one or two other projects, including a film based on American correspondent George Polk, who was found in a Greek harbour shot through the back of the neck, probably on the orders of the CIA and the then right-wing Greek Government. Mel got very excited over the Polk project, buying film rights to a book about the case before it had reached the shops, and persuading controversial Greek director Costa-Gavras to commit to the picture. He had won two Academy Awards for his no-punches-pulled political films *Z*, about the Greek Fascist Colonels, and *Missing*, set in El Salvador.

Other projects were said to include the role of a Sydney photographer who was the only cameraman to get on the island of Grenada when the Americans invaded in 1983.

And besides all this, reaction to *Hamlet* had been so favourable that Mel's asking price for a mainstream movie was now estimated to be $10 million. His investment in making that film for a very modest fee was already paying dividends.

Forever Young – in which Mel co-starred with Jamie Lee Curtis, Isabel Glasser and 12-year-old Elijah Wood – was hardly Mel's most dashing performance, although it did feature his naked rear running through a building protected only by a strategically placed child's jacket. That provoked countless newspaper articles speculating on just how much his nude bottom might add to the box-office takings, but little else. One journalist from the American magazine *Redbook* witnessed an embarrassing moment on the set of the movie when Mel forgot his lines and ended up being comforted by his schoolboy co-star.

The film's biggest publicity coup was to encourage journalists to run countless photo spreads on the efforts of *Forever Young*'s special effects department to age the handsome star from 37 to 80. Headlines like 'SEXY MEL TURNS CRINKLY WRINKLY!' summed up the impact of the movie on the public. And when *Forever Young* did reach the cinemas in late 1992, movie critics gave it a. lukewarm reception.

Box Office magazine in the US knocked it for 'dripping with the kind of gooey sentiment and melodrama at which Jane Austen would have smirked'. And Georgia Brown in the *Village Voice* dismissed the film as 'my candidate for the most inept movie of the year. The final scenes are absolute howlers. Most of the credit goes to the thoroughly absurd, charmless and fraudulent script by Abrams.'

277

Yet, as usual, Mel avoided any criticism of his role in the film. He could get away with being in a poor movie. It seemed as though his charm and charisma would always pull him through. One of the most memorable things about shooting the film for him was that he became unrecognisable after make-up artists had aged him 50 years, and could eat out in restaurants without anyone realising who he was. The bottom line on *Forever Young* was that its inoffensive plot and obligatory naked backside shot of Mel helped it soar above the critics and take in nearly $100 million around the world.

As one British housewife, Debbie Bettridge, from Taunton in Somerset, commented, 'I can honestly say that, apart from a rather far-fetched plot, this was very good, all-round family entertainment. There was no gratuitous sex or violence, just an innocent film for adults and children alike to enjoy, which makes a nice change.'

The film also gave Mel an opportunity to hold a Los Angeles première and raise some much-needed funds for two charities that both he and Bruce Davey had become involved with. Hollywood's Recovery Center is a drug and alcohol rehabilitation centre and Mel, presumably in a thinly-veiled reference to himself, admitted that it was a problem near to his own heart. 'Alcoholism is something that runs in my family. It's something that is close to me. People do come back from it, and it's a miracle, and I like to be part of that.'

The other charity that benefited from the première for *Forever Young* was Santa Monica's Homeless Drop-In Center, which boasts both Bruce Davey and one of Mel's lawyers, Nigel Sinclair, on its board of directors. In all, $70,000 was raised towards both charities.

In the middle of all this, Mel astonished *Forever Young* writer Jeffrey Abrams by inviting the young scribe to join him at the Glendale office of the California Department of Motor

Vehicles while he retook his driving test! It was an experience Abrams says he will never forget.

'When we arrived, Mel threw on a big cowboy hat and dark glasses and did an incredible thing – he turned off his charm,' recalled Abrams. 'His shoulders dropped a little and he became expressionless. The place was packed with all kinds of people. Many looked right at Mel and didn't even notice him.'

It turned out that the only reason Mel was having to retake his test was that he had blinked for his licence photo. Somehow, this was not the sort of thing one expected to happen to movie stars. He passed the test after driving his Mercedes around the test route with a charming examiner called Mona whose only concern at the end of the examination was whether Mel would be appearing naked in his next movie.

Warner Brothers at this time were carefully nurturing Mel, whom they considered their number-one star. After all, he had made the majority of his hit movies with them and there was the not inconsiderable matter of making sure the star was 'tied in' for *Lethal Weapon 3*. The next step was no surprise inside Hollywood; in February 1991, Mel's lawyers in Los Angeles finalised an astounding $42 million four-picture deal which would make him one of the most powerful – and richest – actors in the film industry. With his per-movie fee rising to $12 million for the last of the four pictures, it was seen in Tinseltown as 'one hell of a deal'. And there was also the promise of a lucrative deal which would give Mel a share of the profits from each film as well. The actor earned around $100 million from the package, and the studio had happily agreed to Mel's most important condition – that he get three months a year off to be with his wife and children. Thrown in is free first-class air travel for him and his family, plus assorted helpers so that they could join him at any time. A

Warner spokesman said, 'Money is not a problem – getting Mel Gibson is.'

Part and parcel of the deal was an agreement that Mel's company, Icon Productions, would develop and produce all four movies, with Mel being paid not only as an actor but also producer or executive producer. He was now a Hollywood player in his own right and considered one of the three most bankable stars in the world. His name on a picture ensures financial backing for any project and his name on a movie poster virtually guarantees takings of at least $50 million at the US box office alone.

'They'd give you money for Mel's film even if it was a screen version of the telephone directory,' said one Los Angeles casting director.

On the Warner lot, Icon was given a fine spread of offices. It must have seemed very opulent compared with their previous base in the Santa Monica apartment Mel had bought years earlier and taken some of his women friends to. Mel himself had a dark, somewhat regally appointed office on the Warner lot, decorated with personal memorabilia. *Lethal Weapon* and *Mad Max* posters took pride of place among a couple of swords, a model fighter plane, two cowboy hats and two top hats. His bookshelves displayed such unusual items as icons from south-eastern Europe and Sinai but, perhaps most significantly of all, there are absolutely no photos of Robyn and the children.

But despite the immense power Mel now wielded as an actor and producer, he still harboured unfulfilled ambitions as a director, and Mel was becoming more and more frustrated. There were increasing numbers of occasions when he felt he could do better than the director he had been working for. With this in mind, and still acutley aware of Kevin Costner's award-winning directorial début with *Dances with Wolves*, he instructed his executives at Icon to look out for a script that he could direct.

In 1991, he found what he considered the perfect début project – a modestly budgeted little movie called *The Man Without a Face*, in which Mel slated himself to direct and star as a badly scarred burns victim who befriends a lonely 12-year-old boy. Each of them draws from their relationship something that neither has had before – understanding and mutual trust. However, they are forced apart after townspeople develop suspicions about the man's past. It was adapted from a novel written 20 years earlier by Isabelle Holland and, in the original, intriguingly, Mel's part was originally supposed to be a gay character, but this was changed on his instruction.

According to cast and crew on the film, Mel achieved a good rapport with everyone. One actress, Fay Masterson, said, 'He just gets down to work without any fuss. He is simply wonderful.'

Piper Laurie – who had previously co-starred with Mel in *Tim*, 13 years earlier – was full of praise for him. And his schoolboy co-star Nick Stahl found that Mel's handling was much more 'normal' than the usual Hollywood treatment of child actors. Mel said, as always, that he enjoyed working with children. He is probably the only major Tinseltown star who really means what he says.

Ever-loyal Bruce Davey – partner, manager and the movie's producer, as well as Mel's one-time drinking companion – reported, 'He seems to have been doing this all his life. He's taken to it like a duck to water.'

Cynics on the set say they never heard Davey voice anything other than glowing tributes to Mel. But then, he did pluck the accountant out of a grey little office in downtown Sydney and turn him into one of the most powerful producers in Hollywood.

It took Mel himself to admit that directing was not easy. 'It was more difficult than I thought it would be. It's a lot more involved, especially if you are directing yourself. If I was going to direct another film, I would not be in it. It drove me crazy because it was too much to do. I had to wear too many hats.'

During an interview on Australian television's *A Current Affair*, the actor was even more candid. 'Sometimes, you wake up in the morning and don't know what the hell you are going to do. I was very lucky to have good people around me. They saved my backside more than once.'

Mel even insisted he had tried to find another actor to play the lead role, to allow him to concentrate on directing. But after three stars had turned him down, he reluctantly agreed to act as well as helm the picture.

Some of the other actors in the $12 million film guessed that Mel hid his innermost fears by behaving the only way he knew how – cracking jokes and making bizarre proclamations. Eventually, he earned a new nickname, 'Demento Boy', although everyone agreed that it made a real change to work for a director who joked half the time instead of being extremely bad-tempered, traditional dictator-director behaviour in Hollywood.

He had Robyn and the children with him for much of the film's ten-week shoot in and around the tiny town of Camden, Maine, and then the seaside community of Bayside. Having been off the bottle for at least 18 months, Mel behaved impeccably in local taverns where he became known as the 'Cappuccino Kid' because he stuck to coffee. When Mel's family travelled back to California shortly before the end of the shoot, Mel attended an AA meeting in the basement of a community centre where he was filming. In the presence of 35 people at the Rockland Community Center, Mel introduced himself in the traditional AA way – 'Hi, my name is Mel. and I'm an alcoholic.' Afterwards, he shot a few rounds of pool with other AA members before departing for his rented house nearby.

After completion of filming, Mel retreated to France with Robyn and the children to begin editing *The Man Without a Face*. Post-production was one area of which Mel had little experience; the success of a film could depend just as much on the editing as the actual direction. Rumours that Mel had yet again given up smoking (this time after he played tennis with Hutton Gibson and discovered, to his horror, that his 73-year-old father was fitter than him) seem unlikely, especially because he was about to begin spending 18 hours a day confined to an editing suite. He told American chat show host Jay Leno he had 'quit the weed' but he was soon back on it.

Having completed editing of *The Man Without a Face*, Mel told one associate, 'I'm not going to hang myself. I don't want to commit myself to say it's a masterpiece but ...' When the film was released in the US in August 1993, the critics seemed to agree. The *LA Times* wrote, 'It is a quality, intelligent production – a moving and substantial achievement.'

Mel's other quest was to make a Western. It had been fuelled not only by the success of Kevin Costner's *Dances with Wolves*, but also Clint Eastwood's Oscar sweep in 1993 with *Unforgiven*. He was absolutely convinced that a Wild West picture could work for him as well. His interest had been well noted, and agents were flooding the offices of Icon Productions with Western scripts and movie treatments, following the $100-million-plus takings of *Dances* and *Unforgiven*. But Mel was nothing if not careful. He surprised Tinseltown by spurning one very high-profile Western project, *Bitter Root*, due to be directed by respected helmsman John McTiernan. Sources say that Mel did not like the political content of the script, which was centred around a bloody battle between the US Government and the Indians in 1877.

Eastwood's success with *Unforgiven* helped give Mel the green light for a pet project based on the hit television series of the late Fifties and early Sixties *Maverick*. At first, it seemed a strange choice, as the TV series had been a notoriously badly produced mishmash.

Mel had quietly and carefully assembled a talented back-up team to get the film off the ground. In 1992, Icon commissioned veteran screenwriter William Goldman to pen a screenplay based on the TV show. As originator of *Butch Cassidy and the Sundance Kid*, starring Paul Newman and Robert Redford more than 20 years earlier, Mel saw Goldman as the perfect man to knock the project into shape. But there was also another, more personal reason behind his decision to get the famous screenwriter on board. Goldman had written *Adventures in the Screen Trade* – the book that Mel says helped him recover his sanity when he was on the verge of a classic Hollywood nervous breakdown a few years earlier.

Goldman delivered his script in early 1993 and Mel and his partner Bruce Davey set about persuading a top director to helm the project. They did not have to look far; *Lethal Weapon* director Richard Donner could see potential in the project even before he read the screenplay and, in any case, the two men had formed a mutual admiration society during the filming of the three *Lethal Weapon*s.

Warners were pleased that Donner and Mel were proposing to join forces once more and immediately gave the project the go-ahead. They saw *Maverick* as *Lethal Weapon* meets *The Wild Bunch*. As one studio executive confessed, 'This is really *Lethal Weapon 4* on horseback, without Danny Glover. We are delighted.'

Mel was attracted to the role of the charming, roguish cowboy and gambler Bret Maverick – it was not that far removed from *Lethal Weapon*'s Marty Riggs. Touchingly, he also insisted that Warners sign up the TV series' original star, James Garner, for a supporting role. Then Jodie Foster came on board and the 'package' was complete.

But it was the hiring of Linda Hunt for a smaller part in *Maverick* that really delighted Mel. He had never forgotten the pint-sized actress who had given that Oscar-winning performance as a man in *The Year of Living Dangerously*. 'Mel was just pleased as punch to get Linda on board,' said one insider.

Insiders on location with the movie in Arizona said that Mel spent much of his time playing cards in his caravan with co-star James Garner. But their off-screen friendship is fast forgotten in front of the cameras, because Garner plays a mean-spirited type who tries to steal Jodie Foster's love from Mel.

Maverick took well over $100 million at the US box office alone in the summer of 1994. It was simultaneously released in Europe in a bid to double that figure outside the lucrative American movie market.

Interestingly, little has been made of the pairing of Oscar winner Jodie Foster with Mel. According to one source on the set of *Maverick*, 'they both kept a friendly distance ...' when not actually in front of the cameras. Another member of the crew explained at the time, 'Jodie and Mel are like chalk and cheese. He likes nothing more than a chat and a joke with the crew while Jodie hardly speaks to a soul.'

Mel also found it difficult to resist interfering in the director's job after his experience helming *Man Without a Face*. 'I had to go into a self-imposed exile. Even when I was screaming to suggest something, I wouldn't do it. Dick [Donner] has been at it so much longer than a nasty little upstart bastard like me.'

Other projects that Mel was interested in around that time included the tragic life story of The Who's drummer Keith Moon. Whether Mel intended to play the lead role himself was uncertain. And then there was the long-running saga of another movie adaptation of a Sixties television series, *The Avengers*. Mel was rumoured to be keen to play the part of John Steed, made famous by British actor Patrick Macnee. In the end, that role went to Ralph Fiennes.

Another rumour concerned a role for Mel alongside the late Marlon Brando in an epic feature project being prepared by *Lawrence of Arabia* director David Lean. Eventually, the project – written by Oscar-winning screenwriter Robert Bolt (who wrote *The Bounty*) – was shelved when Lean died. Then there was *Hiroshima Joe*, which was attached to British director Tony Scott, who'd made *Top Gun*. But again, initial discussions fizzled out and the project was shelved. There was even talk of Mel making the perfect Rhett Butler for the sequel to *Gone with the Wind*, but that was nothing more than an entertaining piece of gossip.

But the one rumoured project that really angered Mel was when that old familiar story about him playing James Bond resurfaced during the 1992 Cannes Film Festival. This time, news that the *Lethal Weapon* producer Joel Silver was discussing a co-production deal with 007 mogul Albert 'Cubby' Broccoli fuelled the fire. Hollywood sources were claiming that Silver planned to sign Mel to the role in order to rekindle the once-popular series of spy movies. But Mel turned down any suggestion of him playing Bond, without even considering a script.

In the spring of 1994, Mel managed to get his second film as a director green-lighted. *Braveheart* was, according to many Hollywood experts, either going to be an enormous success or an almighty flop.

For Mel, it was a project he could not resist. *Braveheart* is the story of fiery Scot William Wallace, who fought bloody battles against the English in 1270. With his thinly disguised dislike for the English and his growing obsession with winning an Oscar, Mel was said to be 'ecstatic' to be doing the film.

'This is Mel's attempt to emulate *Dances with Wolves*,' said one member of his production team at Icon. But, with a $40 million budget and a series of difficult locations in the Scottish Highlands, *Braveheart* promised to be a very stressful experience for all concerned. 'If Mel gets this one right and it makes a fortune at the box office, then he will be in a position to direct anything he wants,' added an Icon source.

Meanwhile, Mel had continued his secretive trips to Alcoholics Anonymous in Malibu throughout the previous 18 months and, by all accounts, he steered clear of booze completely. However, he was still capable of flaring up when the glare of the public spotlight became intrusive. During a low-key trip to New York City in early 1993, the actor's bodyguard assaulted local photographer James Edstrom when he tried to snap a photo of Mel outside the Tatou nightclub. Sources inside the club say that Mel was drinking Evian water throughout his two-hour visit and he was unaccompanied. But Edstrom believes that the actor's bodyguard reacted against him because he 'did not want anyone to know he was in New York'.

During the incident, Edstrom says the actor turned to his bodyguard and said, 'You know what to do.' The bodyguard then allegedly punched Edstrom, stomped on his foot and sent his camera crashing to the ground.

Edstrom intended to serve a writ on Mel as soon as he could track him down and he insists he did nothing to provoke the attack.

Ironically, a few weeks later, Mel was photographed in London stepping out of a limousine exposing what looked suspiciously like a bald patch on top of his head. One New York hairdresser who has cut Mel's hair in the past revealed that Mel is 'very concerned about losing his hair'.

But his fears have little to do with vanity. 'He could not stand the thought of being made to wear one of those ridiculous toupées.' And the star has dismissed claims that he wants to be forever young as mere gossip.

In February of 1993, Mel had the satisfaction of hearing that he was the second-biggest earner in Hollywood after Tom Cruise. Edging rival Kevin Costner into third place was a major breakthrough for Mel. In Australia, the actor made the 1992 list as one of the country's richest residents with a fortune estimated to be in the region of $37.5 million.

But he was more concerned with the plight of sick and needy children. In early 1992, he began secretly visiting sick youngsters in hospitals in Los Angeles. Mel agreed to the voluntary work after being contacted by soap star Emma Samms, who runs the Starlight Foundation which makes dreams come true for sick children. At first, he was reluctant to get involved as he believed that people would publicise his hospital visits and that would simply cause inconvenience for all concerned and do little to help the children. He was also particularly sensitive to accusations that he was using the visits to gain some positive publicity.

After a pledge from Samms that his involvement in the foundation would be kept secret, Mel started making visits to the Los Angeles Children's Hospital. At the bedside of leukaemia victim Adrianna Cervantes, he appeared like a guardian angel and sat and talked with the eight-year-old, even agreeing to pose for a snapshot for her family alongside the airtight bubble in which the youngster is forced to spend her entire time.

Then the star moved on to visit other children on the ward, including one terminally ill teenager, who told Mel he was a big Rod Stewart fan.

'He was obviously shocked by the children's condition but he didn't show it to any of them,' said one nurse.

The moment Mel got home to Malibu that evening, he called Rod Stewart at his London home and told him about the boy. Stewart followed up Mel's call by sending an autographed soccer ball and a written promise that he would visit when he got back to Los Angeles. Ever since, Mel has continued visiting children in that hospital.

TWENTY-ONE

'THE HEIGHTS ATTAINED BY GREAT MEN REACHED AND
KEPT WERE NOT ATTAINED BY SUDDEN FLIGHT, BUT
THEY, WHILE THEIR COMPANIONS SLEPT, WERE TOLLING
UPWARD IN THE NIGHT.' THE LADDER OF ST AUGUSTINE,
HENRY WADSWORTH LONGFELLOW (1858)

The relentless drizzle seemed almost horizontal, dark clouds rolled overhead altering the light from minute to minute and, when the weather finally cleared for a while, midges bit anything that moved.

'CUT!' screamed Mel for the umpteenth time on that grey and miserable afternoon by the remote Scottish mountain.

His toughest directorial test to date, *Braveheart,* was proving an exhausting process. One minute he was charging on horseback towards masses of extras, the next he was behind the camera checking to see how the shot had come out. As star and helmsman of *Braveheart*, there were many moments during the shooting of this epic movie when Mel wondered if he had taken on a challenge which might end in disaster. The conditions during the gruelling six-month shoot in Scotland and Ireland were nightmarish for any kind of film, let alone a movie epic on a similar scale as the classic *Ben-Hur.*

In the summer of 1994, visitors to Glen Nevis, near Fort William in Scotland, reported that Mel appeared tense, angry, overworked and completely exhausted. Any suggestions that the movie might scoop a bucketful of Oscars were met with disdain by cast and crew. They were just trying to survive the shoot. Nothing else mattered.

The dice seemed loaded against *Braveheart*. At $40 million, it was an expensive movie for a second-time director, and it featured a name that was obscure to non-Scottish audiences – the 13th-century rebel hero William Wallace. Mel had somehow convinced Paramount that *Braveheart* could work at three hours in length, with a script containing spectacular and gory battle scenes, an invented love affair between Mel as Wallace and actress Sophie Marceau as the French princess Isabelle, and a finale showing the hero being hanged, drawn and quartered.

The script had been a huge problem for Mel and his team of writers. To make matters worse, those who read it immediately compared it with *Rob Roy*, another Scottish rebel movie being shot simultaneously. *Rob Roy* was pronounced as being more concise, literate and historically accurate. *Braveheart*'s main writer, American Randall Wallace (no relation), had television credits but had never scripted a produced feature film before. Yet more reason, said the Hollywood grapevine, why the movie would end in disaster.

Mel was very nervous even before *Braveheart* went into production. He had been fretting over the script for almost a year. He admitted, 'It's not there yet ... the execution could have been better. We sat for months and worked on it – knocked the dents out, patched up a few holes.'

But Mel was convinced that the success of *Braveheart* hinged on its entertainment value rather than historical accuracy. He intended to trim the film and move all the pivotal scenes around until it flowed in true Hollywood adventure-story style.

In the end, he found himself defending a string of accusations about inaccuracy. At times, Mel became defensive about his 'baby'. 'This movie falls somewhere between fact and legend. But there's some basic truth in it,' he insisted to anyone who would listen.

Mel knew perfectly well that, if *Braveheart* was a success, then no one would care about the historical inaccuracies. But success was by no means guaranteed.

Then there were the location problems that haunted *Braveheart* from the moment it started shooting. Mel dearly wanted to film the movie's two epic battle scenes in Scotland but they couldn't find the right locations. In the end, cast and crew decamped to Ireland, where the Government provided army-reserve volunteers as extras. They also promised Paramount some useful tax concessions in exchange for filming in Ireland.

Shooting in Scotland and Ireland was gruelling, with constant rain turning the set into a sea of mud and causing major hold-ups in the film shooting schedule. It was also freezing cold and Mel found himself moving from one damp miserable castle to another together with at least 1,500 extras – many from the Irish Army – in tow.

But Mel wasn't hanging around to suffer for his art. He might have wanted the battle scenes to be the most graphic ever shot but, as he later stressed, 'We didn't linger. We established what was happening and then moved on.' Mel even discovered an editing trick that helped increase the apparent amount of violence in Braveheart. He explained to writer Paolo Black, 'Shall I tell you a little trick? For instance, at the point at which my fist hits your face [he raises his fist to Black's face], you go back just two frames, and you take those two frames out. [There are 24 frames per second of film.] And then – Whack! [He slaps his own face, and his head snaps back]. You put in the sound-effects, and it's incredible the difference those two frames make. The computers we use for editing are fantastic.'

As one member of the crew recalled, '*Braveheart* was organised chaos from start to finish. The weather was appalling and the accommodation was pretty awful, but throughout the shoot cast and crew worked together, ate together and socialised together, which is very unusual on a big Hollywood movie.'

During the making of *Braveheart*, macho Mel discovered the wonders of a ladies' moisturiser called Skin So Soft, by Avon. Mel ordered several cases of the £4.49 moisturiser after hearing that its Woodland Fresh fragrance could ward off repeated attacks by swarms of Highland midges. He'd already tried most insect repellents and found them completely ineffective. But Woodland Fresh Skin So Soft successfully repelled wave upon wave of attack.

The key to this stability was Mel. In the past, he had always got on as well with movie technicians as actors, and during *Braveheart* he managed to make everyone feel as though they were part of the team. But, most significantly, he knew that by shooting *Braveheart* so far from California he could avoid the constant interference of studio executives. In other words, he was on his own – and he much preferred it that way.

By the time Mel had finished shooting and then editing *Braveheart*, he swore he'd take a year off to be with Robyn and the children. He reckoned that the project had proved more costly to his health than filming three *Lethal Weapon*s back to back!

There were more problems to come – Paramount released the film in the United States in May 1995, too early for it to stay fresh in the minds of the Academy of Motion Pictures voters, who would be deciding that year's Oscars. However, *Braveheart* took off on its own and achieved something virtually unheard of in Hollywood movie history. American critics, viewing it with low expectations, bestowed begrudging praise on *Braveheart*, and conceded that somehow Mel had wrought indefinable movie magic. Audiences responded to what Mel called 'the insanely heroic' aspects of the story, word of mouth spread and the movie remained in America's cinemas all summer.

Paramount eventually woke up to the fact that they had a surefire hit on their hands, relaunched the movie in September 1995, and spent a fortune – $16 million in the United States alone – on marketing. This was more than was spent on any film in the whole of 1995, except for Disney's *Toy Story*. But it paid off handsomely: *Braveheart* grossed more than $40 million in America and over $70 million at box offices elsewhere in the world. To Mel, the film's success was doubly sweet because he had, in effect, put his own career on the line by agreeing to undertake the project.

In January 1996, Hollywood was stunned when *Braveheart* received ten Oscar nominations. This proved to be a signal to Paramount to relaunch the movie for a second time, and to conduct an especially vigorous campaign to woo Academy voters to back *Braveheart*.

Behind the scenes, Mel recognised that his movie had a great chance of Oscar success and he started lobbying his own friends inside the industry to devastating effect. Discreet dinners were organised at some of LA's finest eateries and Mel hit the phones in the crucial last few weeks before Oscar time in March 1996.

The previous September, Mel had moved back to his vast home in the hills above Malibu beach after promising Robyn that he would only consider movies to be shot in the LA area following his one year away on *Braveheart*. It meant that, for the first time in his career, he had a chance to do some 'meeting and greeting' rather than movie-making. He relished it.

The coaxing and cajoling worked like a dream. The Academy voters, conservative as ever, opted for an old-fashioned, swashbuckling movie with a charismatic Hollywood star. Of the other Best Picture nominations, only *Apollo 13* came into this category. *Sense and Sensibility* was considered too English. *Il Postino* and *Babe* were too off-beat.

Mel insisted all along that his aspirations for *Braveheart* were modest. 'Producing and directing offer satisfaction, but you can't just grab it right away. You must establish a credit rating. We're getting there.'

Braveheart scooped Oscars for Best Picture, Best Director, Cinematography, Special Effects, Editing and Make-Up. It was clear that Mel was well on his way.

And typically, Mel found a just cause to toast when he hopped and skipped on to the Oscar podium to accept the Best Film award minutes after getting the statue for the Best Director. 'We could not have done it without you,' yelled Mel, thanking his cast of thousands provided by the part-time soldiers of the Irish Reserve Army. He had not forgotten the unnamed heroes. Those warrior extras earned just $300 a week for 14-hour days, and many were injured by the violently realistic battle scenes.

Mel even managed to crack a joke when asked what he was planning to do with his Oscar statues. 'I'm just going to carry them around for a while – for a few days, months maybe, until I figure it out.'

On a more serious note, Mel commented on the reasons behind *Braveheart*'s phenomenal success. 'I can only presume that they [the Academy voters] saw in the story what I saw in it – it's one that sort of touched me in a deep spot. And I also found it very compelling visually at the same time. I loved the material. I guess they responded to it the same way that I did.'

When asked at the Oscars about Australian-made *Babe*, one of the chief rivals to *Braveheart*, Mel quipped, 'Hey, that film did all right at the box office. It brought home the bacon.'

Following Mel's impressive victory in the Oscars, Australian writer Paolo Black wrote an insightful article about how he'd presented Mel with an acting award for *Mad Max* at the Whisky-a-Go-Go nightclub in Sydney's King's Cross back in the early 1980s. There, girls had glistened in silver stilettos, G-strings and gyrated in cages that swung above the dance floor.

Sixteen years later, when Mel met the same writer in New York, he claimed he couldn't even remember receiving that award. Talking about how he stumbled upon the *Braveheart* script in the first place, Mel recalled to Black how he had teams of readers who looked at hundreds of scripts each week and that *Braveheart* came recommended. Although, at first, Mel had read it and rejected it.

Mel explained, 'But it wouldn't go away. I kept thinking about it. I'd be working on another project, and – Wham! – ideas from *Braveheart* would creep into my head, and I'd think, Yeah, I could do that.' And so, a year after rejecting it, he got it the green light.

Just before Mel's Oscar success with *Braveheart*, he accepted an offer from respected *Apollo 13* director Ron Howard to star in *Ransom*, a hard-hitting thriller about a wealthy businessman whose son is kidnapped. His co-star was to be Rene Russo, who had starred with Mel and Danny Glover in *Lethal Weapon 3*.

For Mel, it was quite a relief to be simply starring in a blockbuster following the stresses and strains of his multiple role in *Braveheart*. Ironically, his $20 million fee was four times more than that which he had accepted for *Braveheart* just 18 months earlier.

While making *Ransom*, Mel worked regular hours on locations and sets in the US, and during the studio work in LA he got home most evenings in time to help put the kids to bed. But that didn't stop the shoot from having some serious problems.

The filming of *Ransom* was disrupted when Mel developed acute appendicitis on a flight from LA to New York just two weeks before the Oscar ceremony at which *Braveheart* scooped so many awards. He had an emergency operation, but declared himself fit just a few days after leaving hospital.

Mel's illness marked the end of a long, bleak stretch during the winter of 1995–96 during which little seemed to be going right on the set of *Ransom*. The worst blizzards in decades had turned the Big Apple into the Big Slushball and, in the middle of all this, co-star Rene Russo seemed to be having problems.

However hard she worked, some on the set felt she could not adequately convey the levels of maternal pain and fear expected from the mother of a kidnapped child. To make matters worse, Mel was making it all look easy. As an entrepreneur – and Russo's husband – Mel had to project the same anguish and dread. But he was still managing to crack jokes and get the whole set laughing between takes.

Seeing her intensity, Mel took Russo aside. 'I used to do that,' he said, referring to the torture she was putting herself through. 'But I stopped. You've got to go on the set with nothing, and when the director says "Action!" just go there.'

Russo listened to Mel's speech, turned to him and said, 'I don't know what you're talking about.' But then she walked back on to the set and gave the performance of a lifetime.

After a three-month break, Mel signed for another action-packed movie called *Conspiracy Theory* with his old friend *Lethal Weapon* and *Maverick* director Richard Donner, co-starring Julia Roberts. To many inside Hollywood, the pairing of hard-hitting, plain-speaking Mel and the sensitive Ms Roberts seemed a potential minefield. On the first day of filming, Mel sent an assistant to welcome Roberts with a gift-wrapped box done up in pretty bows. As the actress walked to her dressing room, she eagerly tore the present open to find ... a freeze-dried rat. Explained director Richard Dormer, 'We got a shriek that brought security and two cops running!'

Later, Julia Roberts got her revenge by stretching see-through cling film over the bowl of his dressing room toilet. Fifteen minutes later, Mel got a soaking when he went to have a wee. Crew members later said they heard Mel laughing his head off and then burst into a chorus of 'Singing in the Rain'.

As filming progressed on *Conspiracy Theory*, Mel and Julia Roberts developed a begrudging respect for each other, 'but it was clear they came from two completely different schools of life,' observed one crew member.

Meanwhile, *Ransom* was released in the United States in November 1996, and predictably pulled in a vast opening weekend at the box office. It was heading for $100 million-plus in takings in America alone.

Ransom received an enthusiastic response from audiences who adored the movie's heartbreaking premise, although some critics insisted that it was too much of a formula-flick. But Mel didn't really care about the criticism. He had already made his point with devastating effect through the success of *Braveheart*. His biggest problem in life was to make sure that his family grew up safe, secure and untainted by the Hollywood lifestyle from which there now seemed to be no escape. Mel was painfully aware of the problems of bringing up children in Los Angeles.

Ransom opened at number one at the North American box office and was heading in the right direction to be one of the year's highest-grossing films. The movie was based around the predicament of a wealthy airline owner whose ten-year-old son is kidnapped and held for a $2 million ransom. The twist in the tale was that Mel's character Tom became convinced the kidnappers would murder his son as soon as the money was handed over. 'I liked the whole equation of the film,' explained Mel, 'And that my character wants to go against the advice of the police and the FBI. He knows he couldn't live with himself if he paid the ransom and his son died, and he's aware of the terrible guilt he'd suffer if he went ahead and tried to do it his way, and the kidnappers murder his son anyway.'

Mel reckoned that *Ransom* was one of the most complex psychological films he'd ever made, and he enjoyed the suspense element that kept the audience and his character on a knife-edge throughout.

One of Mel's main motivations in taking the role in *Ransom* was a chance to work with Ron Howard, the former *Happy Days* star, who had carved out an impressive career as a director, making movies such as *Splash*, *Cocoon*, *Backdraft* and *Apollo 13*. But *Ransom* turned out to be a tough shoot with the set plagued by the worst winter to hit New York in 20 years and the script needing several re-writes during filming, causing the production to run more than a month behind schedule.

Shortly after completing the filming of *Ransom*, Mel secretly bought a 27-room Tudor-style mansion set on 31 hectares near Greenwich, Connecticut, for $9.25 million. He installed a security fence which, to the consternation of the local horse enthusiasts, cut off access to several riding trails.

He then spent more than $800,000 remodelling the kitchen, adding a screening room and other improvements. The stone and timber house is 'absolutely stupendous' according to a local real estate agent.

Mel was still striving to live the perfect life and he genuinely believed that, as long as he and his family remained a tight, happy unit, they would get there in the end.

But then, from Mel, little is predictable. Despite an army of advisers urging him to star in more multimillion-dollar movies for vast fees, he still remains quite capable of one day turning around and walking away from Hollywood. He has certainly considered it in the past. Mel has frequently referred to his cattle farm in Australia as his 'back-up plan'. There are also the children to consider. Various stages of school and college are still a consideration, and Mel wants to keep his pledge not to leave the family for long periods of time.

The notion of Mel eventually retiring is not so far-fetched. He has always (despite the occasional diversion) remained steadfastly committed to family life. He has even hinted that he would be perfectly happy if Robyn had another six children by him. And he has never hidden the fact that he considers the film industry as a job of work and nothing more. Only time would tell.

TWENTY-TWO

OH YEAH, YOU BET MONEY'S IMPORTANT – I NEED
SOMETHING TO PAPER THE WALLS WITH AND MONEY
MAKES ME LAUGH. SOMETIMES I JUST SIT THERE AND
LAUGH ... ROLL AROUND IN IT, COUNT IT.

In early 1997, Mel was staying at the family's Sydney beachside mansion when a female fan forced her way into his home. In a scene straight out of one of Mel's own movies, the woman dragged herself through a fierce storm, climbed up a hazardous beach to Mel's front door and then calmly let herself in. Mel later christened her 'Loopy Lipstick', saying, 'There was an electric thunderstorm going on and I was at the house with a few friends. We'd turned out the lights and opened a few beers as we watched the lightning streak across the sky. Suddenly, the lightning illuminated this wet figure outside. There was no way she could have got to where she was without climbing up the beach and across the spiky grass. She walked over to the unlocked door and walked right in. So we switched on the lights and she said, "Oh, hi!"

'She was from Canada and she was drenched by the rain. She wasn't wearing any shoes and refused to leave when she was asked. She absolutely refused. I said to my friend, "Be nice to her and escort her outside," which he did. I went to the back of the house and the windows were closed and I looked out and she was staring right through.

'She scared the shit out of me! It was like a horror movie or something. I shouted, "Go home," and went upstairs to bed. But she climbed up the wall and ended up balancing herself on the roof.' The woman eventually disappeared before the local police showed up but she'd left weird messages sprawled across the windows in lipstick.

But Loopy Lipstick wasn't the only close encounter for Mel around this time. When in Florida filming – also in 1997 – Mel answered his hotel room to a girl who begged him to let her give him a massage. He recalled, 'She literally jumped on top of me and I was shouting, "Get off me!" The guards had to drag her downstairs and she was really undignified about the whole thing. I found it all really embarrassing, really for her more than me.'

Also in 1997, Mel bought up a British film distributor called Majestic Films from the Italian entertainment conglomerate RCS Films. There was also talk of Mel making a follow-up to *Braveheart* starring Arnold Schwarzenegger as a mad half-German duke who slaughtered more than 9,000 Scots in 40 minutes in the Jacobite rebellion of 1745.

And throughout all this, Mel continued to hide all his everyday insecurities behind the façade of acting. He explained, 'All my insecurities as a person are completely healed by acting. I view my characters as separate entities. You use yourself in everything you do, but at the same time you've got to have a very clear idea of another person. Otherwise, I don't see how you can hand yourself over to the role. Every part has to have its own life. It isn't just me wiping myself across the screen.'

Still, Mel hadn't starred in one single romantic love story. Did he care? 'Those films don't appeal to me,' he explained. 'I'm not comfortable acting that way. I'm not interested in projecting that side of myself on film. I like exploring different kinds of stories and maybe a love story is too easy, too insignificant for me ... I don't feel pushed by something like that.'

Joel Silver, producer of *Conspiracy Theory*, summed up Mel's Hollywood status in September 1997 when he said, '$20 million for Mel is fine by me. If that's what it takes to get Mel, then I'm totally OK with that. He's the greatest partner you could ever wish to have in your life – he's no trouble, he's smart, he's capable, he sees the big picture and he gets your jokes. Mel is your dream movie star. And that's not bullshit.'

But Mel, for all his tens of millions, hadn't changed much. He was still chain-smoking Marlboro reds (not Lights) and still feeling a tad self-conscious off set. Sometimes, it seemed as if those sparkling blue eyes were all that really shone. However, on the publicity train for *Conspiracy Theory*, Mel was happy to play the game like a true professional. 'Do I believe in conspiracy theories?' He asked reporters. 'Yes, I do, and they scare the shit out of me.'

In *Conspiracy Theory*, Mel played a paranoid New York taxi driver who was obsessed with such theories. He read sinister undertones into every event and tried to get a wholesome Justice department lawyer, played by Julia Roberts, to believe him. Many in Hollywood were surprised that Mel had gone back to such a mainstream, traditional blockbuster after his highly acclaimed, Oscar-winning acting and directing success with *Braveheart*. Mel's reply was, 'Well, Hollywood is full of conspiracies, but everyone there is a willing participant. There's more backstabbing and cross purposes going on than they had in the Roman senate. It's a game – even war games – and it can be the most dangerous place on the planet.'

But the dynamics behind Mel's working relationship with Julia Roberts weren't just summed up by that dead rat joke. 'You know, she's really very nice,' said Mel. 'She's witty, smart, and she's fantastic to work with. You just watch her from close up and she conveying truckloads of information with the bat of an eyelid. She's the queen of the subtext. We worked well together.'

As Mel's director Richard Donner pointed out, 'The only thing that's changed about Mel in 13 years is that he has a little bit of grey hair. He's a little more secure and happier. But basically, he's just Mel. He's the guy you really want to hang out with. He's a friend, he's a confidant. He's a really special human being.'

In late 1997, Mel made a point of telling the world how wife Robyn had helped saved him from a nervous breakdown when his heavy workload and intake of alcohol threatened his health back in the late '80s and early '90s. Mel explained, 'I felt I was in hell. I hated work and felt lost. I had been driving myself crazy worrying about who I was and what I was doing. Robyn ordered me to take a year off to recharge my batteries ... Robyn made me realise what I was doing to myself and my family and life became easier. Now I laugh about what an idiot I was. Maybe it's a question of getting saner with the years.'

But Mel wasn't that calm. He stormed out of an MTV movie awards ceremony after being allegedly insulted by a wacky comedienne called Janeane Garofalo who was interviewing him on stage at the Disney Studios in Los Angeles. Fellow prize presenter Jamie Lee Curtis told the audience, 'Mel is Australian and I guess they don't do so well under pressure.' Garofalo, 31, explained, 'I feel responsible. I asked Mel questions about me and since he's never met me before he didn't know what to do. It wasn't funny. I'll be up all night worrying about it.'

Meanwhile, Mel was being linked to numerous new movie projects, including a £75 million film about Edwardian explorer Sir Ernest Shackleton, as well as a remake of the wartime classic *The Dam Busters*.

Macho Mel was also forced to meet the Hollywood gay community after being accused of being homophobic following some of those earlier, controversial public statements and specific scenes in some of his recent movies. Mel eventually met with delegates from the Gay and Lesbian Alliance Against Defamation, led by Cher's daughter Chastity Bono. 'I've been chased by automobiles doing dangerous things on motorways. It has made me totally paranoid,' Mel told one reporter. Another reason Mel 'towed the line' could have been a genuine fear that talented gay members of the movie industry might start refusing to work with Mel unless he 'clarified the situation'.

As one Hollywood insider claimed at the time, 'Hollywood is in the grip of a powerful gay Mafia. They wield a tremendous amount of influence in this town. To be perceived as a gay-hater can be a career-breaker. Mel was forced to listen by their complaints. He feels that there has been a massive over-reaction, but the time had come to straighten out a few issues.'

One scene in *Braveheart* in which Edward I killed one of his son's male lovers by throwing him off the castle ramparts was continually highlighted by the gay protestors. When Mel had initially been confronted by gays over the criticism, he'd exploded, 'I'll apologise when hell freezes over. They can fuck off!'

Protestors had even picketed cinemas across the United

States branding the *Braveheart* scene as a 'typical homophobic caricature'. Other alleged examples included Mel changing a homosexual character in the book of *A Man Without a Face* into a straight one for the film; earlier remarks about how he could be construed as being gay himself, because he didn't look or talk 'like them'; and Mel's demeaning characterisation of a hairdresser in the 1990 film *Bird on a Wire*.

One newspaper gossip columnist waded into Mel by writing, 'It's awful to find out that mentally he lives in the Dark Ages.'

In the summer of 1997, Mel made an audacious attempt to hire Princess Diana's butler Paul Burrell. Mel had first heard about Burrell's skills when he was in Britain filming *Braveheart*. The 37-year-old, who later hit numerous headlines after Diana's death, told one reporter, 'I've no intention of leaving the princess. It's ludicrous even to think that. I am loyal and thoroughly enjoying working for her. I'm happier than I have ever been.'

As part of his publicity work for *Conspiracy Theory*, Mel agreed to let British-based Aussie presenter Clive James follow him around Hollywood for ten days. In reality, this 'unparalleled access' meant Mel could get in as many plugs for his new movie as possible. London *Evening Standard* writer Geoffrey Phillips described it thus: 'As soon as he meets his new buddy, Gibson switches on his smile and does not turn it off for the duration.' Even when Clive insists on fondling Braveheart's mighty broadsword. Then it was off to the gym with Mel to watch him doing abdominal exercises and pelvic thrusts. Mel even admitted to James that he didn't often go to gyms.

Mel then took James for a short stroll around a Hollywood studio where they 'bumped into' George Clooney before heading off for his smoking club in Beverley Hills. In a room as secure as Fort Knox, Mel and other stars keep their prized cigars in humidors. Writer Phillips observed: 'Clive then politely selects something small from the cigar hoard but Mel's taste runs to the hand-rolled Zeppelin. As he puffs away, even his manly jaw seems to be challenged by its weight and girth. Maybe this is how Mel works out his smile-muscles.'

In 1998 came Mel's rather dark starring role in *Payback*, a loose adaptation of Donald Westlake's classic crime novel *The Hunter*, which was filmed as *Point Blank* by British director John Boorman back in 1967. Mel played Porter, a heist specialist intent on reclaiming $70,000 from the local mob, and he chain-smoked his way through double-crosses with a twisted grin on his face, cracking jokes like he cracks heads. It was a refreshingly cynical, occasionally brutal role which seemed to counterbalance perfectly the slightly po-faced *Ransom* and the glum *Conspiracy Theory*.

Mel and the studio backing *Payback* – Warners – had to part company with first-time director Brian Helgeland before the film was released because he refused to reshoot parts of it to make Mel's character Porter more likeable. Mel explained, 'He was not fired. Changes needed to be made, the studio wanted them, I wanted them and we asked Brian if he would make them. He opted not to, because he felt it compromised his artistic principles. And that's fine. If that's where he's at, that's where he's at. I happen to disagree and, as a responsible producer, I felt I had to step in and make the necessary changes to make the film work. He left his name on it, it was fairly amicable, it wasn't a screaming ego thing.

'It's bad because it makes Brian look bad and it makes me look bad. And that's not the case. I take care of people who work for me.'

Mel was even sensitive enough not to direct the reshot *Payback* scenes himself. 'I thought that would be like an insult to Brian,' explained Mel, who hired his former hairdresser Paul Abascol instead. 'He's through playing with people's locks,' added Mel, without a hint of irony.

Mel's power in Hollywood was now indisputable.

TWENTY-THREE

WHENEVER I'M TEMPTED TO GO BACK TO MY DRINKING
DAYS, I KNOW I CAN TURN TO ROBYN. ONE LOOK AT
HER AND I KNOW IT'S NOT WORTH IT.

The success of the *Lethal Weapon* series meant a fourth
and final episode was inevitable and, in 1998, Mel
teamed up with director Richard Donner and co-star Danny
Glover for 'one last shot at it'. Mel and Glover had spent
some time together socially since the last *Lethal Weapon*
movie. Mel explained, 'We get together and go for dinner, you
know, swap war stories. You know, lie to each other! And we
talk about heavy stuff, too. Really heavy stuff, you know,
marriage and everything. It's interesting, though, because it's
a kind of Middle Aged Men's Therapy Group with just the
two of us sitting there. And we are more alike than I initially
thought. When we started, he was already nearly 40 and I was
still growing up and now we are both these middle-aged guys.
So we have a better connection and understanding of one
another. I mean, with Danny, what's there not to like?'

In *Lethal Weapon 4* the usual mix of breathtaking action

coupled with humour promised to attract vast takings at the box office. Mel genuinely believed that his character Riggs had travelled a long way from the wild-eyed loony of the first movie. 'When we did that first film, most of the action guys of the day were two-dimensional cardboard cut-out dudes who went around killing a lot of people. But Riggs in the first *Lethal Weapon* was seriously insane and seriously dysfunctional. He drank and in a lot of ways he was trying to kill himself. And there was a kind of truthfulness about that. And he was juxtaposed against the other, more normal, plodding kind of guy who wants to get through the day and put a meal on the table for his family. But Riggs is now a much calmer man. He's got a woman (Rene Russo) he loves and he discovers he's about to become a father. Now that gives us a lot to play with in terms of story.'

Of his co-stars, Mel said, 'I like working with these guys. It's something we all associate with being a pleasant and a fun experience. You go on some film sets and they're like a funeral. But *Lethal Weapon* sets are full of life and there are people having fun. When you work in that sort of atmosphere, not only do you have a great time, but you're better able to come up with good ideas ... with someone like Richard Donner, well, I just think the sun shines out of his ... erm ... ear.'

As usual, *Lethal Weapon 4* was also packed with heart-stopping stunts. Mel remembers, 'We've invented a sport in this one called table-surfing. They're moving a house on the freeway and Riggs gets up on to it and drags some guy out the window. Of course, its going really fast and they fall out, and land on an upside-down table, still being pulled along by the house. So it's kind of water-skiing, on the freeway and we're hitting bumps and slamming into cars. It's insane.'

And Mel performed yet another practical joke on a co-star.

This time it was Italian tough guy actor Joe Pesci. Mel and another co-star comedian Chris Rock 'borrowed' some of Joe's cigars, stuck them up their bums and took photos. When they later saw Pesci smoking one of the cigars in question, they proffered the photos. Pesci, not surprisingly, spat out the cigar.

Meanwhile, back at the Gibson family home, Mel was finding handling teenagers far from easy. He explained, 'Four are now teenagers and that's no fun. It seems everything is a lecture you're ear-bashing them with. They're going, "Oh, shut up," and you just want to say, "If only you'd listen because I've been there." But, God willing, they'll survive.' And with a nine-year gap from youngest to oldest, there are certainly a few phone lines in the Gibson family household. Mel says, 'We've got three or four. But there's a curfew hour. After that, nobody is on the phone.' Mel then paused while having tried to sound like a tough parent. 'At least, there'd better not be,' he laughed.

In August 1998, Mel was reported to have had a severe falling out with fellow Hollywood megastar Tom Cruise. Scientologist Cruise was set to star in a new sci-fi thriller called *Fahrenheit 451*, to be directed by Mel. But all hell broke lose when Mel told Cruise he wouldn't live long enough to understand the script. Cruise then stormed out of a meeting and Mel was told to find himself another star.

A source told the *Daily Star* newspaper in London, 'Now we don't know who's going to be cast in the starring role. Tom lost his cool completely. He took the remark as an insult to his intelligence. Unfortunately, Mel couldn't stop laughing at his own joke, and this made it worse. Tom then told Mel to "Fuck off". He also made it abundantly clear he wanted nothing more to do with the movie. Everyone thought he'd cool off after a couple of days, but he's quit completely.'

Mel was discovering the downside of wielding such immense Hollywood power – dealing with mega movie stars!

However, Mel did also have other things on his mind – he was waiting for Robyn to give birth to a seventh child, as well as prepping a new movie called *Million Dollar Hotel*, with German art-house director Wim Wenders at the helm. The impending birth of yet another child certainly sparked a few raised eyebrows in Hollywood, but Mel didn't give a damn what anyone thought.

On a professional note, Mel was keener to scotch rumours he was in the next *Batman* film than answer questions about why he seemed set on fathering an entire football team. He joked, 'I don't want any more dialogue with Robyn, I get enough of that at home. That's a terrible thing to say – I'm trying to be a smartass. I don't really mean that, dear.'

Mel and Robyn's seventh child, Thomas, was born in the middle of 1999 while the star was on a break from shooting and the couple even opted to make do without a full-time nanny. It was all part of Mel's battle to set boundaries. He later explained, 'We live in a world that says, "Take whatever you want," but I think ultimately it's like being a spoiled child. You're going to get disappointments no matter what you do, and you might as well learn how to deal with them.'

At the Cannes Film festival in May 1999, Mel took a swipe at the aged Hollywood male stars still hanging on to younger, prettier co-stars. Clint Eastwood and Sean Connery, both 68, had just taken Hollywood's long-standing love of older leading men to new heights in two new movies *Entrapment* (Connery with Catherine Zeta-Jones) and *True Crimes* (Eastwood with a selection of beautiful young actresses). Mel told journalists in the south of France, 'I'm very conscious of that, though we are all trudging that way.' He then jokingly cringed over the young actresses who, in being cast opposite the older generation of actors, 'get to floss the teeth of 78-year-old men'.

Around this time, Mel also agreed to be the voice of Rocky the chicken in an animated movie called *Chicken Run* to be made by Aardman Animation, based in Bristol in the UK, who'd struck up a £150 million deal to create five such films for Steven Spielberg's DreamWorks studio.

Mel was feeling highly reflective by the turn of the new century; he found there were definitely moments when he looked back on his life and wondered where it had all gone. He explained, 'It seems like the last 20 years have gone like that [he snaps his fingers], let alone the last 14. And you start thinking, Well, all right, the next bit is going to go just like that, too. And so I'd better be careful not to mess it up! Because it's all going to be over in an instant. I know I'm getting a little metaphysical here, but imagine when you are on your death bed and you go, "That was it? That seemed like a second." It's really weird and frightening to think about that.'

Yet Mel still puffed away on cigarettes despite 'millions' of attempts to give up. However, the hair was still mainly dark, the blue eyes still twinkled and the body, usually fitted out in jeans and a sports shirt, remained lean and fit. Mel had tamed those demons that haunted his earlier life. He was earning a fortune for every movie. What more could he ask for?

In February 2000, Mel became the first actor to be paid $25 million for one film role. Many saw it as a financial Rubicon which the Hollywood studios hoped they would never have to cross. The fee had been secured by Mel's agent for his role in *The Patriot*, an upcoming epic about the US Civil War. It undoubtedly sent shockwaves through Tinseltown thanks to a long list of other stars including Julia Roberts, Tom Cruise and Tom Hanks, who were expected to demand wage parity with Mel. And this $25 million bonanza did not include a so-called 'perks package' of personal trainers, pet-minders, yoga instructors and flights in private jets.

The Patriot grabbed the number-one spot at the US box office, at the expense of *Chicken Run*, and Mel saw similarities in both movies: 'They're both about freedom fighters ... one's got a beak and the other has a musket.' Each film looked set to do well, with *Chicken Run* already earning a respectable $41.1 million before *The Patriot* came on the scene. The *New York Times* proclaimed that *The Patriot* was 'a mix of sentimentality and brutality that suggests a *Lethal Weapon* movie directed by Norman Rockwell.' *Entertainment Weekly* added, '*The Patriot* is a brutish, compelling broad canvas entertainment.'

Mel's portrayal of an American soldier in *The Patriot* caused consternation in the UK. *The Patriot* was accused of portraying George III's redcoats as Nazi-style SS troops, burning towns and villages and torturing and murdering innocent civilians. One local historian complained, 'This is a crass interpretation which is a travesty of the truth. I am sure that Mel Gibson's portrayal of Rocky in *Chicken Run* bears more relationship to reality.'

But Mel was happy to lap up the controversy as usual. But the fact remained that *The Patriot* featured scenes of the British burning down a church filled with people while all the black characters in the movie – set in slave-owning South Carolina – were free, well fed, happy and grateful to Mel's character, naturally. One critic even went so far as to cite a passage in the film which showed British soldiers committing an atrocity closely resembling the massacre of 642 people by the Waffen SS in occupied France in 1944. No such atrocity took place during the War of Independence. Mel's response was to say, 'It's the movies, after all. You need to juice these things up a bit.'

In truth, Mel loved all the fuss. *Braveheart* was similarly criticised and the massively violent *Payback* was dubbed by some as a crass, over-simplistic version of one of Michael Winner's *Death Wish* movies. Interestingly, Mel steadfastly refused to allow his children to see any of these films. He also admitted to one reporter that he believed John and Robert Kennedy were killed because they wanted the US out of Vietnam. And then there was his unshakable Catholicism – Mel still openly opposed birth control, abortion, divorce and the theory of evolution. The family *really* did still come first for Mel, as he explained, 'There's nothing more important than your family. If you ruin that part of your life, what's left? Work? Money? Screwing around? I see a lot of people living like that who tell themselves they're having a good time but, if you look under the surface, you see lots of corpses masquerading as human beings.'

The Patriot ended up under-performing at the US box office, making Mel's $25 million fee look like a gamble by the movie's producers which didn't come off.

Back in the real world, Mel's neighbours at his Connecticut house were not happy with his two donkeys and six sheep which he'd been keeping in the garden. Mel just shrugged his shoulders at that little problem. He was certainly calming down with regard to his attitude towards life in general. As he told one journalist at the time, 'When I was younger, I was tortured. But then I decided it just wasn't worth spending my time on.'

It then emerged that Mel had turned down *Gladiator* (it went to rival Russell Crowe instead) and *The Perfect Storm* (George Clooney) in the space of one week before going for *The Patriot*. Once again, Mel found himself trying to convince British journalists that he did not hate their country. He explained, 'Well, hey, we're giving the Germans a break. What can I say? Somebody's got to be the bad guy and, you know, every country did something horrible to somebody else. The Vikings used to beat up the English, and God knows who beat up the Vikings. Then the Germans beat up the French, and the French used to crap on the Romans. I mean, the Americans used to burn Vietnamese villages.'

Back in Australia, Mel regularly continued to spring unpredictable responses on journalists. Asked whether he believed in his home country becoming a republic, Mel replied, 'I am a little conservative. I tend to favour the monarchy, or the idea of the monarchy. Up until now, it's done a pretty good job of maintaining people's independence and freedom. I just think you can't throw it away without thinking it over.'

Mel said he definitely backed the Queen to open the 2000 Sydney Olympics and took a swipe at the politicians trying to oust the Royal Family. 'Politics is the filthiest business of them all. There is so much skulduggery.'

Around the same time, Mel turned up on a holiday in Florence, Italy, sporting a Kojak-style bald hairstyle much to the shock of many of his fans. Mel's regular hairstylist Daniel Gavin insisted to reporters that Mel was not trying to hide any impending baldness although many were surprised that he would have such a severe 'snip' voluntarily.

Mel then announced he was going to direct so-called Hollywood bad boy Robert Downey Jr in a stage run of Shakespeare's *Hamlet*. Downey had just been released from prison after serving a sentence for drug offences. The two had first met during the filming of *Air America* ten years earlier.

Meanwhile, Mel was getting a tad fed up with the question of his massive $25 million-plus fee for *The Patriot*. He told one journalist, 'Do you think they would give it to me if it wasn't worth it to them? We are dealing with killers in this town and it's really worth it to them. And so am I. I earn every cent.' And Mel insisted he was definitely one of Hollywood's most lucrative commodities. 'Once you get that idea into your head and don't get offended about it, you try to work it to your advantage.' But he continued to insist that his sex-symbol label was 'a device to sell magazines'. Even his considerable celebrity status was, he joked, 'taken very seriously when I want a table at a restaurant'.

Mel's next project, *What Women Want*, with Helen Hunt and Bette Midler, was supposed to help the star come closer to solving the riddle posed by the film's title. But Mel admitted he was still baffled. 'Freud spent his whole working life trying to figure out what women want and he died without an answer – don't expect one from me. After about 20 years of marriage, I'm finally starting to scratch the surface of that one. And I think the answer lies somewhere between conversation and chocolate.'

Other Mel observations prompted by his new movie included such classics as, 'Women are much dirtier than men. They're just dirtier in the way they think. How can I say that any clearer? It was very surprising.'

While making *What Women Want* in 2001, Mel put himself on a bizarre daily diet of raw meat, avocados and olive oil. He even admitted to close family and friends that he believed it would make him live longer and look younger. But medical experts warned that his diet could actually dramatically shorten his life. One of Mel's closest friends told one reporter, 'Mel's under the impression that eating raw beef will boost his immune system and slow down the ageing process because once meat is cooked it loses some of its nutrients. He says if tigers can eat raw steak, then so can he.'

On the set of *What Women Want*, Mel even persuaded co-star Helen Hunt to try his new diet but she got sick soon after drinking one of Mel's avocado, olive oil and algae drinks. Meanwhile, Mel was seriously considering playing the lead role in a movie based on the story of the man who helped compile the *Oxford English Dictionary*.

What Women Want – Mel's first romantic comedy since the less-than-thrilling *Bird on a Wire* with Goldie Hawn in 1990 – made almost $200 million at the UK box office which was even more than his *Lethal Weapon 4* had earned. Mel himself was a little surprised by the film's success and even admitted for the first time that he didn't always get it so right. 'There are so many scripts you read and few which are any good. *Bird on a Wire* was awful. It didn't work for me – it was bread at the time.' Mel's confidence was now so high that he could even admit his past professional transgressions.

TWENTY-FOUR

I THINK THAT WORD 'FEMINISM' IS BULL – IT'S A TERM
INVENTED BY SOME WOMAN WHO GOT JILTED.

I n the summer of 2001, Mel began work on a $70 million
Vietnam war epic called *We Were Soldiers* which he
claimed would be the most accurate portrayal of America's
most controversial war. The film's makers had been granted
access to one of the best accounts of the conflict, by
Lieutenant-General Harold 'Hal' Moore, which had been
under lock and key since elements of it were used in 1979 for
Francis Ford Coppola's *Apocalyse Now*. *We Were Soldiers*
writer and director Randall Wallace – who had been
responsible for the writing of *Braveheart* – spent many
months persuading Moore to allow him to use the book for
the basis of his movie.

Mel's role as Moore's character in the US Air Cavalry
centred around a campaign in which 400 American soldiers
were dropped into enemy territory and found themselves surrounded by 2,000 Vietcong troops. Moore, the

Commander of the 1st Battalion 7th Cavalry troops, and Joseph Galloway, an Associated Press reporter assigned to cover the story, held their ground for a month in the most hostile circumstances. The movie also starred Madeleine Stowe, Sam Elliot and Greg Kinnear and was scheduled for release in early 2002.

At his Icon offices in LA, Mel met journalist Sylvia Patterson, who gently coaxed him into discussing his sex appeal.

'I'm not a kiss and tell kinda guy … it's not conducive to a good working relationship.'

But Patterson wouldn't let go. 'When did you first realise you were so good-looking?'

'I never did.'

'Women must have been fainting all over you.'

'No, they weren't. It wasn't like that. Nope.'

'Rubbish! Not having it!'

'It's true,' guffawed Mel. 'I had a couple of girlfriends and just wondered why they were there. I had a self-esteem problem, I think. I knew I wasn't ugly. But I never thought I was extremely good-looking, and I still don't. I look in the mirror and it's "Woah!"'

'You were an extraordinarily good-looking man.'

'Well, that's what they would tell me.'

'You didn't look in the mirror, see those electric blue eyes and think, Blimey, that's good?'

'Well, it was interesting,' Mel conceded. 'You'd be at a party and some girl would come up and say [he rolls his eyes], "You have the most beautiful eyes," and I'd get all embarrassed, look at my shoes. I was not outgoing and confident about that stuff at all. I had the same hang-ups that every young fella did. You'd get on the front of magazines and even then you'd go, "Man, that's a horrid picture."'

'No one's ever fainted after you looked them in the eye?'

'No. Sorry. Well, I'm not saying people haven't flung themselves at me. It's happened a few times and I'm always alarmed by it. Man, does she really think I'm that stoopid to fall for that shit, y'know? But I think I'm protected from a lotta that – it's some air I give off, some ... field force.'

Now, more than 20 years after first finding fame, a more reflective Mel looked back on his career. 'There's no degree you can take for fame. There is nobody who comes with this contract, "OK, you are now a public person, you have no anonymity whatsoever and if anybody tries to insult you or defame you in a public place they have a perfect right to do that, because you're a celebrity and you got it coming." So when this first started to happen, I was outraged. I was like, "How can they get away with that? I think I'll just walk into the Toronto *Times* and machine-gun everybody ..."'

Mel believed that his self-destructive instincts still lurked somewhere below the surface. 'I think everyone has a degree of it because we're born to die. I think a lot of us are compelled to dip into degrees to get to it faster than others. It's absolutely true. How many times have things been going just swell so you decide to ruin it on purpose? What's that all about? That's self-sabotage. And that's human nature.'

Mel even admitted publicly that he'd had a minor spat with oldest child Hannah over her decision to have her belly-button pierced. Mel said, 'I didn't dig it but she did it anyway. C'mahn!'

But on another level, Mel became virtually misty-eyed as he told Patterson how he'd watched Hannah develop from a child into a woman. 'I've had the blessing of seeing her become a young woman who I am extremely proud of. She knocks my socks off sometimes with the things that come out of her mouth and the actions she performs. Absolutely fantastic.' Mel even admitted that his teenage sons Edward,

Christian, William and Louis had introduced him to bands such as Nirvana and Pearl Jam in the early 1990s.

Mel took *We Were Soldiers* as an opportunity to insist that his father Hutton had not taken him and the rest of his brothers and sisters out of America to avoid the draft for the Vietnam War. 'That story was wrong. It never would have worked if Dad wanted us to avoid the draft. Australia was in the war, too, and I would have been called up,' insisted Mel. But the rumours persist to this day.

Mel screened *We Were Soldiers* for Hutton, who'd of course served with the US Army in the Battle of Guadalcanal in the mid-Pacific. Mel explained to one reporter, 'Dad was there a long time. It was a nasty place. He never talks about it much; that generation doesn't talk about their war experiences, really. He liked *We Were Soldiers*. I heard him laugh at the funny bits and I heard him cry. Well, he didn't cry. He sort of sat there and got emotional.'

In preparation for the role, Mel and other cast members had spent time at Fort Benning, the base for the US Army Rangers featured in the film. 'It was gruelling. They made us do ten days of Ranger training. I stayed in the barracks one night. I put up with 24 hours of smelly socks and snoring and thought, OK, I'm out of here. I'm getting a hotel room! But I was running and training every day. They taught us army protocol and how to use weapons. Then we started on the physical exercise. After the first four-mile run, I was gasping. I might have been able to do it at 22, but now? No way! If I had carried on, it would have killed me.'

And Mel put paid to rumours that he might be considering plastic surgery to try and stay looking young. 'I have a few wrinkles but I'd never have surgery. I don't think I could live with myself afterwards, it would be too weird. I'd feel as if I was giving away part of myself.'

Mel also made a point of telling interviewers that he was determined to make sure his children did not turn into 'spoiled brats'. He explained, 'I don't lavish millions on my children but I don't let them starve either. You have to make sure your children are healthy and they have a roof over their heads and that's it. Beyond that, they have to strive to make things happen. My children understand that. And they also know that I'm not being stingy or mean, I just believe that if they really want something, they have to go out and work for it.'

And out in the real world, Mel remained, he claimed, constantly on his guard for frisky women trying to take advantage of his fame. He explained, 'I must admit, I'm more careful about who I'm photographed with now. There is a type of woman out there who will come up and throw their arms around me and – Bingo! They can say anything. I can spot them a mile off. I'll be at a film première or a function and a scantily clad girl will come up to me with a pimp-like guy who says, "Can she have her photograph taken with you?" I'll say, "Uh no, I don't think so."'

Mel also felt some sympathy for the actor many saw as stepping into his shoes – Russell Crowe. 'When you first become famous, it's weird. Look at Russell Crowe. Russ is doing OK, he can handle it because he's an adult. But he's got a reputation for being a hellraiser that he probably doesn't deserve. We all let off a little steam now and then. You wouldn't be normal if you didn't. As much as people say to you, "Well, you saw it coming," in reality, you didn't.'

On the subject of his 20-odd years of marriage to Robyn, Mel remained philosophical. 'Of course, I would be a liar if I said I never felt like running for the hills and ripping my hair out. That happens. And every relationship takes work. I know that I have a lot at stake in this marriage. I just keep telling myself, "Don't throw in the towel." Everyone is going to be tempted at some point. My parents' generation got married for life. They made vows they meant and they had long-term commitment. Mum and Dad were together for 50 years so I look to their example.'

Next on the Mel movie merry-go-round was *Signs*, a thriller about crop circles written by *The Sixth Sense* writer and director M Night Shyamalan, which was due for release in the summer of 2002. Mel played farmer Graham Hess, who becomes a celebrity when strange 500ft crop circles began appearing in his fields. Mel raved after working with the 31-year-old Shyamalan, 'He was really inspiring. I shut up and watched him work. *Signs* is an extraordinary piece of work and an extraordinary piece of writing.'

Signs proved that Mel truly could blow away all pretenders to his Hollywood crown when it took an impressive $140 million at the US box office within weeks of release. It also enabled Mel to tell the world all about his own supernatural experiences. 'There's a lot of weird stuff that happens to me,' he told one journalist. 'I had young brothers who were twins and one of them woke me up about four in the morning once. I had a driver's licence and he didn't and he wanted me to drive him somewhere. He said, "Christopher's in trouble" and, sure enough, our brother was in a bad way. That's kind of paranormal.'

And Mel told another journalist about how he was driving along the freeway with Robyn discussing an important decision. 'It involves somebody else and it's grave,' he says and, while looking up into the sky, Mel and Robyn saw what he later described as 'a huge sign'. Mel explained, 'It was like a comet and it flew across the night sky and illuminated a cross. I didn't say anything – but I saw it. Then my wife asked, "Did you see that? Do you think that's a sign?" I actually made a decision based on that. We'll see the results of that – we're in the middle of it now.'

But Mel dismissed claims that crop circles were evidence of alien landings. 'I think, if they wanted to make contact, they simply would. They'd drop in for a cup of tea. I'm sceptical when it comes to these things. I think it's probably all an elaborate hoax but some of those patterns do seem a little complicated. They're very intricate designs and so seem inexplicable as to how they could appear overnight.

'The scariest thing to me is the unknown. The expectation of something horrible is far worse than actually knowing what it is. Knowledge dispels fear and all that stuff. But I would definitely be under the bed.'

Meanwhile, Mel the protective father continued to dominate domestic issues. He recalled, 'It's amazing what will motivate you in a family situation. Some guy put his hands on my daughter when we were walking around and I just heeled him with my hand in his chest and knocked him away. My only thought was, You'd better back off, guy. I didn't know where it was going and I wanted to put a stop to it straight away.'

Mel was still haunted by a childhood incident that occurred when he was 15. He explained, 'I woke up to the sound of my sister screaming. She said there was this guy out back, beating up my father. I ran out, and there was some intruder. The guy took off, and I found myself chasing him – in my underpants – with a frying pan. I wanted to kill this guy. It offends you so badly that anybody would come and try to fuck with your family.'

But Mel still refused to keep any guns in his homes across the globe. He explained, 'I don't want any of my kids to find them and blow their heads off.' And Mel believed it was 'highly unlikely' that any of his brood would follow him into

Tinseltown. 'I don't think my kids will become actors. They're interested in other things, which is great. I'm just glad that they have some interests, and are not simply opting for something they might see as easy.'

Oldest child Hannah briefly worked for Mel as a production assistant but then switched to being involved with a Christian missionary. 'She was working as a runner in the production office, bottom of the totem pole. I think she got sick of that stuff. Now she's going through her own university. There's no formal institution – she's learning to take her own path.'

The only career path Mel was determined for his kids to avoid was the armed forces. 'Even in a just cause, I'd still hate to send my kids to war. I'd rather go myself than send them. I believe there are just causes for defending or bring aggressive. I mean, if people hadn't been ready to defend all those things we take for granted, then where would we be? But I couldn't face sending off my children.'

A reflective Mel added, 'I used to butt heads with the guys when they were younger but I quickly discovered that it doesn't do any good because I scared them – and that's not good. Now, it's mostly about trying to stay calm, seeing what the problem is, trying to look behind it and ignoring your own ego. If you're getting angry at someone, it's because your ego is involved.'

TWENTY-FIVE

WHEN YOU BECOME FAMOUS, YOU DON'T KNOW
THAT YOU CAN'T GO BACK TO A NORMAL LIFE ANY
MORE, THAT YOU'VE WALKED INTO A FLYTRAP, THAT
IT'S DARK DOWN THERE AND THAT THERE IS
REALLY NO WAY OUT OF IT.

M el had been nurturing the idea of making a biblical epic
entitled *The Passion of the Christ* for 12 long years,
from around the time when his own boozy, womanising
lifestyle was threatening the very fabric of his family life.
Besides joining Alcoholics Anonymous, he'd also started
reading the Old and New Testaments and focused on images
of Jesus's suffering. 'I began to imagine what that must have
been like. I mean *really* like. No man could have survived
this torture,' he later explained. The script for *The Passion*,
which Mel co-wrote with Benedict Fitzgerald, was also
based on *The Mystical City of God* written by the 17th-
century nun Venerable Mary of Agrede and on the
apocalyptic visions of the 17th-century stigmatic Venerable
Anne Catherine Emmerich.

Mel began shooting *The Passion* in Italy in October 2002
and finished in February 2003. He even built a two-and-a-

half-acre replica of Jerusalem on the back lot of Rome's Cinecitta studios, complete with Pontius Pilate's palace. Most of the exteriors were shot in Matera in southern Italy. Mel had a priest on set the entire time, to take confession and to perform Mass in Latin.

Mel also insisted on the utmost authenticity, in particular for the crucifixion scenes. Jim Caviezel, playing Jesus, had to endure, quite willingly, it seems, up to eight hours a day in make-up 'to have the look of a man who has been scourged, beaten until the flesh hangs in shreds from his body'. He was also strapped to a cross, practically naked, in freezing winds for 15 days. Caviezel turned out to be a natural for the role of Jesus. He was an extremely devout Catholic and professed his conviction he'd been divinely chosen for the role. 'The fact that Mel came to me when I was 33 years of age ... I believe Our Lord meant it.'

Meanwhile, the beautiful Italian actress Monica Belluci – who played Mary Magdalene – insisted that the film would appeal to a wide audience. 'Everyone knows the story of Jesus, so you'll understand what's going on.' Mel himself explained the appeal of the film by saying, 'There is no greater hero story than this one about the greatest love that one can have, which is to lay down one's life for someone. *The Passion* is the biggest adventure story of all time ... God becoming man and men killing God – if that's not action, nothing is.'

In the summer of 2003, at a small movie theater in the Sony building in Manhattan, New York City, Mel was distinctly unrepentant about what some people had already dubbed a potential 'career killer'. Dressed in jeans and a Hawaiian shirt, Mel bundled his select band of guests into the viewing theatre in New York and sat back with them to watch what was about to become the most controversial movie of his entire career.

The dark screen filled with the printed words of prophesy

from the Old Testament *Book of Isaiah*, written 400 years before Christ – 'He was wounded for our transgressions; he was crushed for our iniquities. By his stripes we are healed.' Most of the viewers admitted afterwards they were both riveted and disturbed by the film. Respected writer Peter J Boyer reflected, 'Gibson's resurrected Christ rises in the tomb with a steely glare, then strides purposefully into the light, to the insistent beat of martial drums. With that, Gibson's *Passion* story, and perhaps even the controversy that has attended it, became clear.'

Two days later, Boyer interviewed Mel at the offices of his production company Icon. Mel suggested to the writer that his script for *The Passion* was the New Testament, and that the film was directed by the Holy Ghost. 'I wanted to bring you there,' he said, 'and I wanted to be true to the gospels. That has never been done.'

The problem was that his critics were already circling; amongst them, the Anti-Defamation League and the Simon Wiesenthal Center, as well as some academics, who worried that Mel was drawing too much upon a literal reading of the gospels, and not enough upon contemporary scholarship that sought to distance Jews from culpability. Mel even admitted using subtitles in the film because he wanted to make it clear that some of the Jews portrayed in the film were sympathetic figures. 'You've just got to have them. I mean, I didn't think so, but so many people say things to me like, "Why aren't there more sympathetic Jews in the crowd?" Well, they're there! But you've got to really point it out to them, and subtitles can do that.'

But Mel was deeply disturbed to find the continuing controversy surrounding *The Passion* impacting on his family – especially his father. Hutton, now 85, was accused in a *New York Times* column of being a 'Holocaust denier'. Mel was enraged. 'I don't want to be dissing my father. He never denied the Holocaust; he just said there were fewer than six million. I don't want them having me dissing my father. I mean … he's my father.'

Hutton, now 85, had been dragged into the controversy surrounding the film and presented Mel with the uncomfortable choice of distancing himself from his own father – which he adamantly would not do. Hutton was still the same devout Catholic he'd always been and now many were dragging up his leanings as if it was the first time anyone realised just how devout Hutton had always been. Hutton had, as earlier mentioned in this book, felt alienated from the church since the 1960s and that was how he'd found his way into Traditionalism. But as he grew older he started explaining his dark theories to more and more people. He even told one reporter that the Second Vatican Council was 'a masonic plot backed by the Jews'.

Hutton Gibson explained to a *New York Times* journalist that he believed the Vatican was filled with Masons 'backed by Jews'. About the Holocaust, he said, 'Go and ask an undertaker or the guy who operates the crematorium what it takes to get rid of a dead body. It takes one litre of petrol and 20 minutes. Now … six million?' Subsequently, Hutton also reportedly cast doubts on whether al-Quaeda was responsible for the 11 September 2001 terrorist attacks in the United States.

As a guide to how important religion still was in Mel's life, he even had a chapel built near his Malibu mansion. The Traditionalist church called Holy Family was built in 16 acres of land in the Agoura Hills, bought through an entity Mel controlled called the AJ Reilly Foundation. Mel would not be drawn about the church. 'It's just a private thing. I just want to worship the way I want to worship.'

In March 2003, the *New York Times* writer Christopher Noxon, who's own family lived near Mel's sacred land, dissected Mel's religious zeal in three ways: that Mel's strain of Catholicism was rooted in the sixteenth century; that Hutton Gibson was representative of an extreme 'palaeo-strain of Catholicism'; and that *The Passion of the Christ* was being used by Mel as a tool to spread the word.

That article was noted with concern by a number of religious leaders, scholars and clerics and they turned on Mel, unhappy at the way he'd ignored them while preparing the script for the movie. One academic was so concerned he wrote to Mel seeking assurances that the film 'will not give rise to the old canard of charging Jews with deicide and to anti-Semitism'. Stolen copies of the movie's script even fell into the hands of certain religious leaders who demanded that Mel remake the entire movie. Mel responded through his lawyer, who warned that they were in possession of a stolen script and demanded its immediate return.

In order to counter this, Mel's marketing man for the movie, Paul Lauer, whose father was Jewish, scheduled a series of screenings and appearances by Mel before Christian groups and conservative columnists, who praised the film to their congregations and readers. Meanwhile, Mel summed up his own attitude by telling anyone who would listen, 'In LA, they think I'm insane and maybe I am. *The Passion* is a project good for the soul, not the wallet.'

Many speculated about what had driven Mel to risk so much for a film that it was presumed few people would ever actually see. Mel explained, 'It was the drama of a man torn between his divine spirit and his earthly weakness.'

At yet more private screenings of the movie to the general public, a hand-picked selection of clergymen and Hollywood power players emerged from the cinema proclaiming, in the words of highly respected (and Jewish) critic Michael Medved, 'Praise for the artistry and power of Gibson's accomplishment proved all but universal.' Jack Valenti, former aide to President Lyndon Johnson and President of the Motion Picture Association of America, hailed *The Passion* as one of the greatest movies ever made and a certain Oscar contender.

Medved himself added, 'The charges that the film emphasised anti-Semitic elements of the Gospel story struck me as wildly overblown. Yet, while the movie hardly qualifies as the hate-filled creed described by its critics, it remains a difficult film for any religiously committed Jew to watch.'

And Medved summed up the situation when he said, 'Sadly, the battle over *The Passion* may indeed provoke new hatred of the Jews. That hostility will centre, however, not on a few figures who play villainous parts in a new film but on the real-life Jewish leaders whose arrogance and short-sightedness has led them into a tragic, needless, no-win public relations war.'

But for Mel, God's name was beyond all the controversy about *The Passion*. And that had prompted many Jewish leaders to question his motivation. Mel responded to his critics by saying, 'This isn't a story about Jews versus Christians. Jesus himself was a Jew, his mother was a Jew and so were his 12 apostles. It's true that, as the Bible says, "He came unto his own and his own received him not." I can't hide that. You can't please everybody, but then again, that's not my goal.' When asked whether the film would upset Jews, Mel answered, 'It may. It's not meant to. I think it's meant to just tell the truth.'

With *The Passion* finally about to open, Mel had only one thing on his mind: 'I think when all this is over, the first thing I'm going to do is go somewhere where no one can ever find me.'

The Passion of the Christ was finally released in the US on

Ash Wednesday, 25 February 2004, to conflicting responses from critics but with heavy demand from ordinary movie fans. The number of cinemas showing the film was increased at the last moment from 2,000 to 2,800 so that the film would be seen on 4,000 screens. Cinema chains even reported $8 million (£4.2 million) in advance sales.

Vanessa Rao, a Catholic from North Arlington, New Jersey, said, 'I'm just kind of shell shocked. I just sat rigid in my seat. It was painful, but I couldn't turn away.' Joseph Camerierii, 39, a paralegal student from Los Angeles, could barely hold back the tears as he left a cinema in Plano, Texas. 'I'm in shock. I'm physically weak. I'm emotional,' he said. 'I think if you are a Christian, it will increase your faith tenfold in what Christ has done for you. If you are not a Christian, you'll probably treat others with more love.'

While the film opened like any other blockbuster in 35 New York cinemas, demand to see it was highest in the South, home of the evangelist Christian movement. Thousands of Christians lined up before dawn at a cineplex outside Dallas that had turned over all 20 screens to the film. Parishioners of the First Baptist Church in Woodstock, Atlanta, bought all the seats at all 53 screenings at their local cinema for $63,000 so that anyone could see the film for nothing. Rodney Sampson, an Atlanta evangelist and businessman paid $20,000 for all 12 screens at a local cinema to spread the word. He said the film was 'a masterpiece that will have a shelf life until Jesus returns'.

The Passion took an extraordinary $40 million on its first day at the US box office. But its success sparked a few jokes on American TV. One pundit on CNN quipped, 'Mel Gibson has denied charges of anti-Semitism over his new movie *Lethal Rabbi*.' Chat show host Jay Leno joined in when Mel said he had poured $15 million of his own money into *The Passion* because Hollywood was not interested. Mel even got a standing ovation from the audience. Leno then said, 'The studios said they would have paid for it but they wanted a more upbeat ending.' And he joked that it was doing so well 'there's talk of turning it into a book'.

The Passion took Hollywood by storm and soon looked set to become one of the biggest-grossing films ever made which could make Mel upwards of £200 million for his original outlay of £10 million. And Mel insisted that he'd held back on the violent content of the movie. 'If we had filmed exactly what happened, no one would have been able to take it. I think we have got used to seeing pretty crosses on the wall and we forget what really happened. We know that Jesus suffered and died but we don't really think about what it means. I didn't realise this either when I was growing up. The full horror of what Jesus suffered for our redemption didn't really strike me.'

But even Mel admitted after completing *The Passion* that he found it painful to watch. 'Making this film is the most difficult thing I've done. Watching it is harder. It's difficult because Christ's Passion was difficult. But in watching it, I've found it actually purged me. It somehow heals me to watch it. It's a strange thing – I have never experienced a film like it. The words of God are what heals my wound. My aim is to profoundly change people. The audience has to experience the harsh reality to understand it. I want to reach people with a message of faith, hope, love and forgiveness. Christ forgave them even as he was tortured and killed. That's the ultimate example of love.'

Mel continued to insist he was 'guided by the Holy Ghost' during the filming and that God was present on set. Mel said, 'This was not your normal movie set,' and he then cited several 'miracles' which happened during the shooting of the film to back his claims. These included a blind cast member regaining his sight and the daughter of one of the crew being cured of epilepsy.

Religious adviser Father Donnie Arrant explained, 'Mel told us he did not set out to make a religious film. He said his goal was to tell a true story that would change lives. "I'm bored with my career. This is important. This is something I'm supposed to do. Let the chips fall when they may." This has been a dream of Mel's. He has been thinking, writing and producing it for 12 years.'

Yet no studio would originally touch the project which was why Mel had to stump up his own cash. Later, Mel interpreted this uphill struggle as 'a test of faith'. He explained, 'There have been a lot of obstacles thrown in the way. Whenever you take up a subject like this it brings out a lot of enemies. It's dangerous material. You're talking about the single event that influenced civilisation. This is big stuff.'

But Mel's faith in himself now stood to earn him a vast fortune. Many Hollywood studios began planning similar religious epics within days of the release of Mel's *The Passion* in the US. And Mel was starting to take a step back for the first time in his career. Some wondered if he might give up acting and just stick to directing. As he told one reporter, 'Jesus died for all mankind. It's time to get back to that message. The world has gone nuts. We could all use a little more love, faith, hope and forgiveness.'

Mel's bravery in backing *The Passion* with his own cash had paid off handsomely. It really did seem that everything he touched would turn to gold.

And while Mel could have done without some of the more salacious attacks on his faith, his interpretation of the gospels and the side-swipes at his own family, Mel clearly relished the controversy surrounding *The Passion of the Christ* and summed up his feelings when he told one reporter, 'I don't know where I'm going to fall. And, quite frankly, you want to hear something? I don't give a flying fuck.'

Not even Mel's old favourite Mad Max could have put it better. Mel's notoriously outspoken views overrode even the Catholicism which underpinned his latest movie. He saw it as an unflinchingly literal film version of Christ's Passion and he was solely responsible for turning it into a Hollywood reality.

After all, he'd sunk £10 million of his own money into a project that not even his father's most outrageous comments could sink. Mel himself continued to insist that there was a distinction between his robust faith and his fiery personality. But many remained convinced the film was Mel's personal testament to his belief that Christianity saved him from those personal disasters in his mid-thirties – booze, despair, self-hatred and that Jesus's suffering was a metaphor for his own afflictions. 'When you get to that point where you don't want to live, and you don't want to die,' he once said, 'it's a desperate, horrible place to be. And I just hit my knees. And I had to use *The Passion of the Christ* to heal my wounds. And I've just been meditating on it for 12 years.'

But there was another side to the success of the film; it showed that Mel had truly learned about the craft of film-making after 25 years as a screen actor and, latterly, a director. As an exercise in cinematic technique, editing, lighting and special-effects, the film was, according to many critics, 'breathtaking', easily the most powerful film of its kind since Pier Paolo Pasolini's masterpiece *The Gospel According to St Matthew*. In short, it was never less than compelling cinema and all agreed that Mel should be congratulated on his achievement. As Matthew d'Ancona wrote in a profile of Mel in the *Sunday Telegraph*, 'The movie amounts to a thunder-clap collision between the ancient and the modern: its primitive physicality and ecstatic obsession with every detail of Jesus's suffering gains extraordinary force from the use of the most up-to-date film technique. This is Matthew via *The Matrix*, a vision for the age of computer-generated imagery.'

Mel had explicitly offered his movie as an exercise in historical authenticity, to the extent that the dialogue was spoken in Aramaic and 'street' Latin. As he told one colleague, 'I want to know what really went down. It is as it was.'

But religious author d'Ancona pointed out, 'Having claimed his film is historical rather then devotional, Gibson runs into trouble; he has invited the viewer to watch the film in a very specific way, and pays an according price. Yet there is no contemporary or near-contemporary source for many of the scenes in the film. There is no historical basis for the claim that Pilate's wife comforted Christ's mother and Mary Magdelene while he was being flogged.'

D'Ancona added, 'I left the cinema feeling that, far from being a work of evangelism, addressed to other people, this is one of the most spectacularly introverted films ever made. Gibson decided not to play the lead role himself – casting instead Jim Caviezel, a brooding figure straight from the canvases of Caravaggio. And yet the man behind the camera is really in every frame of the film. This is Gibson's Passion, a religious meditation rather than a quest for the historical Jesus. It is a labour of love, but also of self-love.'

Mel insisted that the incredible box-office success of *The Passion* was neither here nor there, because larger powers had been at work. He explained, 'Fortunately, God is helping me.' In America, God's name was regularly invoked by those in the headlines. Bush invoked God's blessing before invading Iraq in 2003, and he meant it.

Mel later admitted he was exhausted by the furore and

controversy surrounding *The Passion*. He explained, 'It's the first time I've ever experienced the fury of anything like this. Even before I'd finished shooting the film, cannon balls were flying over the bows, and then the film was summarily pre-judged and condemned before I could even edit it. It's been a rough year. I have been silent while people have done character assassinations on me, written nasty editorials and called me names. I could have got nasty and got into a clawing match with these guys, but I'm not supposed to. I'm supposed to exercise tolerance and take the hits and be a man. They say, "Who killed Jesus?" I believe we all did. He died for the sins of all men. It's not about blame ... it's about faith, hope, love and forgiveness.'

Back on the film itself, he insisted, 'The scriptures have been pulled apart and put back together and looked at and turned over and ripped down and reinterpreted for 2,000 years, and they've stood the test of time. It's not like I did this in a vacuum. I read volumes on the scriptures and I talked to biblical scholars and Talmudic scholars until they came out of my ears. This is not the gospel according to Mel, although, in some respects, it is my interpretation and my vision. I mean, the gospels don't mention a maggot-ridden donkey and they don't mention the mother of Jesus wiping his blood up. But I don't think I've betrayed the gospels.

'Now it is being said that the people who wrote the gospels had an agenda. Well, if I had an agenda, if I wrote something that I knew to be false, I wouldn't want to die for it. All these people died for it, so it's true. I believe every line in the gospels. Critics have a problem with the gospels, not with me.'

In response to the Jewish lobby, Mel even took out Caiaphas's inflammatory line from Matthew 27:25 – 'His blood be on us, and on our children – which has long been used to support claims that the Jews killed Jesus. Mel's solution was to remove it from the subtitles but leave it on the soundtrack in Aramaic.

But had making this film helped Mel conquer all those inner demons which had always seemed to haunt him? He replied, 'I'm not courageous – I'm terrified. I've been terrified my whole life. When I was a kid, my family was persecuted for being Catholics. It happens to everybody – they are persecuted for what they are by somebody else who's not them, and it's horrible.'

Self-analysis and his religion, Mel believed, had made him well aware of his faults. 'We're all damaged goods, but there's something better out there if we reach for it. There are episodes in my life when I've done things I'm not proud of, but everybody's got good and bad in them. I'm still a work in progress. I have so many faults. I have so many weaknesses, as do most people, but focusing on the story of this film has enriched me to a great degree. It's actually focused me on my flaws and not on other people's, and that's been a gift.'

In France, cinema owners initially refused to distribute *The Passion* because of fears it would spark a new outbreak of anti-Semitism. The French were wary of its impact on audiences and wanted to wait and gauge its reception elsewhere in Europe before buying the rights to the movie. The debate over the film was highly sensitive in France, where a spate of fire-bombings of synagogues and Jewish schools and attacks on rabbis over the previous year had led Israel to denounce it as the most anti-Semitic country in Europe.

The French newspaper *Liberation* described Mel's faith as 'a Shi'ite version of Christianity … imbibed with blood and pain' which 'reduces the message of Christ to his death by torture … The cult of the martyr is a dangerous combustible in which fanatics burn. It can feed intolerances and religious wars.'

A spokesman for Unifrance, the official promotional

organisation for French films, blamed Mel for the distribution problems, claiming he had imposed 'difficult' conditions on the release of the film. 'I don't think Mel Gibson's people have been making it very easy for the distributors,' said a spokesman.

On 23 March 2004, a one-page advertisement was published in British broadsheet newspapers entitled 'An Open Letter to Mel Gibson from a Jew for Jesus'. The advertisement began:

> *Dear Mel (is it OK to call you Mel?)*
> *I hope you won't feel like this letter is an intrusion, but with all the flak you are experiencing right now over 'The Passion', I just had to write. Anytime anyone makes a statement about Y'shua (Jesus) they stir up a controversy. When he walked the earth, no one could take him lightly. Some were attracted to him and not only believed him but loved him as a best friend. Others were suspicious and all they could let themselves feel was fear or hatred – and if his statements were untrue, who could blame them? After all, Jesus did make some incredible (some might say outlandish) claims:*

The open letter then quotes the Bible before ending with the following:

> *So how can anyone be blamed for the death of a person who is in fact alive? Messiah's willing sacrifice and resurrection bring hope to a world that is desperately in need of some good news. Jesus stands ready to be our helper and redeemer and friend! Not everyone wants to hear that. Maybe they've never read the records of his life for themselves. Or maybe they've heard things about Jesus that are wrong.*

342

Whatever the case. I just want to tell you to hang in there, Mel. There are lots of us Jews for Jesus who are grateful that you made this film. Because of The Passion, this important topic is being discussed passionately – and that's a good thing.

The open letter was signed 'Susan Perlman' A Jew for Jesus.

Some tried to speculate that the entire open letter was a clever bit of publicity generated by the movie's public relations team, but the truth was that Mel had created such a stir that all manner of people were now coming out of the woodwork. There was also the matter of the so-called 'sickening' souvenirs that were being sold across the world thanks to the success of the film. As well as mugs and T-shirts, there were necklaces bearing two-and-a-half inch Crucifixion-style nails on sale in the US for under £9. On the side of the pendants was the inscription Isaiah 53:5, referring to a Bible verse that began, 'He was pierced for our transgressions.'

Some church leaders were sickened by the spin-offs. The Rev Forrst Church, of New York's All Souls Unitarian Church told reporters, 'I expect the prominence of the nail reflects the prominence of the gore in the movie itself. That becomes the icon for identification.' A link in the film's website took the fans to a company that sells official merchandise, including the nails.

Outside Mel's control were the plethora of religious, quasi-religious and political organisations that used the film for their own purposes. Distribution for the film was not helped when Richard Butler, the Idaho-based founder of the extreme right-wing Aryan Nation movement said he would use *The Passion* as a recruitment video. He said, 'I think it'll be a good wake-up call for our people. It'll cause people to ask themselves what Christianity is and what Judaism is. They're true opposites. A lot of so-called Judao-Christians may finally get an idea of who the enemy is.'

For the moment, Mel still found it hard to keep a straight face when talking about his ongoing success. 'I've lied, cheated and stolen,' he says with a grin. I have no idea why I've been a success. Well, I try and keep moving around. It's like boxing, you have to keep bobbing and weaving and throwing the odd hit now and then. That's all.'

Mel even dropped another hint in public that his days as a screen heart-throb might be numbered. He told one reporter, 'I don't feel I want to get in front of a camera any more. I just like being a slob behind the camera and watching other people look good.'

In Britain, *The Passion* received an '18' classification because of its graphic scenes of violence against Jesus. The decision disappointed Icon which expected the same '15' rating it received in Ireland, which would have enabled it to reach a far wider audience.

One of the few people to see the film before its release in the UK was Steve Chalke, a Baptist minister who'd recently written a book called *The Lost Message of Jesus*. He said, 'It was the most violent film I've ever seen, and I'm including *Reservoir Dogs* and *A Clockwork Orange*. This film is an hour-and-a-half of unmitigated violence against Jesus.'

Most UK critics were as bland in their condemnation of *The Passion* as their US counterparts. Respected *Vanity Fair* writer Christopher Hitchens in the *Daily Mirror* commented, 'Gibson is evidently obsessed with the Jewish question, and it shows in his film. It also shows when he's off-screen.' Hitchens added, 'He [Mel] went to some trouble to spread alarm in the Jewish community, which rightly suspected that the film might revive the old religious paranoia. He showed the film at the Vatican and then claimed that the Pope had endorsed it – a claim that the Vatican has flatly denied, but then every little helps.'

Others, such as Dr John Casey, Fellow of Gonville and Caius College, Cambridge, said, 'This is an atrocious film about atrocity and little else, and one that lacks any sense of the spiritual. It is ostensibly about Christ's Passion, yet it conveys no understanding of the meaning that Christians have attached to the sufferings and death of Jesus.'

Jewish writer Melanie Phillips in the *Daily Mail* saw the movie and concluded, 'Whatever Mel Gibson's intentions, this disgusting film leaves the Jewish people once again vilified and the oldest hatred resuscitated.' This was counter-balanced in the same newspaper by movie critic Christopher Tookey, who pointed out, 'At the end of the film, I felt so bludgeoned that I wanted to say, "Yes, Mel, I understand what you're telling me – Christ suffered a lot – but you don't have to keep yelling that over and over again in my ear."

As the controversy over *The Passion* raged on, Mel sat back and watched tens of millions of dollars rolling into his bank account, knowing that he had now reached the pinnacle of his profession. Even his harshest critics could not deny that he was still – after all those years of hard graft and hard living – one of the most talked-about, respected and powerful Hollywood players.

EPILOGUE

IF YOU CAN EQUATE LIFE WITH AN AUTOMOBILE TRIP, I GET LOST WHEN I'M DOING THE DRIVING. THAT'S ALL. YOU HAVE TO BE A PARTICIPANT IN THE TRIP, YEAH, BUT DON'T TRY TO DRIVE THE CAR. AND THAT'S THE HARD ONE TO GET, BECAUSE WE'RE CREATURES OF EGO. I'VE GONE OUT AND DONE THE DRIVING MYSELF FOR A WHILE, AND I FOUND OUT IT DOESN'T WORK.

As Mel comes towards the end of his forties, an earlier lifetime of drinking, womanising and frenzied overwork has taken its toll. A fine latticework of wrinkles is becoming visible at the corners of his eyes and deep vertical grooves are starting to form at the corners of that famous mouth.

Mel may well be, by any definition, an original, and one of the most popular actors of our time. His funny/sad persona has already spanned more than two decades of filmgoing.

He is the sturdy, lower-class kid from the wrong side of the tracks who burst onto the movie scene by playing, essentially, himself. The well-read drama student who can talk like an outback farmer or a Los Angeles cop; the shy, reluctant railroad worker's son identified in the public mind with every woman's fantasy; a cowboy-boot-wearing, rugged-looking character with the down-to-earth tastes of a simple man; the Hollywood heart-throb who preaches about God but refuses to attend the house of the Lord because of his father's feud with the Catholic Church; the irredeemable part-time misogynist who admits he prefers the company of women; the redneck homophobe who earlier dabbled in non-emotional relationships; and – most intriguingly – the flagrantly anti-social film idol who rose to global fame by being like the guy next door.

Mel is the quintessential quick-change artist, moving from accent to accent and country to country so easily that he defies categorising. In many ways, that is what fascinates so many of us.

In that sense, Mel has always managed to keep one step ahead of what was happening in the lives of his contemporaries. In a generation filled with families comprising a manageable number of children, he has gone one step further and bred a mini-army. The arrival of the button-down, money-mad 'Just Say No' 1980s made no difference to Mel. He remained the same old-fashioned character who believed that a woman's place was in the home and that his children sometimes required physical punishment if they misbehaved.

Closer to home, the luck of Mel has become legendary. Apart from the sad death of his mother in 1990, such family tragedies have rarely touched this remarkably fortunate actor. And, all along, Mel has painstakingly chosen the projects he wishes to be associated with.

To promote his obsession with starring in a Western, he appeared on NBC's *Saturday Night Live* in 1989. In one skit, he donned a stetson and a bootlace tie to portray a sheriff. Afterwards, he urged his associates to watch a video recording of the show because he wanted them to be convinced.

The commercial and (surprisingly) partial critical success of many of his films has not deferred his voyage into middle age. To be fair, there is no suggestion that Mel fears old age. There are more dreams to come true first ...